D1035034

A SECRET SOCIETY HISTORY
OF THE CIVIL WAR

A

SECRET SOCIETY

HISTORY
OF
THE
CIVIL
WAR

MARK A. LAUSE

UNIVERSITY OF ILLINOIS PRESS

Urbana, Chicago, and Springfield

SOMERSET CO. LIBRARY
BRIDGEWATER, N.J. 08807

© 2011 by the Board of Trustees
of the University of Illinois
All rights reserved
Manufactured in the United States of America
C 5 4 3 2 1
∞ This book is printed on acid-free paper.

Library of Congress Cataloging-in-Publication Data
Lause, Mark A.
A secret society history of the Civil War / Mark A. Lause.
    p.   cm.
Includes bibliographical references and index.
ISBN 978-0-252-03655-2 (cloth)
1. Secret societies—United States—History—19th century.
2. Secret societies—Influence—History—19th century.
3. Government, Resistance to—United States—History—19th century.
4. United States—History—Civil War, 1861–1865—Societies, etc.
5. United States—History—Civil War, 1861–1865—Underground movements.
6. United States—Politics and government—1861–1865. I. Title.
E458.8.L38   2011
973.7—dc22   2011014504

CONTENTS

ACKNOWLEDGMENTS

Aspects of this study began as papers presented not only at gatherings sponsored by the Labor and Working-Class History Association, but those of the Centre for Research for Freemasonry and Fraternalism at Sheffield, UK, and at an international conference on the history of Freemasonry. I am indebted deeply to the Charles P. Taft Memorial Fund for the opportunity of attending the international conferences. I am grateful to Ken Burchell for his advice on secret societies. Nikiki Taylor, then a colleague in the Department of History, assisted my making my way through elements of antebellum black history. Janine Hartman has, here as on other projects, cast a copyeditor's eye on some of the initial drafts. Laurie Matheson at the University of Illinois Press helped shape the project into something of use to modern scholars and readers, and her coworkers there have been, as always, superb.

INTRODUCTION

This is a secret society history of the Civil War period in American history rather than "the" history of the subject. American conditions at the time gave rise to a broad range of these kinds of organizations. More important, perhaps, the social and political circumstances in the United States encouraged a set of assumptions about the role of clandestine voluntary associations in shaping the course of history.

Massive new secret societies arose this side of the Enlightenment to cast their shadows across what would follow. One could argue that the sort of articulate, educated, successful, and politically active middle-class gentlemen who joined a secret society would try to influence events regardless of their membership. However, from the days of the American and French revolutions, critics and some supporters have emphasized the importance of secret societies in making revolutions, waging wars, and shaping events across the Western world.

Such bodies certainly occupied much of the rare leisure time of mid-nineteenth-century American gentlemen. Freemasons themselves assert the order's importance, as in Allen E. Roberts's *House Undivided* and, recently, Michael A. Halleran's *Better Angels of Our Nature*. Halleran reproduces data indicating that the country had more than two hundred thousand Masons on the eve of the conflict, and this seems to have counted only a few of the major bodies. There were a series of unrecognized rites of "fringe Masonry," or Prince Hall Masonry, among African Americans, and this is without considering the large rival organizations, such as the Odd Fellows, the Sons of Temperance, or other fraternal orders for social and mutual aid purposes.[1] No antebellum community of any size failed to cultivate a lodge of some sort or other.

Yet the discussion of the numbers in a way that assumes something coherent misses the point. Notwithstanding Roberts's triumphalist title, neither antebellum Masonry nor fraternalism generally was "undivided." Just
as abroad, Freemasonry and related secret societies drew members from
diverse social strata and often remained independent of institutionalized
political and spiritual authorities. The order provided the earliest model
of widespread voluntary self-organization, and it brought together those
with the general desire to foster secular republican governments. The lure
of promised secrets made the dream even more interesting and marketable.
The meaning is anything but straightforward.

Certainly, secret societies abroad proved essential to the making of the
modern world. They formed the mortar of the nation-building process, the
catalyst for new political parties, and the means to mobilize constituencies for
or against reforms by which these new governments would foster the well-
being of ordinary citizens. Such orders crystallized around the ideas ranging
from the nationalism of Giuseppe Mazzini to the artisan insurrectionism
of Louis Auguste Blanqui. By the time of the continent-wide upheavals of
1848–49, such orders expressed dissatisfaction ranging from the regime to
governments, from thwarted national aspirations to the injustices of class
society itself. In short, they contributed to shaping broader notions of nationhood, republicanism, and the social order, in part perhaps, as ruling elites
reacted to their fears of pervasive conspiracies against their power.

On this side of the Atlantic, too, the importance of Freemasonry among
the nation's founders is well established. Tracing its influence through the
war years would involve a fruitful exploration that would surely lead, among
other places, into very influential mass veterans' organizations. Here, as
abroad, fraternalism embodied and structured the way middle-class men
grappled with identities of community and gender.[2]

American mythologies mediate some of these assumptions. Based on the
alleged lack of repressiveness in the United States, the molders of its national
self-perception have tended to posit an American exceptionalism that pre-
cludes the need for and discourages clandestine organizations. The vaunted
openness of mid-nineteenth-century Americans politics not only failed to
resolve those tensions around national identity and republicanism but also
proved insufficient to keep those tensions from causing a civil war.

In fact, open public political organizations were also possible in mid-
nineteenth-century Britain and Switzerland, which also gave rise to secret
societies, so it should come as no surprise that we find them in the United
States. Crystallized around the idea of an associative power, participants
may also have had little reason for confidence that they would be free of

repression or that their open organization would have much of a prospect of shaping policy. European radicals brought their associations and their norms of association to America after the repressions of 1848–49. Although often segregated from a general understanding of political history, African American fraternalism independently provided a similar model of a secret society with implicitly radical social criticisms. Nor have we done well in understanding such formations among homegrown white Americans such as the Brotherhood of the Union.

Despite the heavy weight of American exceptionalism, close students of the Civil War should be able to suggest several cases where secret organizations and conspiracies seem to have had a major impact on the broad flow of history. Talk of circumventing and resisting the official institutions of power and their policies ripened through the 1850s. The decade closed with John Brown's armed abolitionist raid on the U.S. arsenal at Harpers Ferry, Virginia, which brought to the fore the sectionalization of sentiment over the subject of fugitive slaves cultivated in Kansas. The identity of Brown's military adviser, the remarkably obscure Capt. Hugh Forbes—who headed a coalition of those European revolutionary societies reorganized by refugee émigrés in New York City—requires a more accurate appreciation of Brown's 1859 raid.

The historical contribution of secret societies to defining national identity raises a logical set of questions, but it is not through Freemasonry that an emergent secessionism makes its primary contribution. Hardly any book-length account of the conflict fails to mention George W. L. Bickley's Knights of the Golden Circle (KGC). Describing the KGC as a secret society of Southern sympathizers in the North essentially smudges it into the Democratic Party, on the one hand, and Confederate secret services, on the other hand. However, the KGC hoped to unite Mexico and the South, using the acquisition of Texas as their example. No less an authority than Horace Greeley wrote:

> Before the opening of 1861, a perfect reign of terror had been established throughout the Gulf States. A secret order, known as "Knights of the Golden Circle," or as "Knights of the Columbian Star," succeeding that known six or seven years earlier as the "Order of the Lone Star," having for its ostensible object the acquisition of Cuba, Mexico, and Central America, and the establishment of Slavery in the latter two, but really operating in the interest of disunion, had spread its network of lodges, grips, passwords, and alluring mysteries all over the South, and had ramifications even in some of the cities of adjoining Free States. Other clubs, more or less secret, were known as "The Precipitators," "Vigilance Committees," "Minute Men," and by kindred designations; but all of them were sworn to fidelity to Southern Rights; while

their members were gradually prepared and ripened, wherever any ripen-
ing was needed, for the task of treason. Whoever ventured to condemn and
repudiate Secession as the true and sovereign remedy for Southern wrongs,
in any neighborhood where Slavery was dominant, was thenceforth a marked
man, to be stigmatized and hunted down as a Lincolnite, Submissionist, or
Abolitionist.[3]

In short, beneath the rhetorical fear of a "slave power conspiracy," prominent
and respectable thinkers discerned a genuine mass secret society.

The KGC has gotten some serious study but clearly merits a more rigorous
look. Most sensationally, perhaps, Simon and Schuster in 2003—the same
year that Doubleday published Dan Brown's *DaVinci Code*—gave us a work
that traces the KGC back through the Freemasons to the Templars and used
aerial photography and surveys that seemed to transpose the same kind of
geometry described around Rennes-le-Chateau into parts of rural Arkansas.
While not drawn into the lineage of Jesus, it discloses the really important
secret protected by the defunct KGC, the location of the missing treasury of
the Confederate government, supposedly tucked away in Arizona's Supersti-
tion Mountains. At the opposite extreme of this popular sensationalism, Frank
Klement's *Dark Lanterns*—the most complete scholarly look at Civil War secret
societies—simply dismisses the KGC as a paranoid fantasy, substantiated only
by Federal forgeries.[4] While the evidence for government forgeries is as thin
as that for hidden treasure, assumptions about the importance of the KGC
seem to parallel the old nineteenth-century nationalist faith in clandestine
planning and its inverse, the predisposition to believe in hidden conspiracies.

Along with the issue of national identity, a look at the secret society tradition
in mid-nineteenth-century America also tests the extent to which the implicit
plebeian dynamic abroad applied to the Second American Revolution. This
study will look in various quarters, including the émigré circles, radical organizations, and African American fraternalism, for which American realities
proved most similar to those of oppressed nations in the Old World.

This study will also have implications for the flip side of this discussion,
an unbelievably pervasive American faith that the unseen hand of conspiracy moves history. The belief in the power of a secret society and the
fear of conspiracy are opposite sides of the same coin. Both see a fragile
and vulnerable status quo, the functioning of which may be disrupted by
secret cabals and the defense of which justifies extraordinary clandestine
measures. The reciprocal nature of this faith usually leaves me unimpressed
by the blanket debunking of conspiracy theories, because those who do so
are rarely consistent in their skepticism.

Fear of secret conspiracies festered in early American history until the 1826 disappearance of William Morgan, a Mason professing plans to expose the order's secrets. A wave of suspicion depleted the order of membership and power, leaving it even more fragmented in the United States than it was abroad. It is interesting that Antimasonry centered in New England, upstate New York, and the upper Midwest, whereas Halleran's figures on state membership indicate that Southern gentlemen joined the Masons in much larger proportions than their Northern countrymen. The sectional implications of this point merit some thought.

In a broader sense, the penchant for seeing secret cabals may or may not be pathological, but it is hardly a simple pathology distinguished from a reasoned and rational world view. The closer one looks, the more the line blurs between an unquestioned fear of an international Communist (or "terrorist") conspiracy, the threat of illegal aliens, and the menace of extraterrestrial aliens. Through my life, the dominant institutions of our society have all fostered world views centered on unfounded fears of secret cabals where the fear suits their policy purposes. At this moment, our TV remotes can dance us across lengthy and repetitive "documentaries" on bigfoot, alien abduction, ghost-hunting, and the afterlife. Interspersed in this muddle are laments about the state of education and the need to reform it by getting rid of teachers. The "news" spares us all sorts of potentially disturbing information about the environment or overseas wars in order to repeatedly revisit allegations of the president's secret foreign birth and his clandestine religious allegiances. An examination of the myth and reality of secret societies in the Civil War period offers us some insight in how the "paranoid style" reaches farther and runs deeper than the popular delusions or aspirations of the unlettered masses.

A SECRET SOCIETY HISTORY
OF THE CIVIL WAR

PROLOGUE: OLD WORLD CONTOURS

Revolutionary Politics and the Secret Society Tradition

In the wake of the revolts of 1848–49, Americans rather quickly faced the proliferation of revolutionaries and revolutionary secret societies that had so disturbed the repressive powers on the Continent. In February 1854, as-yet-unconfirmed U.S. consul George Nicholas Sanders hosted some of the most prominent émigrés in London at a dinner marking the anniversary of their republican outbreak. Ambassador James Buchanan, about to become the president of the United States, joined the festivities that brought together Giuseppe Garibaldi, Giuseppe Mazzini, Felice Orsini, Lajos Kossuth, Stanislaw Worcell, and others. At the banquet, Sanders toasted the "world republic in Kentucky whiskey," which Alexander Herzen found so intense that he warned Alexandre Auguste Ledru-Rollin. (Sanders replied that only Americans and Russians actually knew how to handle strong drink.)[1] At the time, it remained unclear to many Americans where the established American republican order could or should fit such figures into their view of the world.

Americans initially shared with Europe the mechanisms by which republicans sought to reconstruct their civilizations. Masonry, the earliest model of a secular voluntary association, emerged from the Old World Enlightenment with unavoidable implications for the political organizations built in its wake and for the revolutionary movements of the eighteenth century. For the defenders of the status quo, the membership, influence, and agendas of secret societies might be unknown, but it seemed wisest to assume them to be massive, pervasive, and insidious. On the other hand, some participants sought to turn a Masonic model to revolutionary purposes, with goals that ranged from the mere displacement of a regime to a thorough social transformation. While these contradictions seemed unimportant before the upheavals of

Prologue

1848–49, the prospect of power spread the would-be revolutionaries across a broad spectrum. These midcentury developments not only had a vital, if subtle, impact on the sectional crisis, but did so through the perceived medium of clandestine organizations.

FREEMASONRY AND THE

EIGHTEENTH-CENTURY REVOLUTION

Craftsmen in the building trades sustained some form of organization for centuries. In the Compagnonage or Herbewege on the Continent, such artisans sustained local "lodges" in the British Isles to provide jobs, a certain level of economic security, and companionship. Men of these generally migratory trades roamed from one construction site to another, as their skills might be needed. In a preliterate age, secret signs and passwords known only to the trained initiates not only controlled admission to the lodges but could also identity skill level and even job record.

By the seventeenth century, the ancient mysteries claimed by these "operative masons" attracted the interests of more privileged and prosperous gentlemen. Enjoying the expanding life beyond the household and eager for recreational association with the like-minded, these new "speculative masons" or "freemasons" joined the older lodges and soon began to constitute entire lodges of their own. On June 24, 1717, members in London established a Grand Lodge to standardize rituals, regalia, and structures. By 1750, it had deputized provincial grand masters for Gambia, Bengal, Gibraltar, and Charleston, South Carolina. The new order also appeared in Ireland, France, Saxony, and what became Italy, with isolated lodges as far away as Spain and Russia.[2]

By then, masonry had become the dominant form of voluntary secular association in the Western world, subsuming a broad spectrum of social, religious, and national identities. If members did not reject religious, nationalistic, or hierarchical values, they generally believed that other, fraternal, values transcended them. Since legitimacy within the order rested on tradition, originality usually came through the "rediscovery" of previously hidden degrees, rites, and rituals. Distinctions over such superficially unimportant matters as origins and structure grew as the order spread on the Continent. The farther from the control of the Grand Lodge the order went, the more it tended to foster fringe variants that often reflected predispositions to differing social and political interests.

On the Continent, a series of papal bulls threatened members with excommunication, inspiring French masons to "discover" more independent, respectably Catholic, Jacobite, and Scottish origins. Of course, the order may well have had some such roots or assimilated some lodges that did. Yet the effort left the order in France with not only its own Grande Loge by 1737 but also a Conseil des Empereurs d'Orient et d'Occident established in 1758, representing a division between the three-degree "blue lodges" and more complex and diversified "red lodges."[3]

The introduction of this fragmented masonry into central Europe became part of both the Aufklärung, the German Enlightenment, and the reactions to it. The latter suspected the rationalizing tendency of Western thought and inspired alchemists, arithmosophists, geosophists, cabalists, and theosophists of all sorts. Old Rosicrucian claims to have inherited secrets from a wandering Templar who had visited the East in the Middle Ages surfaced in the 1750s when an "Order of Gold and Rosicrucians" emerged among the masons. Others insisted upon Templar origins. Codified in 1764, the largest number of German lodges began arguing for a "Strict Observance" of Teutonic rites allegedly older than the Scottish; by 1770, their "United Lodges" spread back into France and continued into Hungary, Italy, Russia, and Scandinavia as the "Swedish system."

In general, the nature of the milieu that gave rise to freemasonry made it a vital force in defining its specifically national character. Traditional elites discomforted by the secrecy responded to freemasonry in different ways. In some places, they joined it, and, in others, they tried to repress it. Masons in different countries responded in various ways, all of which shaped an institution with a peculiarly national character.

In England, the order became the common ground associated with a creative renegotiation of social and political duties. The year 1776 marked the opening of the Freemasons' Hall in London and brought hints of the order's utility in terms of political action. More than this, though, freemasonry provided a model of organization that permitted politics in societies that discouraged their more open expression. Secrecy represented a strength, the safeguard of vulnerable memberships and plans. The mechanisms of signs and passwords provided means of identification essential to collective self-identity.

However, whether intended or not, the composition of freemasonry in France, Germany, and America predisposed it to often subversive purposes. The same year that the hall opened in London, some masons in the American colonies helped compose their Declaration of Independence. By then, English-speaking Masons had themselves divided between the "Moderns" and the more unorthodox "Ancients," who, like their peers elsewhere, claimed an older structure and ritual with a fourth mystical Royal Arch degree. Boston, the first political battleground of the American Revolution, had lodges of both Moderns and Ancients. While the former included some of the most prominent local Loyalists, the latter had the rebels like John Hancock, Paul Revere, and Joseph Warren and also shared its meeting place—the Green Dragon Inn—with the Sons of Liberty. At Philadelphia, the destruction of its records for 1776 hints at a more significant role in a local revolution, which not only toppled British authority but also displaced the old government of Pennsylvania with a radically more representative government. Based on a broadened suffrage, the radical new government eliminated slavery, acted against profiteers, and considered a bill of rights declaring unlimited accumulation of private wealth dangerous to the liberties of the people. In addition to the cosmopolitan Benjamin Franklin, their ranks likely included the revolutionary agitator Thomas Paine, the later author of an essay on the origins of Masonry.[4] Their Revolution established a new nation with a civil religion imbued with Masonic symbolism.

In the same year, on May 1, Adam Weishaupt, a faculty member at the Jesuit-dominated University of Ingostadt, launched what became one of the most famous secret societies using the Masonic model. After repeated and unsuccessful battles to introduce "enlightened" French writers into the curricula, he took a page from his opponents' organization and formed the new Order of the Illuminati, structured by degrees through which the thinking of the member became progressively enlightened to the social and political implications of their rationalist values. As a rule, initiates required an acceptance of generally secularist values, while those admitted to the "Minerval Illuminate" sensed the political implications of those values, probably advocating the abolition of monarchy and hereditary political power by a representative government, and the "Areopagus" extended equality into social and economic relations. After three years of marginal success, the order struck on the idea of going into Masonic lodges, where they found many predisposed toward their secularism, and grew to the hundreds. At the 1782 Wilhelmsbad Covenant, the Illuminati denounced mysticism in the order, as a resurgent Catholicism. Soon after, the Bavarian authorities issued escalating bans, ending with the March 1785 outlawing of the order.[5] Although Weishaupt recanted, faith in the power of secret societies and fear of the dreaded Illuminati spread into the rest of the world, alongside the German variations of freemasonry.

Indeed, the Illuminati had less an impact on the political world than those mystical currents in Masonry to which they objected, such as Martinism and Mesmerism. Louis Claude Saint-Martin proselytized for the ideas of Martinez de Pasqually, who posited a higher spiritual plane of reality, perceived through cabalism and popular mystical beliefs with which the living needed to be "reintegrated" as a prelude to regeneration. At about the same time, the 1784 Bayonne experiments with hypnosis hinted at the existence of an "invisible world." Franz Anton Mesmer, an Austrian Rosicrucian, introduced *le magnétisme animal* to Paris, promising treatments with magnets and water to influence fluids in the body. When the Academy of Sciences, the Royal Society of Medicine, and the medical faculty of the University of Paris refused to take his work seriously, Mesmer became something of a cause célèbre, and his followers founded the Société de l'Harmonie Universelle, affiliates of which called themselves "lodges."[6]

On the Continent, Illuminatism, Mesmerism, and Martinism soothed different kinds of disaffections with the ancien régime, but each reflected and contributed something to the Revolution that erupted in 1789. According to some accounts, an exiled Illuminatist initiated Nicholas Bonneville. His 1788 *Les Jésuites chassés de la Maconnerie et leur poignand brisé par les Mascons* (The Jesuits expelled from Masonry) certainly repeated the Illuminatist charges that Jesuit influences lurked beneath the appearance of occultism within freemasonry. During the fateful summer of 1789, Bonneville published *Le tribun du peuple,* looking beyond the turmoil around him toward "a revolution that is being prepared" and leading toward "universal regeneration." Through Paine and Étienne Dumont, another of Honoré-Gabriel Riqueti, Comte de Mirabeau's secretaries, the Cercle Social had close ties to foreign participants in the Revolution, including English-speaking radicals such as Eleazor Oswald, James Rutledge, and John Skey Eustace.[7]

The Cercle Social provided the springboard for the movement launched by François-Noël Babeuf. Although born to a large, poor family, he had acquired an education that enabled him to serve as a minor government functionary and seek admission to the Freemasons. With the Revolution, he helped to write the local cahier, cataloging popular grievances. He also led a crowd to the land records on which he had worked and burned them. After a brief visit to Paris, he returned to Roye and in 1792 moved to Amiens to take an archivist post in the Department of the Somme. The Thermidor of 1794 caught Babeuf on the Food Commission in Paris and eventually landed him in a prison at Plesis. There, from March into October 1795, he lingered with his cell mate, Filippo Giuseppe Maria Ludovico Buonarroti.

In hindsight, attempts to build a society grounded in the wisdom of initiates rather quickly polarized what kind of wisdom might be the most important. Some envisioned a future built upon the politics of building national institutions, while others saw the only real measure of a revolution's success as the realization of human equality, which required a kind of cooperative internationalism. These currents continued to function alongside each other through the first half of the nineteenth century.

Over at least the next half century, whether the revolutionaries themselves realized it or not, they aspired to a level of organization and power attributed to Buonarroti.[8] His shadow haunted the nightmares of the powers that be for decades. Born into a noble family at Pisa and a direct descendant of Michelango, Buonarroti enjoyed the benefits of education and training but nevertheless earned the disapproval of his elders and superiors by such behavior as a youthful flight to Marseille in 1780, where his first encounter with urban poverty drove him into a deep depression and serious thought. A few years after his graduation from the university and his marriage to Genoese woman, he was already a Mason, and the authorities raided his library, confiscating books judged to be seditious and anticlerical. The year 1789 found him on the French island of Corsica, where his *Giornale patriottico de Corsica* hailed the Revolution on the mainland. He was in and out of the service of the Revolution in various capacities, including as a *commissaire national* at Sardinia, before returning to Paris in March 1795 and landing in a cell with Babeuf.[9]

Babeuf and Buonarroti gained release when the authorities responded to an attempted royalist coup by releasing imprisoned radicals. The newly released political prisoners rallied many surviving democrats into a new Society of the Panthéon and launched the *Tribun du Peuple.* In February 1796, the Directory closed the *Tribun,* leaving the society to dissolve into a small insurrectionary committee that issued tracts such as Sylvain Maréchal's *Manifeste des egaux* (Manifesto of the Equal) and tried to infiltrate the army, police, and other arms of the government. On May 8, 1796, the insurrectionists agreed upon a scheduled seizure of key public buildings and officials, but government informants had already reported their plans. Two days later, the authorities rounded up two hundred of the leading Babouvists, bringing the chief culprits to trial in February 1797, eventually executing Babeuf and Augustin Alexandre Darthé in the spring. The involvement of foreign Babouvists helped erode the last traces of internationalism in the French Revolution, leaving Buonarroti's vision a quaint throwback to the Enlightenment.

Then, too, despite his incorrigibly radical and egalitarian hopes as an end result, Buonarroti seemed to have involved himself in revolutionary circles of even the most modest goals. From his prison at Cherbourg from 1797 to 1800, he maintained old contracts and established new ones. Such activities continued after his transfers, to Oléron and, later, to Sospello in the Alpes Martines. At this last place, he found what may have been the most important republican secret society of the early Napoleonic years, the Philadelphes. In the spring of 1806, he gained his freedom on the condition that he move to Geneva, where the prefect of the police reported his alleged organization of a group of Philadelphes within the Amis Sincéres. Even as the police closed the Amis Sincéres, the Philadelphes renamed themselves the Amis de Moreau. However, the prefect apparently heard nothing of Buonarroti's 1809 organization of the Sublimes Maîtres Parfait, the "Grand Firmament" of which he hoped might coordinate the development of such societies all over Europe.[10] However, "Philadelphes" was a particularly common name, and we may never know how much of this has substance or consisted entirely of smoke and mirrors.

These alleged activities did coincide with the growth of secret circles in the army opposed to Napoléon Bonaparte. Alleged to be prominent among the Philadelphes was Jean Victor Moreau, earlier implicated in the circulation of anti-Bonapartist literature. The sensationalist writer Charles Nodier, in his fanciful *History of the Secret Societies of the Army,* associated with Jacque Joseph Oudet. In 1812, with the emperor in Russia, Claude François de Malet and others back at Paris announced Napoleon's death and attempted to seize power. The only real link to Buonarroti was that, after Malet's defeat, the Geneva police drove Buonarroti from the city. In January 1813, he turned up at Grenoble, where he remained until the fall of Napoleon.[11]

More substantively, Buonarroti translated the perceived conspiratorial legacy of the French revolutionary process back into his native Italian. Partly because of the politically fragmented nature of Italy and the way in which French revolutionary goals arrived, often on the bayonets of Napoleon's army, organizations were many and varied. After 1802, the Raggi came to be known as the Astronomia Platonica or the Centri, and claimed thousands of members a few years later. The Guelfi in the North had peculiarly British origins, and Charles Nodier questionably asserted that no fewer than three secret societies shared the name Adelfi or Filadelfi, and Napoleon himself feared a Ligue Italique. Republican societies took up the protective coloration of freemasonry and influenced the Spilla Nera, the "Knights of the Sun," the Decisi, and the "Society of Universal Regeneration." Gioacchino Paul di Prati claimed that, in 1810, Milan had a "masonry in masonry" governed by a "Great Firmament" apparently derived from the French Philadelphes and tied to societies at Paris and Geneva, said to have been involved in the Malet intrigues.

Most famous of all, however, were the Carbonari. By 1789, an informal association of charcoal burners—a vestige of the old craft *compagnonage*—

existed in the Franche-Comté. Its forest *ventes* had only two degrees of membership, apprentices and masters, referring to its members as *bons cousins*. Like the old "operative masonry," it admitted bourgeois and professional men as well as soldiers into its ranks, and the new Charbonnerie of the France-Comte had ties to the Philadelphes. By 1806, Pierre Joseph Briot worked with friends of Buonarroti to establish one of the first Carbonari lodges in Italy among Scottish-rite masons, although others formed. After the fall of Napoleon, the edict of the king of Naples against the Carbonari clarified the practical shortcomings of a simple Italian nationalism.[12]

Buonarroti's adoption of the Illuminatist tactic of operating through Masonic lodges provided greater security. After the Restoration, he returned to Geneva and threw himself into the work of coordinating the reorganization and reorientation of conspiratorial activities throughout Europe. As early as 1817 or 1818, the Sublime Maîtres Parfaits had virtually swallowed the remnants of the Adelfi, and the French Philadelphes. On this basis, he renamed the order Le Monde, although it was still known by its old name for some years to come. The Austrian crackdown after the risings of 1819–21 in northern Italy seemed to confirm old suspicions that something like Le Monde possibly lurked behind all popular disorders. In 1821 and 1823, the authorities intercepted correspondence among revolutionists of different nations. However, they lacked evidence of Le Monde's Supreme Aeropagus, a name more than vaguely reminiscent of the governing body of the Illuminatists.[13]

The subsequent repression in Switzerland drove Buonarroti to Brussels. There, he associated with many of the exiled lesser lights of the French Revolution, something that lent luster to his reputation among younger revolutionaries, and revived Le Monde. By 1828, he published his *Conspiration pour l'égalité dite de Babeuf* (Babeuf's Conspiracy for Equality) and made a final clean break from a central strategy of infiltrating freemasonry. A few years later, his legacy had an indeterminate influence on the revolutionary risings of 1830, particularly the successful Belgian revolution for national independence against the United Kingdom of the Netherlands.[14] In the wake of these revolutions, Buonarroti attempted another international revolutionary organizations, the Charbonnerie Réformée, which jettisoned entirely the complicated hierarchy of quasi-Masonic grades for the more plebeian two-grade structure of the original Carbonari.

Meanwhile, the Mediterranean contributed its variations to a somewhat political "fringe Masonry," focusing on mythological ideas about antiquity to transcend contemporary national preoccupations. Along with Hermetic, Templar, Rosicrucian, and Pythagorean degrees and orders, eighteenth-century groups such as the "Initiated Brothers of Asia" offered the mysteries of "the Orient" (a term encompassing everything from the former Ottoman domains east to Japan), which aspired to something as radical as that of the "Philalethes," the perfection of the human race. In 1779, Count Alessandro di Cagliostro, an affable Palermo peasant-turned–confidence man, launched an Egyptian Rite open to women and well as men. Some of the forty thousand French soldiers who invaded Egypt had been freemasons, some survivors of which returned with various synthetic rituals. In 1810, when one such Ancient and Accepted Rite at Milan failed to offer more degrees, the Bédarride brothers proposed to offer ninety degrees in their new the Order of Mizraim—*Mizraim* being another name for *Egypt*.[15]

The Egyptian mysteries that Samuel Honis (or Hennis) brought to Montauban in southern France "about 1814" or 1815 may have originated with Cagliostro, Napoleonic freemasonry, or the Bédarride brothers. Honis's claims seemed stronger for his alleged nativity in Cairo, further bolstered by his swarthy complexion. With the Bourbon Restoration of 1815, his nephew Gabriel Mathieu Marconis de Négre took the responsibility of quickly putting the order into mothballs, though Gabriel's son Jacque Étienne Marconis reestablished the order in 1838, building at least two lodges ("Osiris" and "Des Philadelphes") at Paris, two more ("La Bienveillance" and "De Heliopolis") in Brussels, and, interestingly, a number of English supporters.[16] Secular radicals with a revolutionary outlook concentrated within this order.

Buonarroti's final effort came in 1833 with the Carbonnerie Démocratique Universelle, the *ventes* of which spread rapidly through France, Belgium, Italy, Switzerland, and possibly Spain and Portugal. Modern radicals and scholars found much to criticize in the various Carbonnerie intrigues of Buonarroti's later years. Nevertheless, he had established the foundations for revolutionary organizations among the French and Italian—and largely among Germans, British, Irish, and others.

The followers of Buonarroti created serious obstacles for themselves with their anachronistic obsessions with degrees and grades, the conspiratorial legacy of Babeuf, and a rigid insistence on clandestine work. Still, the weaknesses in his orientation and perspectives grew in part from his lifelong commitment to the internationalist and egalitarian visions associated with the legacy of secret societies like those of Bonneville and Babeuf. His redoubled efforts to revive that legacy in the 1830s came not only from his own eagerness to leave his imprint on the world but also from an ongoing ideological struggle against the narrower, if more practical, patriotism of the European conspirators deprived of nationhood by the arrangements of 1815.[17]

NATIONAL REVOLUTION AND SOCIAL REVOLUTION

Different circumstances inspired different aspirations for different revolutions. Those facing essentially feudal practices inspired critics, activists, and leaderships drawn from the lesser gentry, nobility, or upper bourgeoisie, who sought to displace the ancien régime with secular republican institutions. Where the demands of a new, competitive marketplace had shaped a social formation with different kinds of inequalities, the hired workers increasingly tended to reach beyond ideas of justice or liberty defined exclusively in business terms. The latter gave substance to what had been Buonarroti's egalitarian vision of a social and economic reconstruction of society.

Few better expressed this ambiguity at the heart of nineteenth-century revolutionary ideas than Giuseppe Mazzini. In 1831, the veteran Carbonari and Mason founded Giovine Italia, an association inspired by messianic nationalism, as he expressed in his 1840 discourse "On the Duties of Man." He asked how one might fill that divine command to love mankind in a world where the individual was so weak and humanity so vast. God himself had "divided Humanity into distinct groups upon the face of our globe, and thus planted the seeds of nations." To love that portion of humanity within reach, individuals needed to rebuild national communities "disfigured . . . by conquest, by greed, by jealousy of the just sovereignty of others; disfigured . . . so much that today there is perhaps no nation except England and France whose confines correspond to this design." The lack of a unified nation-state meant oppressed and divided peoples would remain "the bastards of Humanity."[18]

There certainly existed a social dimension to Mazzini's nationalism. "Do not beguile yourselves with the hope of emancipation from unjust social conditions," he continued, "if you do not first conquer a Country for yourselves; where there is no Country there is no common agreement to which you can appeal; the egoism of self-interest rules alone, and he who has the upper hand keeps it, since there is no common safeguard for the interests of all." So, too, he saw "no true Country where the uniformity of that right is violated by the existence of caste, privilege, and inequality—where the powers and faculties of a large number of individuals are suppressed or dormant—where there is no common principle accepted, recognized, and developed by all." Moreover, "in the name of your love for your Country," declared Mazzini, "you must combat without truce the existence of every privilege, every inequality, upon the soil which has given you birth."[19] In short, some prospect of national revolution seemed even more attainable, and it seemed to incorporate Buonarroti's social *illuminismo*.

Still, the aging Buonarroti remained unimpressed. He countered Mazzini's "Young Italy" with a Veri Italia, emphasizing the egalitarian and internationalist goals essential to a "true Italy." The old man tried to build his new order within Mazzini's group. Buonarroti's radicalism had greater influence among the French radicals. A student named Louis Auguste Blanqui entered this conspiratorial struggle for the international social republic. His Société des Saisons urged an ongoing revolutionary overthrow of ruling classes until the process left the working class alone to exercise power.[20] By the time of Buonarroti's death in 1837, a new generation of Blanquists had taken up his ideas and would carry them into the 1870s.

The Blanquist tradition took root deeply among émigré German workers in Paris. Divided into numerous independent states, Germans faced national problems similar to those among the Italians. Despite the repressive policies in the larger of these states, such as Prussia, and the suppression of such insurrectionary efforts as those in 1830, driving thousands of Germans into exile, organized secret societies continued to form and grow. In 1833, émigrés at Geneva formed a Junges Deutschland with ties to Mazzini's "Young Europe." At Paris, Theodore Schuster organized a particularly militant association of Rhenish secularists into the Bund der Geächteten. This "League of the Outlaws" organized members into regional and provincial tents, as had Buonarroti's Carbonnerie Démocratique Universelle, and advocated the unification of Germany as a "cooperative republic." With an unsentimental objectivity, Friedrich Engels described the Bund der Gerechten simply as "a German outlier of French working-class communism," that was "in reality not much more than a German branch of the French secret societies, and especially of the *Société des Saisons*," with goals "the same as those of the other Parisian secret societies of the period."[21]

On the other hand, Schuster's politics always left many of the more plebeian admirers of Blanqui uninterested. No sooner had the Bund attained almost a hundred members at Paris and seventy or eighty around Frankfurt am Main than it began to disintegrate. Schuster formed some of the more middle-class republicans into a new Bund der Deutscher, a simple nationalist League of Germans. Meanwhile, the more plebeian "Outlaws" formed the Bund der Gerechten—the League of the Just—and embraced the moral leadership of Wilhelm Weitling. Born and bred into poverty, the self-educated tailor from Magdeburg concocted a particularly combustible blend of plebeian Christianity, and the 1836 effort of "the Just" provided a mechanism to foster such values. In 1837, after a short stay in Switzerland, he returned to Paris, where he began explaining his insights in *Die Men-*

schheit wie ist es und wie sie sein sollte (1838), *Die Garantien der Harmonie und Freiheit* (1842), and *Das Evangelism eines armen Suenders* (1845). The new Bund shared that vision of "humanity as it is and as it ought to be" and advocated political guarantees of social harmony and freedom.

As among the French or Italians, expectations about the extent of the coming European revolutions continued to create tensions within the Bund der Gerechten. One wing, called the "cabinetmakers" or "carpenters," advocated agitation for political reform to achieve the social republic, while another wing, the "tailors" or "shoemakers," saw the overthrow of the existing political system or its displacement by a new system as an essential prerequisite for a proletarian reconstruction of society. This latter section followed the leadership of Weitling and Johann Hoeckering, the former protégé of Buonarroti, a veteran Masonic conspirator and then editor of a Franco-German journal.

Blanqui's attempted coup against the French monarchy on May 12, 1839, set the Bund der Gerechten on its own course. The authorities repressed not only the Société des Saisons but also other implicated associations from the Bund to Egyptian freemasonry, which drove a wave of refugees into London. There, the Bund reached beyond conspiratorial work with a public Arbeiterbildungsverein. Severed from the influence of Blanqui, the German workers' movement turned to education and propaganda, establishing libraries, organizing classes, and sponsoring public festivals. This, in turn, brought them together with men of learning interested in the social question. Engels recalled its members as "the first revolutionary proletarians I had met" and encountered Dr. Karl Marx. The two established one of the most fruitful intellectual collaborations in history, applying a rigorously materialist standard to political radicalism. Wedding the ethical aspirations for a society unfettered by capitalism to the tangible struggle of the social classes, the Bund der Gerechten became increasingly distinctive until its June 1847 metamorphosis into the Kommunist Bund.

Similar divisions took place among the radicals of other nations as well. Early as 1844, the Germans had joined William Lovett and other "moral force" Chartists to establish the Democratic Friends of All Nations, which reorganized in 1848–49 as the People's International League, embracing Mazzini's vision of cooperative nationalist revolutionary groups. On the other hand, "physical force" Chartists established a loose body of Fraternal Democrats in 1845, joining with the German, Polish, and French allies, even as the local German Workers' Educational Societies became an international organization in its own right, establishing affiliates at Brussels and elsewhere. After failing to establish an international association, the Fraternal Democrats merged in 1850 with Bronterre O'Brien's class-conscious National Reform League, aimed at nationalization of land.[22]

The rise and repression of the 1848–49 revolutionary upheavals diffused such ideas. In France, the February revolutions inspired and mobilized workers and radicals. Under Louis Blanc, they pushed the government to promise the opening of new socially owned National Workshops, for which 100,000 workers quickly applied. Terrified, the authorities turned against these innovations and sent some 40,000 troops against an indeterminate number of workers during "the June Days," which left between 4,000 and 5,000 dead workers, with an unknown number of wounded and thousands more facing imprisonment or flight. Similar repressions drove thousands of Germans as well as French to cities in Switzerland, Belgium, the United States, and, most notably, England. By 1853, London authorities counted 2,500 refugees from Poland, 1,000 from France, and 260 from various points in Germany.[23] The émigrés quickly aligned themselves with radical English masons engaged in propagandizing free thought in the *Free Thinker, Reasoner,* and *National Reformer.*

In London, exiles made repeated efforts to rebuild their organizations. By 1850, Mazzini, Ledru-Rollin, Arnold Ruge, Albert Darasz, and others founded the European Democratic Central Committee, with Italian, Polish, German, Austrian, Hungarian, and Dutch subcommittees. Among the French, Ledru-Rollin's followers maintained La Société la Révolution, but Blanc, Étienne Cabet, Pierre Leroux, and others offered an alternative in the Union Socialiste in May 1852. Later that year, Blanqui's followers started their own Commune Révolutionnaire, which called for a "universal democratic and social republic." Implicated in the coup of 1839 and the revolution of 1848, the Conseil Supreme de l'Ordre Maconnique de Memphis established at least ten lodges in neighboring countries. Most important, it established La Grand Loge des Philadelphes at London, chartered in January 1851, and began to evolve into what became a quite nonrevolutionary plebeian version of English freemasonry.[24]

More important, German, French, Italian, Polish, and other émigrés in England, refugees from the Continent, encountered proponents of the "People's Charter"—the demand for universal manhood suffrage—which had already built a mass working-class movement. As among the Germans or French, experience with the repressive power of the state created distinctions between "moral force" Chartists, who believed the rulers of England could be rationally persuaded of the merits of suffrage and were predisposed to the cooperative nationalisms Mazzini envisioned, and "physical force" Chartists, who were increasingly allied with the Arbeiterbildungsverein. In 1845, the German and English radicals sought to launch an international organization called the Fraternal Democrats.[25]

In short, the experience of Western societies generally gave rise to alternative visions of the future. Schuster and Mazzini or the English proponents of the Great Reform in the Parliament and French critics of monarchism sought a solution in a new kind of state centered on the nation. It would establish a unified secular state with organic roots in "the people." On the other hand, Marx and Buonarroti or the Chartists and Blanquists espoused internationalist politics to establish egalitarian and democratic social republics by those sharing a common social identity at the base of civilization in all nations.

Revolutionists generally shared the desire to challenge feudalism, monarchy, the established church, and the values these institutions promulgated. The power those institutions enjoyed often mandated clandestine organizations, and the nature of secret societies of any sort predisposed them to emphasize the most conservative version of their politics. For this reason, perhaps, the contradiction between form and function seemed less for Mazzini and the advocates of national revolution. In the end, after all, their goal was the displacement of one minority class, the feudal nobles, by another, the bourgeoisie, while Marx and his allies discussed the displacement of all minority classes with the rule of the majority class, the workers, and related social groups.

Even among the former, though, fostering a revolution secretly became increasingly problematic with the development of established republics, where government required more than the simple coercion of an unarmed and unorganized majority by the armed, wealthy, empowered minority. In places such as the United States—and other countries moving that direction—government involved a ritualized popular mandate or its appearance, which would require the mass organization of politics. There would be an American translation of these ideas, organizations, and tensions.

AMERICAN IMPLICATIONS

In the United States, fraternal orders had provided the base for the first perfectly respectable political parties. Such associations as New York's Society of St. Tammany provided a quasi-Masonic form that tweaked government paranoia about unseen conspiracies masterminded by the Bavarian Illuminati. These contributed to the Federalist Party's passage of the unpopular Alien, Sedition, and Naturalizations Acts, the backlash to which fueled the Democratic-Republicans victory in the strictly electoral "Revolution of 1800."[26] Still, the Democratic-Republicans did not so much defend freedom of association as debunk charges of their involvement in a conspiracy, and the Federalists ultimately countered with their own fraternal Washington Benevolent Associations.

Although no evidence existed for the Federalist paranoia, some Illuminatists, Martinists, or Mesmerists made it to the United States. Members of the Cercle Social, the Sublime Maîtres Parfaits, Le Monde, the Charbonnerie Réformée, and Egyptian-rite freemasonry did so. After the Restoration, Robert Babeuf—the eldest son and cothinker of the 1796 conspirator—came to the United States, as did Nicholas Bonneville in 1815–19. At Newburgh in upstate New York, a Masonic veteran of the revolutions in France and America, John Skey Eustace, helped transform the local Masonic lodge into "the Druids." So, too, when Thomas Paine returned from France in 1803, he gathered about him a circle of radical freethinkers that his enemies called the "Columbian Illuminati." Decades later, Egyptian freemasonry would, eventually, cross the Atlantic rather publicly.[27]

Although the United States needed no movement for national independence, the political and social tensions leading to 1848 elsewhere assumed an overtly political course in a nation that had largely realized the Chartists' ambitions. Electoral revolts by "Workingmen" and "Locofocos" in the 1820s and 1830s mobilized such veterans of Paine's "Columbian Illuminati" as Alexander Ming, John Fellows, and Thomas Herttell. Almost as soon as propertyless white men began exercising the right to vote, labor organizations launched Workingmen's Parties to capture public offices. At New York City in 1829, Ming's son published Thomas Skidmore's *Rights of Man to Property!* which spoke in language reminiscent of Babeuf and the Cercle Social of confiscating and dividing property and of cooperative industry, as well as a rather offhanded assumption that the new order would establish equality for blacks, Indians, and women.[28] Generally, small groups tended to coalesce around such radicalism.

Nevertheless, the secret societies and fraternal orders that emerged from the local and regional agitation remained apparently short-lived. In 1841, upstate New York craftsmen in the building trades—clearly influenced by the Odd Fellows—formed a fraternal order of Christian workingmen, the Mechanics' Mutual Protection Association. Including artisan employers as well as hired men, the association functioned as a mutual aid society, in effect insuring members and encouraging health. Its embrace of temperance, however, was a moral choice as well.[29] At times, and around specific issues, the order effectively functioned politically.

More important, the United States wound up being as much a refuge for exiled revolutionaries as London. Among the thousands of French, Italian, and German émigrés reaching the United States in midcentury were veteran revolutionaries who had decided to take a step into the unknown beyond London. The Germans, perhaps more used to organizing in exile, had established the most radical wing of the movement even before 1848. During those years, a veteran of the old Communist League, Hermann Kriege, had established a Social Reform Association, which spread from the New York City area into Newark and also had affiliates at Philadelphia, Cincinnati, Milwaukee, Chicago, and St. Louis. Communist tailor Wilhelm Weitling launched an Arbeiterbund in 1850, which had affiliates in the same places (except Chicago), but also added branches at Detroit, Rochester, Dubuque, Trenton, Maysville (Kentucky), Williamsburg, Louisville, Baltimore, Pittsburgh, and Buffalo.[30]

As well, some Americans in Europe at the time of the revolutionary upheavals there shared these radical politics, observing and sometimes participating in the movement around them. Margaret Fuller and George W. Rose threw themselves into assisting the Italian revolutionary movement. Albert Brisbane, the foremost American proponent of the socialist ideas of Charles Fourier, had the resources to travel widely against the backdrop of these revolutions and witnessed the agitation in Germany. Such revolutionary tourists may have followed the course of Fourierist army officer–turned–Unitarian minister William Batchelder Greene, who had joined politicalized freemasons in France.[31] These Americans came home with ideas of political self-organization and the possibilities of a new kind of republic, grounded in human equality.

While some Americans did not like the idea that newcomers found the American Republic as unjust, in its way, as the French monarchy, a few had witnessed the revolutions abroad and found their course particularly discomforting. After aiding in "the suppression of disturbances among the Sioux tribe of Indians," the family of the wealthy and powerful Charles Lucas Hunt of St. Louis went to Europe with Father Pierre-Théodore Verhaegen, a prominent Jesuit and educator. They watched the movement break out in Paris and in Ghent, where Belgian politics pitted the liberalizing revolutionary movement that had secured national independence in 1830 against the church.[32]

Hunt acknowledged the "distress" that caused the revolts, but the prospect of change terrorized him. He feared the possibility of a French invasion of Belgium and fretted over a "European liberty" very different from that in America. "The Europeans do not know what liberty is even in theory much less in practice. Their general idea of liberty in this country, is the right to appropriate another man's goods + chattels to your own benefit." (He admitted, though, that the destruction of property had mostly been due to "boys of from 10 to 18 years old.") It became too much, though, when "a party of forty of fifty persons, hoisted a red hand kerchief on a cane and started off under the rallying cry of '*A Bas les Jesuits*.'" Hunt started to pray for "energetic measures" to rescue civilizations.[33]

In short, Americans responded in various ways to the prospect of revolution in the Old World and to the kind of secret societies that professed to advocate them. In part, these differences reflected what became the immediate political crises that led to the Civil War. Moreover, among those eager to embrace revolution were some who remained preoccupied with a national destiny and others hopeful for a social republic.

* * *

Nothing better demonstrated these tensions among American advocates of revolution than George N. Sanders, the host of that 1854 banquet for European revolutionaries in London. The bravado ultimately cost him confirmation by the U.S. Senate. As appreciative of irony as well as anyone there, Herzen recalled the Sanders soirée "the *red* banquet given by the defender of *black* slavery." Later, Sanders ranted on behalf of "Red Republicanism" before a New York City audience, assuring them that he favored "death to tyrants. He was for the guillotine, and he would work it by steam, by G-d." However, he warned listeners not to confuse fervor for the rights of man and republicanism with abolitionism and reminded them that they had been holding "a meeting for white men, and not for niggers in Europe."[34] His white supremacist national chauvinism expressed a uniquely American fearlessness about purging a new nation of its impurities. However, the only other white American present at that gathering, William J. Rose, took to his feet to challenge Sanders.

America's 1848 also embraced Greene's libertarian socialism and his commitment to a Blanquist organization. In America as in Europe, the tensions between these two perspectives—the nationalism of the middle class and the nascent internationalism of the labor reformers—played out in the familiar organizational setting of the secret society. In fact, even as the European authorities had acted ruthlessly to suppress the workers in "the June Days" of 1848, one of America's most popular fiction writers, George Lippard, launched his new Brotherhood of the Union, an order that claimed roots going back to the *Illuminati* for its project to revolutionize America.

ALTERNATIVE

PART I

MEANS

1. THE BROTHERHOOD OF THE UNION

George Lippard and the Palestine of Redeemed Labor

The Brotherhood of the Union gave its initiates a well-choreographed experience. At the opening of the ritual, a costumed herald announced, "Behold the enemies of mankind!" The curtains opened before them to reveal a tableau with costumed representatives of privilege and power gathered around an altar. This was a "table covered with scarlet, on which a dim taper is burning. Beside the taper appear a skull, a goblet filled with red liquid, a copy of the Declaration, the Gospel of N[azareth], and a Map of the Continent of America." In a memorable ritual, they expressed their contempt for the ethics of the gospel and the values of the Declaration, drinking the symbolic blood and discussing their plans for the conquest of America's soul.[1] Such a mystification of nation reflected an idealization worthy of Giuseppe Mazzini, and it inspired exactly the kind of association he would have found familiar.

The Brotherhood represented a particularly American version of the radical nationalist idealism characteristic of the European revolts of 1848–49. Unlike such associations abroad, it functioned within a civilization, paradoxically free in terms of a republican ideology but politically shackled to human slavery. In founding the order, Gothic writer George Lippard sought to create a mutual aid fraternal order that would play the same sort of role widely attributed to the secret political societies in Europe. Known members—a rather limited proportion of the entire order—included some of the leading socialist and radical land reformers, people with ties to the antislavery Free Democratic Party. Nevertheless, Lippard amalgamated the rhetoric of a social visionary with a pragmatic practice balking at any explicit opposition to the Democratic Party. No less than kindred associations abroad, the

Brotherhood of the Union blended abstract romantic humanity and social love with political goals that required blood and iron.

Born on April 10, 1822, Lippard was the fourth surviving child of a sometimes officeholder struggling to maintain the family's Chester County, Pennsylvania, farm. The family sent him, when only a few years old, with his three sisters—Sarah, Mary, and Harriet—to live with a grandfather and aunts Catherine and Mary in Germantown on the Wissahickon. Later, the parents lost the farm and moved to Philadelphia, without reclaiming the children. Not surprisingly, adults found Lippard introverted, dreamy, and studious. They sent him at age fifteen to Duchess County, New York, in order to study for the Methodist ministry. He later told the tale of how an uncharitable and gluttonous act by the minister training him moved him to disgust, and he returned to Philadelphia, but it seems just as likely that he came back to reconcile with his father when the latter sharply declined to his death in October 1837.[2]

Lippard "inherited little, if any, property from his family" even as the panic of 1837 devastated the economy. In desperation, he joined other squatters in "a rusty dilapidated old house" near Franklin Square. Over the next few years, he slept on four chairs with an old valise for a pillow, spending his days in whatever jobs he could, though eventually he was reduced to a point where he kept his clothes together with twine. The experience cultivated a genuine sense of class injustice. "You cannot give one man the fruits of the labors of a half a million of his brothers without blaspheming God," he insisted. "It matters not whether you give these fruits by custom or by law: the result is the same. The half million deprived of the means of life are tempted by necessity to all manner of crime." After a brief attempt to take up the study of the law, he met John S. DuSolle of the *Spirit of the Times* and began writing for the press.[3]

Once Lippard took up the pen in seriousness, his experiences and those of the other poor people of the city poured luridly across the page. His 1845 book *The Quaker City; or, The Monks of Monk Hall* dramatized the seduction of a young local woman by a fashionable dandy, his murder by the woman's brother, and the refusal of the jury to convict the killer. As one of his admirers recalled, the novel "divided society into two parties, one justifying the 'Quaker City,' the other execrating it and the author. The laborers, the mechanics, the great body of the people, were on Lippard's side." Demand drew the story to the stage only a few years after clashes between the Nativists and Catholics bloodied the cobblestones of Philadelphia. Scorning changes of fashion, the author turned up on opening night with his long hair falling almost to "an ample cloak, and carrying a sword-cane to repel assaults." Lippard imitated the style of a proper bohemian of Paris or London, but when the mayor told him that the authorities feared a riot, Lippard withdrew the play.[4]

Success brought prominence, respectability, and some financial security. In 1847, the Reverend Charles Chauncey Burr married him to Rose Newman in a romantic moonlit ceremony on the Wissahickon, with Lippard's sister Harriet as the second witness. His love of the area inspired his writing of the two-volume *Paul Ardenheim, the Monk of Wissahikon* (1848 and 1855). Clearly, too, he felt a kind of social responsibility with his good fortune and actively assisted and encouraged less appreciated writers, such as Edgar Allan Poe or the future New York bohemian R. H. Stoddard.[5] Lippard's version of the Jacksonian success story helped move the writing of American fiction from the parlors of the wellborn or well-heeled to a profession in which one could make a decent living.

A Mason and an Odd Fellow, Lippard had long been familiar with—and drawn upon—the lure of the transatlantic secret society tradition. He greatly admired Charles Brockden Brown, that pioneer of American letters who had, a generation before, woven his own stories of clandestine schemes to transform the world for the better. The perspectives of the authorities and their accomplices in the press persuaded many that the social and political rebellions of 1848–49 abroad had actually resulted from the conspiracies of a small number of radicals. For his part, Lippard embraced the romantic view that "the greatest movements which mark the history of the world have been the work of Secret Societies." Through the summer of 1849, his *Quaker City* mingled translated pieces by Louis Blanc on the Illuminati, Alessandro di Cagliostro, and Franz Mesmer. "The mystery of Combination," wrote Lippard, "is well learned by studying the Secret Societies of the Past—of the old World and of the New."[6]

This faith in the power of hidden truths coincided with a mass interest in spiritualism, the proponents of which experimented regularly with secret societies. Cincinnati's "True Brotherhood" or "Spiritual Brotherhood" included radicals such as Josiah Warren, and Augustus and John O. Wattles associated with the upriver community of Utopia. By the mid-1850s, Stephen Pearl Andrews, John Murray Spear, John Orvis, John Allen, Ellen Lazarus, and other radical spiritualists back East established the oddly named ultra-feminist Order of Patriarchs, followed, toward the close of the decade, with the Sacred Order of Unionists. Many of these members also gravitated to Lippard's Brotherhood, notably Philadelphia's Isaac Rehn and Rochester's Eliab

Wilkinson Capron and Henry Barron, two of the most nationally prominent promoters of spirit communications.[7]

Land reform had also given rise to such fraternal efforts. George Henry Evans's National Reform Association (NRA) sought to transform local working-class movements into a national movement for radical land redistribution. Although they offered a far more radical vision than Mazzini and "Young Europe," they adopted the term *Young America*. (Continually befuddling to scholars, a circle of expansionist writers and their supporters also embraced this term.) The radicals used *Young America* both for their newspaper name and for a proposed new fraternal secret society, one that would coexist with the projected Industrial Brotherhood.[8]

Lippard had cooperated with the NRA at the June 1848 National Industrial Congress, which met at Philadelphia. He later hinted at the existence of a new secret society that came out of that gathering, though there is no evidence for its existence for another year. Indeed, in June 1849, he announced the existence of the organization, and added, "Not yet will we reveal the name of the Society: there is a time for all things." By the end of the month, though, Lippard wrote that "the Society is known to the world as THE BROTHERHOOD OF THE UNION." He unfolded his plans for the order in a series of short pieces and regularly reprinted excerpts from the order's constitution, the platform, and statements on the order "encircled in the H[oly] F[lame]."[9]

Like the European orders the Brotherhood emulated, it spoke the language of plebeian radicalism. *Quaker City* published articles and commentary titled "Social Aristocracy" and "Social Slavery." John Greig—a veteran Fourierist "long known as an able and untiring advocate of humanity"—urged Lippard to write a book titled *The Crimes of Capital*, complaining of a utopianism "praying to capitalists for aid—bah! they might as well ask them to go and preach the Gospel of Jesus—apostle-fashion—without scrip or purse; or ask Satan to go and break the yoke of the captive, and heal the broken-hearted— God help us, none else will." The Brotherhood's solution lay in its appeals "to those who work." "The Few have been *organized*," wrote Lippard. "The Masses have *not* been *organized*." The order "will work by the combination of half a million Hearts, Arms and Minds—to say nothing of the congregated Pennies of Labor, which in the Society will grow rapidly into Capital." A sympathizer from distant Wisconsin wrote that he hoped the Brotherhood would "be decidedly *the* society of *the* age."[10]

The Brotherhood declared itself "a secret organization, which embraces all that is good in other secret societies, such as Masons, Odd Fellows and Sons of Temperance, with the addition of many an important factor." Membership required a belief in God and added a commitment to the federal Union.

Depending on one's age, initiation fees ran from one to five dollars, with dues set locally, depending on the desired level of benefits, rental costs for meeting rooms, and whether the circle wanted its own library. The Brotherhood sought "correct views of the relation of Capital and Labor, so that the Capitalist may no longer be the tyrant, nor the Laborer the victim." If possible, its local circles sought a practical and cooperative "union of capital."[11]

A closer look at the larger, more documented urban circles brings the meaning of these ideas into sharper focus. At Philadelphia, the Pilgrim, Jefferson, Progress, Richmond, and other circles included members such as John Ferrall, who helped lead the citywide general strike of 1835, as well as the former Chartist tailor John Sheddon, Yorkshire shoemaker Thomas Phillips, and veteran land reformers and Fourierists. By the end of 1849, these local circles began holding joint ceremonies. In March 1850, they called a mass meeting at the Chinese Museum to raise money and publicize the effort to organize local seamstresses into a cooperative "Industrial Union." In addition to Sheddon, the former Chartists on the platform were John Mills, Edward P. Powers, John Campbell, and Scots radical George S. McWatters, later a pioneering bohemian in New York City. With them stood socialists Pascal Coggins and Thomas Speakman.[12]

The Brotherhood pursued similarly radical goals in New York. The National Reformers' *Young America* declared the order "formed on the model recommended by the [1845] Convention which formed the Industrial Congress, its form of organization and its objects being almost identical with that recommendation, its object being to convert the soil of America into Free Homes for all its inhabitants." The Powhattan and Nazarene circles formed at, respectively, Yonkers and New York City. John Commerford, a leader of the Workingmen's movement a generation earlier, joined, as did other leading land reformers—Benjamin Price, William V. Barr, John H. Keyser, Joshua K. Ingalls, and Parsons E. Day of *America's Own*. The most prominent national spokesman of the Fourierists, Albert Brisbane, spoke for the order, and the cooperationist printer Keyes Arthur Bailey assumed a leadership role.[13]

The city already had some vigorous cooperative organizations comparable to Philadelphia's Industrial Union. Ira B. Davis had arrived earlier from Massachusetts, discontented with the Fourierist project of starting underfunded communities. Like many others, he turned to cooperative "protective unions" as a transitional measure to introduce the merits of socialism to urban workers. Starting in 1848 with a cooperative store, Davis had expanded into a bakery by 1850, when he took up the cause of the Brotherhood, as did the book printer Bailey and newspaperman Donald C. Henderson. By early March 1850, the Nazarene changed its name to the Ourvrier Circle, reflecting its affinity for émigré radicalism in the city. The society sparked what the *Quaker City* called "a magnificent movement" in favor of land reform at Tammany Hall, but went on to organize a citywide labor association, the New York City Industrial Congress. The body briefly combined dozens of local craft organizations and inspired the formation of many more.[14]

Lippard and his supporters sometimes embraced the European word to describe their goal. He described what the order had been doing as "nothing but Socialism—pure Socialism—French Socialism—the very thing the Tories and Money Grubs have been blaspheming these twelve months." As to the meaning of this, he added, the antisocialists "have no more definite idea, than a black hat has of a sky rocket." The term, he declared, had been "often ridiculously misapplied. Nothing is more common, than the injustice and ignorance of the daily papers of the large cities, which so often link Socialism with all manner of robbery and crime."[15] Yet Lippard seemed to think of socialism more as an ethical preference than a political principle and would not have the opportunity to learn from his mistakes.

Workers joining the Brotherhood had to take their membership seriously enough to invest money and time into the order. Lippard announced one of the Baltimore members "prepared to manufacture and furnish all the Insignia, etc., etc., needed for a Circle of the Brotherhood—his terms are very reasonable—and his workmanship correct and beautiful." The founder recommended him "heartily to the patronage of every Circle of the Order."[16] Few would have invested in the costumes and badges unless they planned to use them regularly.

Still, beyond the rhetoric and the very tangible ventures at New York and Philadelphia, the significance of the Brotherhood of the Union merits a critical assessment.

AMBIGUITIES OF THE BROTHERHOOD

The problem of what the Brotherhood of the Union actually did or could have done as an organization begins with its scale. The order experienced a steady growth after the first group coalesced at Philadelphia. *Quaker City* began reporting the formation of circles in September and mentioned at least fifteen by the year's end. By early March 1850, the Brotherhood announced interest in the organization from Maine to Georgia, adding that "already have the laborers of California and Oregon reached forth their hands to join us in the holy bonds of Brotherhood." In less than four years, the order was establishing Circle No. 200 at Laurel Factory in Maryland. True, after launching Circle No. 1, Lippard chartered the second as No. 56, and other gaps in the record may reflect his likely desire to exaggerate the order's scale and influence.[17] Even allowing for the shameless puffery, though, the Brotherhood chartered a not inconsiderable 139 to 146 circles.

Such circles appeared in a wide variety of communities. Members organized in cities across the North, including Boston, Providence, Buffalo, New York City, Rochester, Schenectady, Philadelphia, Pittsburgh, Cleveland, Cincinnati, Columbus, Dayton, Chicago, and Milwaukee, as well as communities in slaveholding states, such as Baltimore, Wilmington (Delaware), Washington, and Tallahassee. Most, however, formed in very small towns and villages, such as Ellsworth, Maine; Noank, Connecticut; Pontoosuc, Illinois; and Perryville, Kentucky. Smaller and smaller organizations in settings that were tinier and less documented further complicate our effort to understand the order's scale.

Because the sources generally name only a few officers, membership is even more difficult to determine. The order required at least ten persons to start a circle, but some of the labor-based urban circles seem to have become large and stable organizations, supplying large petitions to Congress for homestead legislation.[18] A reasonable estimate of the numbers involved—with a liberal allowance for turnover—would be between five and eight thousand, with roughly half in Philadelphia, New York City, Rochester, and other large cities.

Not only did the Brotherhood eschew a disciplined approach to political work, but it never even sustained an official organ for the internal deliberations necessary to define their goals and place within the wider society. Lippard launched his *Quaker City* as a repository of his legends, stories, and social commentary, but it failed after "some internal difficulties—perhaps dissensions." In July 1851, he launched what he intended to be a more irregularly published periodical, the *White Banner,* but apparently managed only one volume of yet another essentially personal organ.[19]

As with contemporary European societies, the Brotherhood mingled a romantic nationalism and the sentimental idea of the United States as "the Palestine of Redeemed Labor." "America was set apart by God as the Palestine of all the poor," wrote Lippard. "His Providence proclaimed at the proper time to the sick and suffering of all races, a new Exodus." He named its inner circle of officers Chiefs Washington, Jefferson, Franklin, Wayne, Fulton, and Girard. In the initiation ceremony, the Chief Washington of the local group drew a circle around the initiate with a sword, offering the protection of the order. The parable of the rods displayed the weakness of "a solitary Son of Labor" and their strength in numbers. The order presented a succession of thinkers from Moses to Washington as "believers in the H. F." and shared with the initiate "the grip, sign and passwords of the Brotherhood." At this point, the older Executive Washington arrived "clad in the garments of poverty and labor" to demonstrate that "the power sometimes resides under the sackcloth robe of Poverty." In one case, the order noted that Revolutionary War general Anthony Wayne's sword was "now in possession of 'Humanity Circle'" and being used in its ceremonies.[20]

Membership required that they "not interfere as a Brotherhood with the *party politics,* or *sectional* or *sectarian* questions of the day." Lippard hoped not "to add another *sect* or *party,* to the ten thousand which already divide mankind," and hoped to make the order "an organization of men of all creeds, sects and nationalities." At some point, "when all Brothers of the Union are fully indoctrinated with the Truths of the B.G.C. the *general plan of action* will not be difficult to find." The first national convocation of the Supreme Circle of the Brotherhood of the Union determined that it would not, "by any pretense or by any subterfuge, be forced into the Maelstrom of politics" or "take any part in the sectional questions of the day."[21] He believed that, at least in the United States, an order need not be directly oppositional and could best advance its goals by attaining respectability.

In some respects, this position dragged rather than led the dynamics of American labor reform. The U.S. war on Mexico placed slavery, its expansion, and the dominance of the southern Democratic policies on the agenda. In response, the land reformers and the abolitionist Liberty Party fielded joint "Free Soil" tickets in New York and Massachusetts in 1846 and 1847. These candidates claimed enough support to exercise a critical balance of power. While politicians sought to launch a national Free Soil Party, the radicals' National Industrial Congresses of 1847 and 1848 voted for an explicitly radical presidential ticket headed by abolitionist Gerrit Smith.[22] Radicals might well have shared a hope that America could become a "Palestine of Redeemed Labor," but only through opposition to expansion and slavery, as well as economic injustices to whites.

Rhetoric aside, Lippard wound up supporting the 1848 Whig presidential campaign, based on Gen. Zachary Taylor's military career and assumptions of national destiny mystical enough to have impressed any of Mazzini's followers. In *Adonai,* Lippard sketches the story of a resurrected early Christian, joined by the spirit of George Washington, to vanquish the evil of Satan himself. The "Risen Washington" transcends even sainted humanity to perform the role of a lesser deity. Moreover, "the Gospel of the Rifle" proclaimed this religion.[23] Although often seen as a demonstration of Lippard's militancy on behalf of working people, it is set not in the squalor of a city but on the frontier, where the rifle would proclaim its gospel not to the bosses but to Indians and Mexicans.

That messianic nationalism erupted to the surface of Lippard's writings on Mexico. In addition to his *Bel of Prairie Eden: A Romance of Mexico* (1848), his *Legends of Mexico; or, The Battles of Old Rough and Ready* (1849) revisited his earlier and very popular *Washington and His Generals* (1847). Particularly in the last two of these books, Anglo-Saxon Protestants strove to advance civilization, while the dehumanized brutes who opposed them failed to understand what was good for them. Lippard's publications also carried regular contributions by Jane Maria Eliza Storms Cazneau, who, as "Cora Montgomery," advocated a ruthlessly expansionist stance toward Mexico, Cuba, and Haiti.[24]

The Brotherhood of the Union claimed to be "the only actually American Order in the World." Lippard believed that "the American continent should be the homestead of the free, the Palestine of redeemed labor," reflecting the often radical social aspirations of militants of the growing working class. However, it also jibed with the southern and Democratic advocacy of an aggressive American expansionism, aimed at neighboring Indians or Spanish-speaking Catholic nations like Cuba or Mexico, which offered Anglo entrepreneurs the romance of individual riches and adventure. In "The Globe, the Sun, and Rosy Cross," Lippard spoke of "the Empire City," New York, as the center of "an empire no less bewildering in the suddenness of its growth than in the god-like glory—or yet the awful gloom—of its Future." Then, too, Charles Goepp and Theodore Poesche offered their appreciation in *The New Rome; or, The United States of the World.*[25] In this light, expansion generously made more peoples beneficiaries of American standards.

Being conquered by the republic-empire of the "New Rome" brought order, modernization, and the "human progress" that the order advocated. In "A Sequel to the Legends of Mexico," Lippard transformed Taylor's army into an imaginary modernizing force. In his mind's eye, he saw legions of marching men with the tools of construction gangs on their shoulders. What he envisioned as "the Industrial Army" would subject social labor to "severe military discipline" to transform the lands it acquired by force of arms from Mexico with irrigation and agriculture.[26] This scenario contained not only an implicit endorsement of the U.S. invasion of Mexico but also a sense of what he seems to have seen as the ultimately positive impact of American military power as a modernizing force.

Not surprisingly, perhaps, the messianic nationalism of the order also inspired the Nativist adherents of the American Party, suspicious of immigrants, Catholics, and, especially, the Irish. Although Lippard and the order had some ties to German immigrants, he had dedicated the first edition of *Monks of Monks Hall* to Nativist writer and politician Augustus Joseph Hickey Duganne. Evan as *Monks Hall* electrified readers with its portrayal of secret criminal societies, Duganne's *Knights of the Seal* offered a fanciful portrait of organized political conspiracies, in part implying that immigrant organizations represented a threat, while Nativist secret societies could thwart that threat.[27]

The Brotherhood's insistence on a national character embraced the standard requirements that tied the Jacksonian Democratic coalition of Lippard's father to the white gentlemen of the slaveholding South. The Brotherhood aspired the unity of "all true men—all the men who desire and are willing to work for Human Progress—from Maine to Texas, aye from the Atlantic to the Pacific."[28] In short, the order chose not to embrace any standards that would alienate the South.

Lippard also exaggerated the order's strength in the South to emphasize its national character. He boasted of its circles' presence in Alabama, Arkansas, Texas, Maryland, the District of Columbia, Virginia, Kentucky, and Tennessee, with new groups recently forming in the last three. From January through early April 1853, Lippard rested his hope for the order's future on the slaveholding states. His journal recorded the activities at Washington, D.C., and Virginia, and five of the last six circles he organized were in the South, the last, on July 8, being Circle No. 200 at Laurel in Maryland.[29]

In contrast, the Brotherhood, as such, avoided associating with abolitionism, which reflected Lippard's own ambivalence over slavery. "We are opposed to slavery of all kinds, shapes and colors," he insisted, but only as a prelude to asserting that many social wrongs eclipsed it. Without comment, he published Cora Montgomery's assertion that "African Slavery is a light stain compared with our Indian policy." He himself wrote, "Multiply the evils of Black Slavery by ten thousand, and they will not parallel the wrongs and atrocities committed by England upon her White Slaves."[30]

Riding the popularity of *Uncle Tom's Cabin*, Lippard wrote an antislavery novel, but the Brotherhood's orientation to "true men" that included slaveholders implicitly excluded blacks. In the spring of 1852, Heman Burr took Lippard, in a singular trip into the South, for a dinner at the Odd Fellows' Lodge at Fredericksburg, Virginia. Murmurings about his views moved Lippard to rise during the offering of sentiments and offer his own with a characteristically dramatic flair: "Here's to the revolving pistol. The best antidote to a Northern scoundrel who meddles with the opinions of a Southern gentleman upon slavery while traveling in the North; and as equally good course of treatment for a Southern blackguard who interferes with the sentiments of a Northerner while a guest of the South." Remarkably cited after his death as an alleged demonstration of hostility to slavery, the tale actually asserts his belief that being a good "guest" in the South required white silence on slavery, even as abolitionists should not verbally "meddle" with the self-esteem of a slaveholder traveling in the North.[31] Such unconcern about slavery, slaves, or abolitionists was the kind of silent antislavery which no slaveholder could actually resent.

This orientation actually required Lippard to tone down radicalism in general within the order. *Quaker City*'s obituary for Baltimore brother Samuel L. Detwiler, who had gone to California, praised him as "a hater of humbugs in politics, and cant in religion." He had "gifts of oratory, for one with no educational advantages, while compelled to toil daily for his bread at his business as a machinist," but the uppity machinist had wanted "to run too fast—to tear down too rapidly—to demolish in a moment." Lippard also published an essay decrying the kind of "Ultra-Democracy" that extended into "uninterrupted brigandage."[32]

Lippard dismissed interest existing in "factions, parties, Presidential electors, or spasmodic Reform societies" as the work of "brawling *Negative* Reformers who pull down, but never attempt to create or build up." Instead, he turned to battling "lukewarmness and treachery within" the Brotherhood. Like many, he regarded the agitation of abolition as strictly such a negative measure and advised members to "have nothing to do with so-called Industrial Congresses and Legislatures" at just the point when these groups had taken up antislavery politics and begun to associate publicly with black workers. He particularly called "a farce" the 1852 National Industrial Congress at Washington, chaired by abolitionist congressman Charles Durkee. For the Brotherhood's founder, far-reaching resolutions for specific radical measures seemed "fragmentary; they feed the masses with sawdust."[33]

On the other hand, there is no indication that Lippard ever directed such criticisms to those circles of the Brotherhood closely identified with the Democratic Party, and such associations emerged more readily as the order expanded. The "Rainbow Circle" of Portsmouth, Ohio—the lowest numbered (Circle No. 121) and likely the oldest in the area—included a range of members. Benjamin Work, one of the old masterminds behind the Portsmouth Mechanics Institute, and John H. J. Friar, who ran for marshal in 1857 as an independent, joined the circle. However, its most well-known members were William P. Camden and Jesse J. Appler, both prominent local Democratic leaders.[34]

Despite Lippard's protestations and occasional independence, very little he did directly and systematically challenged the Democratic Party, per se. In a prolonged stint in New York, he served as the literary editor for the man who had performed his marriage ceremony, Charles Chauncey Burr, who ran the *National Democrat,* and Lippard also boarded with his brother, Heman. The author regularly praised politically connected partisan writers, as when he noted the presence at Towanda of "our friend" John Wein Forney, a partisan Democratic editor.[35] Many members may not have realized it, but any organization embracing "all creeds, sects and nationalities" in "every part of the Union" had to reject the impulse "to tear down too rapidly—to demolish in a moment" injustices such as slavery.

FREE DEMOCRATIC TEMPTATIONS

Lippard's Brotherhood took no disciplined approach to politics, and the radical land reformers and socialists in and around the order remained undistracted by its ambiguities. For them, the society was but one of a number of manifestations of the movement, and their annual National Industrial Congresses of 1849, 1850, and 1851 at, respectively, Cincinnati, Chicago, and Albany pursued a trajectory of their own. Their resolutions reached beyond land reform to advocate the shorter workday, cooperatives, and the equality of women. Increasingly, they took explicitly antislavery positions and discussed resistance to the Fugitive Slave Law. Indeed, the last of these congresses seated a black delegate, representing an African American housing cooperative, and that of 1855 chose a black newspaper editor to serve as one of its officers.[36]

Conversely, abolitionists had incrementally broadened their platform to include land and labor reform. The *National Era* realized that "we, who are ourselves under the ban of good society, as incendiaries and fanatics are not ready to cast the same unmeaning epithets on those who apply our own principles to other objects." It expressed confidence that "the disfranchised in our country, immigrants, women, and colored men, will feel that our cause is theirs, so soon as we make their cause ours." Most substantively, the *National Era* asked whether abolitionists were more likely to fine reliable recruits and allies "among the holders and minions of power, or among its victims."[37]

The *National Era* believed this required more than more protest voting and urged the formation of a "League of Freedom." As the presidential elections approached, it revived its call, adopting Masonic terms for proposed local, state, and General Lodges. It suggested avoiding the pitfalls of an independent party or direct action by simply soliciting a written pledge not to vote for any candidates who did not favor repeal of the Fugitive Slave Law, trial by jury of anyone claimed as a fugitive, a ban of slavery in the territories and the District of Columbia, and no further extension of slavery.[38]

From May into August 1852, known working-class radicals of New York's Ouvrier Circle badgered the existing parties over a homestead bill. Democratic presidential candidate Franklin Pierce heard not only from several parts of the movement but also from New York Democrats who sent him a confidential report. It estimated that six thousand votes turned on the question in the state and warned of Whig inroads into "a large and secret state organization of Mechanics," likely meaning the Mechanics' Mutual Protection Association. The party's national leaders, however, even ignored its own supporters, and working-class discontent exploded late in the summer at a series of mass meetings. These took place at the Military Hall on Bowery and Spring, where some had been going for more than twenty years when it regularly hosted gatherings of the Workingmen's Party.[39]

These meetings reflected not only the prominence of Ouvrier members but also its inability to provide coherent leadership to the grassroots. Ira Davis stuck to the Democrats and avoided the meetings, leaving Parsons Day alone to single-handedly defend Pierce before their old comrades. However, even Day capitulated when the Democratic vice presidential candidate vociferously attacked the Homestead Bill and Senate Democrats defeated the measure, even as some Whigs such as William H. Seward and Benjamin F. Wade defended it. In response, Alvan E. Bovay (the NRA's former secretary), Lewis W. Ryckman, William West, and former Democratic editor Thomas A. Devyr urged them to use Winfield Scott's candidacy as "the club to bat Pierce's brains out with."[40]

More persuasively, though, the Free Democratic Party emerged from the shambles of the old Free Soil coalition as an increasingly strong alternative. Evans (the NRA's founder), Bailey, William V. Barr, and Dr. William J. Young, and other mainstays of the movement favored joining the radical antislavery party. As these meetings went on, several of the more prominent Ourvrier attended the city convention of "Independent Democrats," which passed land-reform resolutions and elected a delegation that included West, Young, and Lewis Masquerier under the leadership of Abraham Levy, a sometime ally of the movement. The best indications are that these meetings—and most of land reformers outside New York—went for the Free Democrats.[41]

The Free Democratic National Convention less resembled a major party gathering than a mass meeting. The two thousand participants who crammed into Pittsburgh's Masonic Hall included many members or associates of the Brotherhood such as Sheddon, Sherman M. Booth, Warren B. Chase, James H. Collins, and James H. Paine. Gerrit Smith submitted a minority report that not only made the most radical land-reform arguments but also expressed "our fraternal sympathies to the oppressed, not only of our own land, but of every other land." It also called for a "Democratic League" to be "organized in every part of the world." Delegates cast three votes to nominate Smith for president and three each for Collins and Evans as vice presidential candidates.[42] The ticket finally nominated—Senator John Parker Hale and Congressman George W. Julian—represented the most radical in an American presidential politics for a generation to come.

The Hale-Julian campaign posed the possibility of winning a more stridently radical voice in the nation's affairs than ever before. Certainly, the *American Whig Review* disparaged the new party as a mere quibble among Democrats, and Greeley's *New York Tribune* remained the partisan Whig operation it had been. Yet members at grassroots meetings and conventions across New England into distant Wisconsin established an organization they hoped would outlast the voting. Hale delivered this message to those in the Brotherhood of the Union active in the campaign at Philadelphia and New York City on October 27 and 28.[43] On one level, the Free Democrats politically expressed the values many associated with Lippard's order.

The Free Democrats did establish a presence in New York City. Many of those active at the Military Hall meetings over the Homestead Bill turned up at Free Democratic gatherings. In addition to those previously noted, Arnold Buffum and George W. Rose joined the local "Independent Democrats," as did some of the long-standing allies among the Democrats, such as Levy and Sanford E. Church. On the one hand, the new party energized Daniel Fanshaw, a printer who had been actively organizing his fellow craftsmen for nearly a half century and, on the other, Russell Thacher Trall, a physician and medical educator whose frank sexual advice would disturb the authorities for decades to come.[44]

Nor were the brothers in Lippard's own Philadelphia immune to the appeal of the Free Democrats. William B. Thomas, a member or ally of the order during its efforts to organize local seamstresses, presided over a June 1852 meeting at the courthouse of those opposed to Whig and Democratic parties. Principal speakers were Lippard, his fellow writers Duganne and Goepp, along with Sheddon. Mullen, another ally of the order, played prominent roles in the Pennsylvania Free Democratic State Convention at Pittsburgh, held quite literally at the threshold of the national convention. During the campaign itself, the press described Sheddon's stump speech as one that "will not soon be forgotten by the workingmen."[45]

In fact, however briefly, Lippard himself seems to have caught fire with the inspiration of the Free Democrats. Despite his abandonment of the more radical options four years before, he began talking in ever more radical terms himself. In October, the Supreme Circle assembled at Independence Hall to hear the clearest message Lippard ever gave about the order's political purpose. He deliberately addressed them "not as Brothers, but as citizens," advising them to "open your halls to the public of both sexes, for the purposes of listening to lectures, or of holding conversational meetings on Land, Labor, and Social Reform." He urged them "to charter a Grand Convocation in every county in the Union." Perhaps thinking of his own wife, daughters, and aunts, he suggested the "most earnest efforts to interest your wives, your sisters, and all the good women of our land, in our movement." He declared, "No order, no organization for any good purpose can succeed without the co-operation of the women of our land." Around this time, he even entertained the idea of starting a "Sisterhood of the Union."[46] Apparently, Lippard quickly found that such a course did not appeal to the gentlemen of standing and power he had hoped to recruit to the Brotherhood.

Indeed, the Free Democrats inspired radicals from New England into the Midwest. Cincinnati Fourierist and NRA spokesman Lucius Alonzo Hine took to the field for the new party. However, few radicals played a more prominent role for the Free Democrats than in Wisconsin, where Booth edited one of the most important papers in the state and Chase stood on the slate of presidential electors. In turn, Free Democratic congressman Durkee chaired the 1852 National Industrial Congress when it met at Washington.[47]

Despite Lippard's own dalliance with the insurgency, the overwhelming shift of the urban brothers to the Free Democrats forced him to scramble to reestablish the balance he believed to be the Brotherhood's proper role. The 1851 admission of a black delegate from Philadelphia to that year's National Industrial Congress and the chairing of the next year's by an abolitionist congressman were simply incompatible with an organization aspiring not to alienate any "true men . . . from Maine to Texas."

Those hostile to the Free Democrats tried to regain control of the movement's dynamic at the 1853 National Industrial Congress, hosted by the Wilmington circles of the Brotherhood of the Union. Robert B. McDonnell, an elderly Jacksonian and an Odd Fellow, battled to keep a land-reform constituency within the Democratic Party, in hopes of actually making "Delaware—A Model Agrarian Republic." While the earlier congresses had adopted increasingly radical resolutions, that of 1853 carefully avoided "any matter that does not legitimately belong to the object of the organization," which was to be "confined to the consideration of the subject of Land Reform."[48] Still, one year did not reverse the movement's dynamic so much as it left the Brotherhood of the Union increasingly marginalized.

* * *

To a great extent, the vicissitudes of the Brotherhood reflected Lippard's personal life and tragedies. He had encountered his demons enough to have become an ardent temperance man, the issue inspiring "the first, last, and only play we know of from the pen of Lippard." However, in quick succession, death took both of his little girls, Harriet (the second of his two sisters to die), and, in June 1851, his wife. In part, he dealt with his grief by wandering off into the West, where John Bell Bouton watched him at Cleveland and concluded, "Nothing, we believe, would have given him greater happiness (had he possessed the means) than to have traveled forever among the circles of the Union, helping the faltering, strengthening the backsliding, and establishing new circles, even to the remotest parts of the land."[49] Formulating a strategic orientation never seemed to enter into these aspirations.

Lippard embodied what historian David Montgomery calls a "sentimental reformer." As he sickened and faced his own death, Lippard chose a kind of internal exile that required a full-scale retreat from politics. Despite all the episodic concern about women's rights in October 1852, the next annual Grand Convocation of the Supreme Circle merely sanctioned the Home Communion as a ladies' auxiliary, comparable to those for the Masons and Odd Fellows. Shortly after, Lippard made his last entry in the Brotherhood's journal, one complaining of "an infamous circular supposed to have originated with John H. Wilson of Baltimore." On March 15, 1854, Orsimus L. Drake took up the document, unused for five months, to note Lippard's death earlier that day at the age of thirty-two. One admirer did not accept the story that consumption had claimed Lippard's life, but believed he had "died mysteriously either of suicide or *mania a potu*," that is, delirium tremens. Yet another writer in Philadelphia later told Walt Whitman that the "handsome, Byronic" Lippard "drank—drank—drank."[50] Either way, America, too, experienced the very early death of a brilliant and talented romantic writer, albeit one whose brilliance and talent did not lie primarily in politics.

2. UNIVERSAL DEMOCRATIC REPUBLICANS

Hugh Forbes and Transatlantic Antislavery Radicalism

By the end of 1854, Americans in both the Ouvrier Circle of the Brotherhood of the Union and the Free Democratic League joined a citywide federation of European émigrés in New York City, many still organized as they had been overseas. The loose coalition included a general Democratic Union of naturalized citizens, organizations of Cuban and Polish Democrats, French and Italian sections of the Universal Democratic Republicans (UDR), and the German Arbeiterbund, Freie Gemeide, and Turnerbund, that is, the overlapping organizations committed to socialism, free thought, and physical culture. At the fringes lurked individual Russians and even a Turk. One of its key officers also provided the link to "a small coterie of clever colored men," interested in the politics but nurturing what one white thought to be "a counter race contempt, antagonism, and rage" against Caucasions.[1]

The development galvanized, in America, an urban, plebeian current within the secret society tradition. The defeat of the 1848–49 revolutions abroad sent émigrés to the United States from many different nations with a common desire to universalize the claims to democratic rights and social justice. The result was an unprecedented and cosmopolitan new social radicalism that could accept African American aspirations for freedom, on the one hand, and repudiate the concept of national conquest and exploitation, on the other.

HUGH FORBES AND THE LEGACY OF 1848

Hugh Frederick Forbes, who masterminded this association, was himself never very forthcoming in supplementing the scanty records of his past. He was born in Scotland around 1808 and supposedly raised, in part, at Forbes

Castle, the seat of the powerful and well-positioned family of that name. Sources describe him as a wellborn "Etonian white-suited" Englishman, and he matriculated from Oxford in 1823 at the age of fifteen. *The University Calendar* in 1824–26 described him as a "gentleman commoner" of St. Mary Hall.[2]

Little is known of Forbes's next fifteen years. Family lore identified his first wife as Hester Hermes, and the *Army Lists* confirms his commission as ensign and lieutenant in the prestigious Coldstream Guards, dated July 11, 1826. A War Office memorandum of May 24, 1831, identified him as the second-ranking lieutenant in the regiment and his promotion: "Unattached—To be Captain, by purchase.—Ensign and Lieutenant Hugh Forbes, from the Coldstream Regiment of Foot Guards." Captain Forbes left the army after five years.[3]

In 1842 or 1843, Forbes went to Italy, where the Austrians, the French, the pope, and various local overlords maintained a piecemeal occupation of the nation. Before or after that move, he remarried, to one Laura Passarini (or Passerini), and entered the silk business at Siena, near where he later ran a mining company in the mountains. He also became involved in the clandestine revolutionary movement and "a co-operator with the patriots around him." When the February 1848 upheavals in Vienna and Paris detonated rebellions across the Continent, he left to participate with his son Hugh. "Being an Englishman, unless I had been thoroughly convinced of the justice of this Italian cause," he later wrote, "I should not have taken up arms in its defense—Such a course being opposed to my private interest; and I most certainly should never have allowed my eldest son to accompany me to the field."[4]

A half century after Filippo Buonarroti began his work in Italy, the fragmented nature of the country framed distinctive revolts in various theaters. Forbes entered the service of the Venitian revolution. He commanded 2,500 volunteers guarding a bridge over the River Piave to the northeast, as an Austrian force five or six times as big converged on them. After nine days of fighting depleted Forbes's men's ammunition, another Austrian force crossed the river upstream, and their superiors ordered them to fall back. As a member of the Military Council of Volunteers, he led one prong of the attack on the Lock of the Sile. After a short time with his family in Tuscany, Forbes was elected to the revolutionary military commission, recalled to duty, and sent to Sicily.[5]

Even before February, the Sicilians had risen against the Bourbon Kingdom of the Two Sicilies. By April, they overran Syracuse and offered the crown to the son of King Carlo Alberto of Sardinia-Piedmont. By May, Forbes helped defend Sicily against the overwhelming might of the old rulers. Meanwhile, agitation in the North had driven the Austrians into fortifications, from which they launched a military counteroffensive, contested by, among others, Giuseppe Garibaldi's small Italian Legion, which had fought the Argentine dictatorship in Latin America.[6] With the stakes so high, Forbes hurried to assist the Romans.

Nowhere did an Italian revolution face a more time-honored power structures than at Rome. There, a revolutionary constituent assembly declared the Papal States the new Roman Republic and drove Pope Pius IX into exile. Back in Siena, "a mob excited by the Jesuits" drove Mrs. Forbes and the children from their home. They hurried to Florence, where English diplomats refused to extend them the protection due them, and they were, "by force, made to go on foot through the street by the police," who essentially held them hostage.[7]

By early 1849, Garibaldi had joined the defenders. Forbes assumed local command when the Austrians attacked the defenders of Urbino against and managed their retreat south to Terni, north of Rome. When Forbes's force joined with the main republican army, he counted in Garibaldi's ranks 150 Poles and 40 French, with about a dozen Germans and Hungarians, a few Corsicans, "and four English," as well as Garibaldi's "negro servant" fighting for Italian liberty. Garibaldi, in turn, was clearly impressed by this "forceful, rich, cantankerous officer of forty-one," a "remarkable Englishman in a thin cotton suit and a white chimney-pot hat." Forbes took charge of training recruits, an experience that inspired his writing of the *Manual for the Patriotic Volunteer.* He saw a future of Europe "decided by the force of arms" and urged revolutionaries to adopt professional military standards rather than rely on inexperienced persons who believed that "mere decrees could create efficient officers."[8]

The defeat of the other continental uprisings doomed the Roman Republic. The Austrians forced the abdication of Carlo Alberto in favor of his son Vittorio Emanuele while the Bourbons in Sicily pounded the island into submission. Meanwhile, President Louis Napoleon Bonaparte of the new French Republic dispatched a force of nearly 30,000 to crush Rome. At noon on July 3, 1849, the Roman assembly adopted a constitution and proclaimed the new order, but the French entered the city by the end of the day. The English and American consuls issued passports to some republicans, and Giuseppe Mazzini—the firebrand agitator—slipped back into exile. However, Garibaldi and his men escaped to the north, joining Forbes's recruits at Terni on July 8. Reduced by desertions to 1,500, the combined column set off for Venice, the last holdout of the revolution. London readers of the *Times* noted the presence of Forbes "at the head of a body of partisans" with Garibaldi. Closely pursued, and hemorrhaging volunteers, only about 230 made it across the mountains, arriving on July 31 at San Marino, which required them to disband to satisfy the Austrians.[9]

The hope of Garibaldi, Forbes, and their comrades dissolved before them. From Cesenatico, they sailed for Venice, hoping to run the Austrian blockade, but the bright moonlight exposed them at the mouth of the Po. Garibaldi leaped overboard and swam to safety, while Forbes and others fell into Austrian hands. After the August 1849 capitulation of Venice, Forbes's wife and the British government helped negotiate his release in October, followed by that of the 160 others.[10]

Forbes's experience confirmed his revolutionary politics. The Florentine authorities allowed him to rejoin his family with "a guard put over him in his house." The London press then reported that they "ordered him to leave Tuscany." Again imprisoned at Genoa, Forbes gained release only in December. With William J. Linton, the Anglo-American diplomat, Forbes made his way to Lausanne, Switzerland, where he met Félix Pyat and other revolutionary leaders. There, "Mazzini and his associates of the Roman Triumvirate" urged him to go to New York and work among the émigrés there. Like other veterans of 1848–49, Forbes became very critical of privileged figures designated as representatives of the people, quipping that Carlo Alberto had gathered votes while the reactionaries gathered bayonets. More substantively, as he later wrote, the Italian people had risen not merely against "foreign foes" but against "the Royalist-Aristocratic-Jesuitical party, and of British diplomacy." At Paris, he met Lamennais, Herzen, and American abolitionist Maria Weston Chapman before continuing on to London, where he established associations that included the Fraternal Democrats and the most radical of the Chartists.[11] There, he raised enough money to get across the Atlantic.

This English Garibaldian traveled to the United States with thousands of other veterans of the European secret societies. Historian George M. Trevelyan wrote of Forbes, "His mental activity took many various directions. He was an engineer, and took out patents for inventions. He wrote poetry, and 'Catechisms' of a highly argumentative character, expressing his own private religion, which was of a Deistic character. Though a strong patriot, and actively connected with the English Volunteer movement, he was not incapable of calling certain sections of his countrymen 'the baptised Pharisees.' He was what is called 'an original.'" Trevelyan thought Forbes "not an altogether wise man, but he had incurred obloquy and laid waste his fortune and that of his large family on behalf of one generous cause after another," usually the sort where even "men who follow the beaten track of life shrink from connection with 'disreputable' associates and 'hopeless' undertakings."[12] This "original" would have a deep, pervasive, and virtually hidden influence at a particularly critical juncture in the history of American radicalism.

New York confronted the veterans of those societies with an entirely different situation than that which had fostered their secrecy, but this was only one aspect of the problem. Forbes found the Italians not only facing isolation by language and by Nativist hostility but also subject, like the Irish, to the reactionary politics of the Roman Catholic hierarchy. Forbes challenged "the intolerance of Popery" on behalf of his comrades less facile in English. When Archbishop John Hughes of New York denounced the "intemperate and untimely zeal for freedom" in 1848–49, Forbes replied in his *Answer to Archbishop Hughes*, followed with *A Few Words on Popery and Despotism* and, in March 1851, *Four Lectures upon Recent Events in Italy*. The abolitionist *Independent* reviewed the latter as written by "a devoted actor in the Italic revolution," who "has had the very best opportunities to know." Theodore Dwight wrote Forbes a letter of introduction when he shifted his operations to New York, recommending him as "my esteemed friend, and the friend of America and of mankind, in my estimation." The *Tribune* thought it noteworthy when Forbes "commenced a tour in the interior of the State of New York . . . under the auspices of Mazzini and other friends of Italian Liberty."[13]

Forbes found not only thousands of other European émigrés there, eager to cooperate with each other, but Americans equally interested in an internationalist radicalism. For a generation, American radicals saw their efforts as part of a broad movement for progress and justice. In turn, *Quaker City* carried material on the French and Italian revolutions. By the end of 1849, assemblies of the Brotherhood of the Union embraced the insurgent forces in Europe as their own, offering toasts to "*Kossuth, Louis Blanc, Ledru Rollin, Jules Lechevalier, Mazzini*—the heroes and apostles of Brotherhood in the Old World."[14]

When the British Chartists made another effort at reorganization, they invited an American "mission of brotherhood" to a "World's Industrial Congress." In February 1851, the New York City Industrial Congress assigned Parsons E. Day to represent them. A descendant of Joseph Warren of Bunker Hill fame, Day met "with inventors, clubs, trade societies, labour associations, &c." Alongside him, radical émigrés from the Continent also pushed the Chartists toward some international alliance.[15] This came to fruition a few years later when members of the Ouvrier Circle entered a coalition of sorts with revolutionary émigrés living in New York City.

REPUBLICAN INTERNATIONALISM IN THE EMPIRE CITY

In the fall of 1853—almost the same time Lippard chartered his last circle of the Brotherhood—Forbes put together a coalition of émigrés of various nationalities in New York. Earlier that summer, a band of Greeks employed by the

Austrians seized Martin Koszta in the city of Smyrna, then controlled by the Ottoman Turks. A Hungarian who had come to America in 1850 and declared his intention of becoming a citizen, Koszta was put in irons and held aboard the Austrian warship *Hussar*. On July 2, U.S. Naval Commander Duncan Nathaniel Ingraham moved his *St. Louis* alongside the Austrian ship, cleared his decks for action, and warned the Austrians to release Koszta by the end of the day or face a storming party. Forbes and other old enemies of the Austrians followed the example of their London counterparts by organizing an "Ingraham Committee" to present the South Carolina–born Ingraham with a medal of appreciation. Early in 1854, the French hosted an anniversary celebration of the February revolution attended by the Americans; the Germans, Italians, Hungarians, Cubans, and Poles who had participated; "that rarity, a Russian Democrat," Ivan Golovin; and a growing number of English Chartists, including Wemyss Jobson, the former dentist to the British royal family, who spoke on "the Secret History and Policy of the English Government."[16]

The Germans have a special prominence in the scholarship, but the French organizations may have been larger and certainly had many prominent revolutionary figures among them. Among the many revolutionary leaders who washed up in Gotham was Marc Caussidiére. A veteran of the old Sociéte des Droits de l'Homme, he had been sentenced to prison twenty years earlier. Yet the revolution of 1848 had swept him into government as prefect of police. After he resisted the crackdown on the workers in the June Days, he faced further political prosecutions.[17]

Garibaldi himself took up residence among the Italians. After arriving in New York, he attended political meetings of Forbes's association but maintained a remarkably low profile and kept his attention focused mostly on affairs back in Europe.[18] Surely, too, Garibaldi had confidence that his old comrade would perform the duties of an English-speaking advocate in America.

As the Europeans organized themselves in New York City, Senator John Parker Hale turned up for a banquet in his honor hosted by the city's new Free Democratic League and, while there, addressed a rally of the émigrés. Neither he, such episodic Democratic allies as John Cochrane, nor any other Americans balked at mounting a platform on which the Stars and Stripes stood beside "the French Red Republican flag" of the Union Socialiste. At one of these meetings, shoemaker Bernard Paul Ernest "Honeste" Saint-Gaudens described it as "the symbol of the solidarity and fraternity of nations. The Carpenter of Nazareth had been clothed with ignominy for having protested against the yoke of the Caesars, and for preaching universal Justice, Liberty and Fraternity against iniquity and despotisms; and as a barrage of ignominy they had placed on him a red mantle. It was the banner which had often been with the people against the power of feudality."[19]

American developments placed unexpected demands on the émigrés. The Free Democrats continued to strive for organization in New York. It held state conventions in February and September 1853. Participants included radical feminists like Antoinette Brown and black abolitionists such as Frederick Douglass, as well as local radical Democrats such as Sanford E. Church. Out-of-state visitors included Senators Hale and Henry Wilson. Douglass closed one session by singing the Hutchinson Family song "There's a Good Time a-Comin.'"[20]

Within days of the September state convention, the Free Democrats at New York City decided to follow the examples of Lockport and Niagara County in launching the Free Democratic League. After some preliminary meetings in John Jay's law office on Nassau Street, the group moved into the Stuyvesant Institute. With Hale and Wilson as observers, participants included bricklayer-turned-historian Henry B. Dawson, as well as George W. Rose, David Marsh, J. E. Snodgrass, and William West, who were members of the Ouvrier Circle of the Brotherhood of the Union or the Universal Democratic Republicans. They secured explicit land-reform resolutions "to encourage emigration from abroad and to provide homes for the homeless, by free grants to actual settlers, in the public domain at the West." The radicals were nominated for office by the league and nearly secured a resolution for a Free Democratic newspaper.[21]

The two-party system in the U.S. Congress dealt itself a final blow with the Kansas-Nebraska Act, establishing the new Kansas Territory that had the option to admit slavery there by a simple vote of the settlers. That February, former NRA secretary Alvan E. Bovay organized meetings at the former socialist community of the Wisconsin phalanx at Ceresco, recently renamed Ripon, calling for a new party around opposition to the bipartisan concession. In Wisconsin, Michigan, and the Midwest generally, the new party began to subsume the Free Democrats into a much broader political movement, but New York's "anti-Nebraska" coalition voted to merge with the remnants of the Whig Party, took on a Nativist coloration, and even declined to affiliate with the national third-party movement. With an eye back to the city, Bovay had proposed "a cherished name with our foreign population of every nationality. They call themselves *Republicans, Republicains, Republikaner, Republicanos*—or by some modification of it in all European countries, and this name meets them here like an old friend."[22] However, conditions in New York made the Republicans initially a less savory option than the Free Democrats.

In April 1854, the German *Freie Gemeide* proposed "a general union of Liberal Societies." Forbes reported to the UDR that the new union would "compare the platforms and candidates of all parties, without being the slave of any," a process with "ramifications from Maine to Texas." This conference expanded into a broad "Union of Liberal Societies," which declared, "The object of this confederation is a radical reformation both in Government and Society in the interest of Liberty, which must lead to the enjoyment and happiness in life in which all are equally entitled." Two seats on the Central Committee required an organization of fifty members, and each additional fifty got another delegate. They also projected a national Central Directory to combine the efforts of radicals in diverse parts of the United States.[23]

By early 1854, the Universal Democratic Republicans formed the core of this union of "liberal societies." The listed participants included both the "Free Democratic League.—(Americans, opposed to the Extension of Slavery.)" and the "Ouvrier Circle.—(American workmen.)."[24] Given that the personnel of these groups overlapped, the Brotherhood of the Union in New York saw itself alongside the revolutionary secret societies of Europe and their successors and, in an American context, as part of the radical wing of the antislavery movement.

This coalition addressed American politics on its own. That July, it recommended Forbes's *Manual for the Patriotic Volunteer* as "indispensable for the Revolutionists" and endorsed the view of American politics reflected in Forbes's "Catechism" that described the Democrats and Whigs as existing "to procure public occupation in the diplomatic service, custom house, post office, treasury, patent office, land office, municipality, police, or any other where salary and profit can be enjoyed," and to preserve slavery. Forbes praised the Free Democrats (and later editions said the same for the Republicans) for their opposition to the two-party system but expected that "substituting themselves, is too great a temptation not to bring corruption." That is, Forbes argued, the price of governing would be placating the powers that be. Brushing the rhetoric of liberty aside, he found "little sympathy in America for the European liberals, because the praise of revolution, and liberty, and progress, must naturally be distasteful to the upholders of slavery." The abolitionist *Independent* not only praised the *Manual* for its contribution to "the oppressed peoples of Europe" but also reported that "a few copies have gone to Kansas." Forbes also serialized his report for the group on social conditions in the United States.[25]

While resolutions expressed political intentions, practical politics often seemed to divide them. Even if the antislavery position was sincere, there remained the question of what emphasis people in a city that did not have slavery should place on it. When Forbes chaired a meeting to prepare circulars "to enter into communication with all such as seek liberty and progress" beyond New York, they thought it essential to avoid "those false Liberal societies, which, under captivating names, assumed merely to deceive, have in view to secure a place for their partisans, at the expense of public morality and the public weal." When Kansas came up, Dr. Louis Szpaczek of the Polish Democrats "objected to any interference with the domestic politics of the United States, which had received them with hospitality as exiles and wanderers." Among the others who replied, Forbes declared "opposition to despotic measures and men on this side of the Atlantic" to be "a service rendered to the cause of freedom universally."[26] Many remained to be persuaded.

The actual conflict in Kansas began demanding the attentions of the Europeans at New York. Forbes argued persuasively that "every extension of Slavery is perilous to Republican Liberty," because it also deprived "the free settler" of a voice in government. However, what others of the UDR found objectionable about the Kansas-Nebraska Act was the fact that it lacked a provision clarifying the right of citizenship in those territories. The body also gave priority to an address responding to appeals for support from their comrades "and the several Liberal Societies in Europe." In September 1854, the appearance of three warships of Napoleon III visiting New York inspired the French societies to charter a steamboat in order to go out into the harbor waving a large red flag, singing revolutionary songs, and unfurling a banner proclaiming "Égalité, Fraternité, Liberté, Solidarité!"[27] In short, events of greater gravity or closer to home would have to focus the antislavery energies of the émigrés.

Nevertheless, these gatherings of revolutionaries often included Democratic partisans. Radicals met beneath not only the Stars and Stripes, the red flag, and the banners of the various European nationalists but also a Lone Star flag "and the banner of the Cuban Junta." In America, aspirations for the liberation of Cuba became inexorably intertwined with the cause célèbre of the southern faction of the Democratic Party, which had its own version of what that liberation would entail.[28] This incongruous association of republican radicalism with what amounted to the conquest and assimilation of Cuba underscored the deep ambiguities at the heart of nineteenth-century American nationalism.

Under the leadership of old-school Democrats such as Capt. Isaiah Rynders, the issue of Cuba united local Democratic rivals such as Tammany Hall and the Irish-based Spartan Band and nationally became the cause célèbre of the southern faction of the party. Other participants included Dr. John V. Wren, also of the Order of the Lone Star, and Daniel Sickles, who had a hand in snubbing the English government, even as he, Gideon J. Tucker, and other local politicians courted the land reformers in the local Industrial Congress.[29] Such officeholders and office-seekers sought to translate revolutionary sentiments into expansionist aspirations.

Democrats in New York had always made a particularly strong effort to recover their credibility among the working-class land reformers. Reactions to the local ascendancy of Nativism in the city muddied responses, as when "Colonel" Alexander Ming (wed to an Irish Catholic) became so disgusted with those who "disgrace the American flag" with their narrow-mindedness that he returned to the Democratic Party. So, too, the bluenose threat to prohibit alcoholic beverages tended to drive the Germans back to the Democratic Party. Hoping for more such reactions, Cochrane, a reform Democrat, enlisted Lippard's old Democratic allies John W. Forney and Thomas B. Florence for an 1855 meeting at Tammany that would hopefully repair the breach with the land reformers.[30]

At one time, the broader radical coalition discussed holding "a weekly Convention till the elections shall have taken place," but West, Ira B. Davis, William Arbuthnot, and some members of the Ouvrier Circle had already taken action. On October 4, Davis presided over a rally of about four hundred "Practical Democrats" after work in the park. After calling for independent political action, the group resolved almost immediately to question those candidates already running. A week later, Davis invited the international organizations to participate in the Practical Democrats. Other members of the Brotherhood of the Union mentioned in connection with these activities were Price, West, Marsh, Keyes Arthur Bailey, Joshua K. Ingalls, William J. Young, William V. Barr, and John Commerford, though numerous other veteran land reformers and Fourierists may well have also been in the Ouvrier Circle. Even the hostile *Herald* acknowledged theirs to be "an organization of some importance." Along with Price, Donald C. Henderson, and William Rowe, they revived the application of NRA principles to municipal reforms.[31] Davis, at this point, may have had a position in the city government himself, which might explain how the Practical Democrats wound up supporting John Wheeler, a Democrat, for Congress.

At the next meeting of the Liberal Societies, Forbes agreed with Davis's position that they should question candidates but insisted that slavery should head the list "as being the most important." Should a candidate not answer that question satisfactorily, argued Forbes, it would be "useless further to question any candidate for the Legislature." Davis disagreed, declaring himself "opposed to Slavery, but wished this question, for the present to be set aside," and his comrade Arbuthnot also "went for the total abolition of all Slavery, but was for deferring, for the present, the particular question of Negro Slavery in the South." After "a protracted discussion," all but two gave priority "to the question of Slavery."[32]

After the election, Davis and the Practical Democrats sought to organize the unemployed. A December 21 rally in the cold outdoors "numbered only a few hundred" but passed land-reform resolutions "without dissent." Young urged the workers to take united political action and "cared not whether they were born in America or in Africa, in Ireland or in Russia," he added. A later rally "numbered at least a thousand persons" braving the cold before taking up the offer of the large hall of the Chinese Assembly Rooms for meetings that began right after Christmas. The incoming mayor, Fernando Wood, ignored their proposal but promised "a plan of my own for the relief of the unemployed workingmen." Into the new year, this attempted movement of the unemployed drew some of the existing trade unions into its agitation for local land reform and its initial exploration of the plans of Edward N. Kellogg for social change through government reform of the currency, an idea that would resurface almost twenty years later as "Greenbackism."[33]

Forbes and Davis battled over direction of the internationalist coalition. Davis encouraged resolutions against a rising Nativist and prohibitionist threat, after which Arbuthnot noted that the antislavery candidates sometimes also favored Prohibition. Forbes, Davis, and Kaufman, a member of the German Turnerbund, formed a committee on platform, which assigned Forbes to "report on the condition of the laboring classes, and the origins of the present distress." At the end of February 1855, Forbes presented his report to what seems to have been a meeting of the platform committee. Despite agreement on many questions, Arbuthnot objected to Forbes's skepticism as to the long-term value of land reform, but the real issue, the primacy of abolitionism, remained unresolved as the fall elections rolled around in 1855. Davis, Bailey, and others of the Ouvrier Circle sponsored a rally of "about 300 persons" to rebuild the Practical Democrats, but many immigrants, particularly Germans, shared their lack of interest in an antislavery party.[34]

The initial course of the early Republican Party in New York hardly encouraged either of these currents. The party's origins in the state had been in an August 1854 statewide protest meeting called to order by NRA veteran and Free Democrat Calvin Pepper; almost alone, Pepper had "opposed a fusion" with the Whigs. The meeting did schedule a September political convention at Auburn to launched a statewide Whig-dominated anti-Nebraska coalition. Its failure even to mention the land question or affiliate immediately with the new Republican Party sparked a radical walkout led by land reformer Leonard Gibbs and others. When a Republican State Convention finally took place a year later, the well-established and tightly led former Whigs and Americans dominated the party and accorded little prominence to the antislavery or reform features emphasized in the Midwest.[35]

Individual NRA veterans joined Pepper and Gibbs in the arduous task of enlisting working-class support for the new party. Jacob Seaman and William H. Fry participated in the 1855 founding Republican meetings on the Lower East Side, while J. H. Tobitt, Freeman Hunt, and Watson G. Haynes participated in launching the party in Brooklyn.[36] Nevertheless, the Republican Party in the state remained a hard sell for radicals of any sort.

Although New York City's Free Democratic League would later recast itself as a precursor of the Republican Party, it initially remained markedly skeptical of the state's early anti-Nebraska coalition. The Free Democrats remained militantly antislavery, and its last state conventions had declared "a natural right to a portion of the soil, and that . . . the use of the soil is as sacred as their right to life itself." Moreover, "The Public Lands of the United States belong to the people, and should not be sold to individuals nor granted to corporations, but should be held as the sacred trust for the benefit of the people, and should be granted in limited quantities, free of cost, to landless settlers." Still, by August 1855, most of the Free Democratic League saw few means of attaining such goals without the Republicans.[37]

Some of the most diehard of the Free Democrats remained determined to make their point. In March 1855, William Goodell, the fifteen-year editor of the *Friend of Man*, reorganized the abolitionist New York Anti-Slavery Society, followed in October by the American Abolition Society. Goodell shared the thinking of Lysander Spooner and others that the early abolitionists and the Republicans had erred in accepting the constitutionality of slavery. On June 26–29, he brought together a racially mixed body that included Dr. James McCune Smith, Gerrit Smith, C. C. Foote, and others at a national convention at Syracuse that launched the Radical Abolition Party.[38]

Forbes's radical coalition at New York hovered on the fringes of both the Free Democrats and the Radical Abolitionists. Some sources indicate that, at this time, he also served on the central committee of a London-based attempt to build an International Association among the émigré radicals. New York's Brotherhood of the Union had this milieu in which to survive, though the order imploded almost everywhere after George Lippard's death.[39] Politics within the United States proved more challenging.

Despite everything, the national trend among radicals beyond New York heavily favored the Republican Party. The 1855 National Industrial Congress (NIC) carried the point even further when "persons favorable to the Land and other cognate reforms" entered Cleveland's Sons of Temperance Hall for the

NIC's tenth session on Wednesday, June 6, 1855. An active milieu of literary reformers had made the city Lippard's favorite western community. Since 1842, John Brainerd had issued the *Farmers' and Mechanics' Journal* with C. T. Blakeslee at nearby Chagrin Falls, passing it on in 1844 to Cleveland, where H. E. Calkins changed its name to the *Spirit of Freedom,* soon transformed by the "Laboring Men's Association" into the *Laborer.* John Bell Bouton, a Dartmouth graduate and lawyer-turned-newspaperman, became the editor of the *Plain Dealer* in 1851. With Brainerd, Bouton gained fame as one of the literary men of the new Midwest.[40]

As well, German émigrés established a succession of organizations that reached into the region. Most notably, Wilhelm Weitling's Arbeiterbund and a succession of similarly named associations led by Joseph Weydemeyer sustaining pro-NRA newspapers like *Der Kommunist* and *Waechter am Erie.* The Brotherhood of the Union publicized the work of these German socialists among English-speaking radicals.[41]

That fall of 1855, Davis got the more skeptical members of the Ouvrier Circle to launch an "American Democratic Party" that shared neither the Nativism of the American Party nor the Democratic partisanship of Tammany or Mozart Hall. In September, it literally battled Nativist rowdies to maintain control of its second mass meeting. Bailey and George joined the group, which provided a platform to émigré Germans. The "party" opposed the effort to prohibit alcohol in the city, private contracts for public works projects, and changes in the naturalization law. They favored local autonomy for the municipality, frugality in city government spending, and cooperative protective unions; it also argued that the government "should enact laws making it criminal to defraud working people out of their just wages for labor performed." Last, but not least, it urged land reform, proposing in particular that the city construct its own buildings to rent cheaply to the landless. They resolved that "for these objects, vital alike to humanity and the Republic, we are ready to unite with all men under whatever name or organization."[42]

* * *

Events would clarify this contradiction not only in New York but in many localities, including the far southwestern border, along the Rio Grande valley. According to some accounts, Juan Nepomuceno Cortina, who rallied a Mexican resistance to the Anglo occupation, formed a new secret society within the older Defensores de la Patria. Said to be called La Unificacion de la Raza or La Santa Raza Unida or just La Raza Unida, it offered a local version of Mazzini's national brotherhood. While the established Chicano families tended to accommodate the Anglos, likely to secure what they could of their land, wealth, and power, some quietly encouraged the popular resistance, which, as one Texas paper noted, rested on "the class known as *pelados,* or *ladrones,* who can be governed only by an iron rod—by force and fear—as much to be dreaded by every American, as they are and always have been by every good Mexican." The movement of local flavor owed much to the mysticism and spiritualism of local healers, *curanderos,* and the imagery of the Virgin of Guadalupe.[43] It would become a strange foil for the bizarre apparition on the Rio Grande of the remarkably famous, bastardized version of Lippard's Brotherhood.

At the same time, some associates of the Brotherhood of the Union participated in several ill-fated ventures to liberate other countries. Richardson Hardy and John McCann of Cincinnati's cooperative *Nonpareil* had helped to organize Kentucky volunteers in the 1850–51 Cuban campaign, with the latter also serving as their chaplain. A young Mississippi printer named John Moore marched with his newspaper colleagues, singing to the tune of "Oh, Susanna":

> Oh Cuba, Cuba
> > Is the Land for me.
> I'm bound to make some money there!
> > And set the Cubans free!

McCann also presided over Moore's funeral, after the Mississippian accidentally cut short his ambitions by shooting himself with a musket.[44] At its root, a messianic nationalism had opened the possibility of conquest in the name of liberation, the conflation of spreading freedom with making money.

George Lippard. The Gothic writer whose idealization of American values formed the foundation of the Brotherhood of the Union, an American order roughly analogous to the revolutionary nationalism of early European secret societies. Source: Ellis Paxson Oberholtzer, *The Literary History of Philadelphia* (Philadelphia: George W. Jacobs, 1906).

Hugh Forbes. The English Garibaldian and adviser of John Brown brought the local Brotherhood of the Union and antislavery groups a loose coalition of radicals of different nationalities that later evolved into the First International. Source: Theodore Dwight, *The Roman Republic of 1849, with Accounts of the Inquisition, and the Siege of Rome, and Biographical Sketches, with Original Portraits* (New York: R. Van Dien, 1851).

George W. L. Bickley. The Virginia-born Cincinnati con artist and member of the Brotherhood of the Union tried to get investors to support his scheme for a traveling military drill team. Source: Harvey Wickes Felter, *History of the Eclectic Medical Institute, Cincinnati, Ohio, 1845–1902* (Cincinnati: Alumni Association of the Eclectic Medical Institute, 1902).

Having leased the hall and raised money for uniforms, Bickley found the drill team project unworkable and decided to use the team as the basis for a new secret society, "the Knights of the Golden Circle." Source: *An Authentic Exposition of the "K.G.C.," "Knights of the Golden Circle"* (Indianapolis: Charles O. Perrine, 1861).

Two scenes of an initiation ritual in an idealized KGC hall.
Source: *An Authentic Exposition of the "K.G.C.," "Knights of the Golden Circle"* (Indianapolis: Charles O. Perrine, 1861).

George N. Sanders. The American mastermind recast Southern secession as an American version of European revolutionary aspirations, something ideologically accomplished through a rigid white supremacism. Source: *Harper's Weekly,* August 26, 1865.

George DeBaptiste, a barber and the cofounder of the African or African American Mysteries with the tailor William Lambert. This genuinely European-style revolutionary and working-class secret society existed to spirit runaway slaves north through Detroit into Canada. Source: Courtesy of Documenting the American South Project, University of North Carolina, Chapel Hill. Permission to publish with this statement: "The original work is the property of the University of North Carolina at Chapel Hill. It may be used freely by individuals for research, teaching, and personal use as long as this statement of availability is included in the text."

Moses Dickson. Farther west than DeBaptiste and Lambert, Dickson's "Knights of Liberty" formed for similar reasons and may well have represented the same secret network under a local name. Source: Frontispiece illustration of *Manual of the International Order of Twelve of the Knights and Daughters of Tabor, Containing General Laws, Regulations, Ceremonies, Drill, and a Taborian Lexicon* (St. Louis: A. R. Fleming, 1891).

Dr. James McCune Smith. The New York–born and Scottish-trained physician argued for the Egyptian and African origins of freemasonry, and his activities hinted at the antislavery role of the order in the black community. Source: Daniel Alexander Payne, *Recollections of Seventy Years* (Nashville: AME Sunday School Union, 1886).

The Knights of the Golden Circle assembling before the Alamo beneath "the Bonnie Blue Flag" of Manifest Destiny and secession. Source: *Harper's Weekly,* March 23, 1861.

Paul Gustave Cluseret. A French Garibaldian and successor to Forbes, Cluseret largely failed to rally the émigré radicals in their revolutionary secret societies behind a Radical Republican agenda. Source: Library of Congress Prints and Photographs Division, LC-DIG-cwpb-04620.

3. LONE STARS AND GOLDEN CIRCLES

The Manifest Destiny of George W. L. Bickley

George Washington Lafayette Bickley became one of the most famous members of the Brotherhood of the Union after he founded his own Knights of the Golden Circle. The news that he had been "the head of some grand order of momentous political import and of specially wonderful mystery" amused those that had known him at Cincinnati's *Scientific Artisan*. However, he had successfully presented himself to the public variously as "Doctor" Bickley, "Professor" Bickley, and "General" Bickley, to the point where an exasperated Horace Greeley referred to him "'Sir George Bickley, K.G.C.' or whatever his proper appellation may be."[1] In a nation of "self-made men," the founder of the KGC so persistently and frequently remade himself that many contemporaries remained at a loss as to who he actually was.

Nevertheless, by any measure, the KGC became much more well known and accorded vastly greater importance than the organizations of George Lippard or Hugh Forbes. That its origins remain murky reflects the character of its founder. The order became, for Bickley, a means to respectability and power. While Giuseppe Mazzini's idea of a mystic national destiny rested, in part, on the cooperation of nations, Bickley worked where nationhood grew pure without feudal or monarchist constraints. In his mind, an American "Manifest Destiny" unfolded in an unbounded fashion that would be not only unique but exceptional. Indeed, the more intensely one might feel that sense of destiny, the more it created the almost irresistible conditions for something like the KGC.

THE MAKING OF A SELF-MADE MAN

The full name of G. W. L. Bickley is used here largely in deference to his own preference, at least some of the time. "George Washington" remained an appropriate appellation for a contemporary Virginian, but he acquired the "Lafayette" at about the time of the 1824 tour of Washington's French protégé. Still, his middle initials are also given as "William" and "Lamb" or "Leigh." For that matter, his last name is sometimes given as "Beckley," likely an affectation on his part, implying membership in the prominent Virginia family of John James Beckley—a close adviser of Thomas Jefferson, the first clerk of the U.S. House of Representatives, and librarian of Congress. Beckley's son, after graduating from West Point, moved to western Virginia and named a town for his father in Raleigh County, near the more obscure Bickley clan.[2] The most likely source of the confusion would have been Bickley himself.

The Bickley family had enjoyed some local prestige in Russell County. Bickley boasted that his great-great grandfather William Bickley had been a Knight of the Garter before emigrating in the seventeenth century, but his own grandfather Charles Bickley had actually been one of the eighteenth-century pioneers of Russell County, Virginia, having fought Indians there at the time of the American Revolution and helped to guard the trails across the mountains into Kentucky. When he later acquired land at Castle Woods (now Castlewood), it included one of the early outposts, subsequently known as Fort Bickley and, later, Bickley Mills. From there, G. W. L. Bickley described himself among "the scenes of boyhood's days . . . on my native soil, and amid the graves of my ancestors," the site of his birth on July 18, 1823.[3]

At the same time, Bickley found that it sometimes suited his purposes to have been born in Boone County, Indiana, or in 1819. In some quarters, a northern birth brought a credibility that a native southern white may not have had. Too, a few more years may have eased his marriage to older women with the resources he lacked, something he did three times. He also claimed to have been "only eleven years old, at which early age he saw his little brother and sister murdered by blacks during a servile insurrection, urged on by Abolitionists," during the 1831 Nat Turner slave rebellion, as indicated in his statement. In fact, three of his four siblings died too early to have been killed in this event, and a fourth reached adulthood by remaining conspicuously unmurdered by anyone.[4]

Bickley's parents, George and Martha, left some record as well. Contrary to his son's claim that George had been a surgeon in the War of 1812, there is no military record of service, and he did not actually take up the study of medicine until at least a decade after the war. The mother, the former Martha Lamb (or Lambe) of Sussex County, pressed for the family to resettle in Petersburg when G. W. L. was a child. There, George earned very little, lost a lawsuit over a brother's estate, and may not even have finished his medical studies before succumbing to cholera on June 10, 1830. At the time, young George—"Lafayette" as his mother called him—had not yet reached the age of seven, rendering half true his later self-description as "an orphan boy in Virginia."[5]

From here, Bickley's childhood went downhill. Martha Bickley hoped to get her son an education but "had to put him out this years for his victuals and cloathes. Next year if wee boath lieve I wish him to goe to school." A disapproving sister-in-law, however, thought Martha a neglectful mother, adding that she "had 2 or 3 men waiting on her and she'd sent Lafayette to her brothers in Southhampton so she is as free as a lark now." If correct, Bickley did live with one of the Lamb relatives there during Turner's rebellion, though he had not quite been, as he said, "thrown on the world penniless and friendless." He also claimed to have left home at the age of twelve for New Orleans and gone from there to Europe, but we have no real evidence of either. While claiming that he returned early, he also wrote that he had not seen "the tender smile of a relative" for many years.[6]

Most impressively, Bickley distilled an impressive professional education. He claimed to have studied medicine in Baltimore under one Dr. Patterson, graduated from St. Mary's College in 1838, taken an 1842 degree in surgery at University College and Guy's Hospital in London, and studied phrenology and toured southern Europe before returning through New Orleans and setting up a practice in Prince George County around 1845. Not only is there no record of any of this, but after he allegedly received this extensive education, he wrote of his hopes that he might eventually attend college. In a flush of unconscious honesty, Bickley later acknowledged, "I educated myself and rose to eminence in the profession of medicine."[7]

What Bickley actually did is almost impossible to tell. He said that when war broke out with Mexico, he followed in his father's footsteps, serving in the war—and in the ongoing conflict with the Seminole Indians as well. However, there is no more record of Bickley's service than his father's. An extant letter from October 1846 located him not in Mexico but in Santa Rosa County, Florida, and that too late for the Second Seminole War and far too early for the third. He later worked as a printer, and that letter mentioned his work in the U.S. "Typographical" (not Topographical) Corps, indicating that he pursued this trade. On February 3, 1848, he married Frances Belle in North Carolina. She died in June 1850, having had one son, Charles Simmons Bickley, whom George left with her relatives.[8] As a widower, Bickley had a real opportunity for self-transformation.

Bickley returned "to my native country (Russell) after an absence of more than twenty years." There, he also helped launch the first Masonic lodge in his community and understood the value of appearances and secrets. Although he subsequently claimed to have been on a second long sojourn in Europe at this time, the 1850 census found him in Russell County with an estate now worth four hundred dollars. He described opening a medical practice out of the Union Hotel at Jeffersonville (now Tazewell) in Tazewell County, but the census listed his occupation as a "phrenologist," that is, a reader of the bumps on the heads of his customer-patients.[9] Very few Americans outside of a major city could have actually made a profession out of being a self-taught phrenologist, and the entirety of Russell County had fewer than eleven thousand white residents.

One of Bickley's closest allies in Jeffersonville would have been the local press. Bickley's most prominent friend there had brought a secondhand press from Abingdon into the town and launched the *Jeffersonville Democrat*. It reorganized in the summer of 1850 and, a year later, became the *South-Western Advocate,* with a circulation of "about three hundred and fifty copies, and with proper caution, might be placed on a firm basis." Bickley's work as a community booster brought him to the attention of the community's "leading gentlemen." In August 1851, he claimed credit for founding the Jefferson Historical Society to "collect the historical material found in traditional form in great abundance in Southwest Virginia." It published Bickley's *History of the Settlement and Indian Wars of Tazewell County, Virginia,* which he began with a promise "to leave myself out of the question, as soon as I have stated why I have been induced to take upon me the labors of the historian—labors more important, and requiring greater skill in their execution, than most persons imagine." The essential argument of the book was the need to raise money to publish at least five more volumes of local lore.[10]

What really elevated Bickley's social position was his move to the Ohio Valley. He came to Cincinnati brimming with confidence, presenting himself as a European-trained practitioner of allopathic—that is, standard—medicine, who had decided no longer to practice. In fact, he told Dr. Joseph Rodes Buchanan of the local Eclectic Medical Institute that his own study and practice had convinced him of the merits of "eclectic" and homeopathic methods—that is, herbal and water cures. Recognizing the value of such a convert, Buchanan brought him onto the faculty in 1852. Bickley not only gained the prestige of being a medical doctor without having to practice but found he could handle teaching what he himself had never studied as well. He later explained that "he would not hesitate to take a professorship in any college, knowing that he was able to study and keep ahead of any class he could be given charge of."[11]

Success included a lucky marriage on January 23, 1853, to the Widow Dodson of Scioto County, Ohio. Rachel Kinney Dodson's grandfather had been in the American Revolution, and her parents had crossed the mountains from Pennsylvania in 1804. She had been born five years later at Portsmouth, the seventh of twelve children that reached adulthood. The later county history included biographies of five of her brothers, prominent as businessmen, land speculators, railroad builders, bankers, and officeholders. One of them, Peter, presided over the city council, and several had business at Cincinnati around the time that Bickley turned up. Rachel's sisters also made marriages of quality, becoming matrons in respectable middle-class households of the county. Her own 1833 wedding to John Dodson made her part of a flourishing and dynamic local bourgeoisie as well.[12]

The Kinneys seem to have been less than happy about Rachel's remarriage. A matron of more than forty-three, she had already gotten her daughter into a suitable marriage, and her relatives had good reason to suspect a smooth-talking, fast-spending newcomer in his twenties. The comment in Bickley's obituary that he had "married and ran through the fortunes of three wealthy women" seems particularly apt in the eyes of the Kinney family, most of whom seemed to think that the new Mrs. Bickley was being victimized by a spendthrift. Years later, when the family supplied her name to the county history, they gave it as "Dodson," as though marriage to Bickley had never happened.[13]

Still, Bickley's newfound financial security permitted him to promote the Brotherhood of the Union. A prominent member of the new order from New York worked in Santa Rosa County, Florida, at the time Bickley had been there. Back in Virginia, Bickley surely had a hand in organizing the Independence Circle, No. 131, at Jeffersonville on July 4, 1850, within weeks of the establishment of lodges of Masons and Odd Fellows. Years later, he described it as having "about twenty members, and is calculated to do much good in the cause of reform." Later, Bickley officered and almost certainly founded Circle No. 162 at Lebanon and possibly No. 104 at Wytheville. One suspects that he also had a hand in the later establishment of recognized circles of the order to the south—five in Kentucky and three in Tennessee—for which almost no members are known.[14]

In Ohio, he played an even larger role in the order. His wife's hometown of Portsmouth hosted No. 121, the "Rainbow Circle," likely the oldest in the area and overwhelmingly Democratic in its proclivities. Most visibly, though, Bickley took the order to Cincinnati, founding No. 192, the Wayne Circle, in that city. Perhaps through the reputation of the order, he claimed a major but undocumented association with the *Nonpareil,* a local cooperative paper that had emerged from a local printers' strike. In March 1853, Bickley delivered a major address to the Brotherhood's Grand Circle of Ohio.[15]

Meanwhile, despite his complete lack of training or credentials, Bickley impressed his colleagues. They recalled him as "a fluent and eloquent *extempore* speaker," though they thought his delivery of medical lectures verbatim from manuscript copies simply careful planning. He produced these by consulting books and dictating twelve to twenty pages an hour to a stenographer and sometimes employing one or two literary assistants to turn the dictation into publishable work. In four months, he had twenty-seven hundred pages for lectures and distilled more than two hundred pages for *Physiological and Scientific Botany.* He also "corresponded with five newspapers," edited the *West American Review,* and "prepared a novel of 300 pages," since translated into French and German. He wrote that he took "never longer than twenty-four hours of actual time in compiling a novel of 100 pages."[16] Any reader of *Adalaska* will surely find such a pace of production far more plausible than its translation into French and German.

That novel, also appearing in 1853, exposed the fictional secret history of western Virginia. The Lippardian story of *Adalaska; or, The Strange and Mysterious Family of the Cave of Genreva* began with an investigation of contradictory descriptions of "a wild man, who was frequently seen in the mountain forests" of Tazewell County. The investigator found an entire family of self-exiled Europeans—as exotic aristocrats as surely as they were revolutionaries—with their entourage. They had not only holed up in an isolated valley but also occupied a vast underground complex there. They had chosen to establish "our colonies in your beautiful country, where man is free, and kingcraft and priestcraft are unknown."[17]

Nevertheless, the flush times could not have lasted indefinitely. Indeed, one wonders how long a self-taught phrenologist masqueraded as a doctor in a community of trained medical people. More important, he reached the end of his tether with the Kinneys, who cut off his subsidy for that editorial staff in Cincinnati. In mid-1853, Bickley's productivity collapsed in an "attack of amaurosis," a temporary, often fleeting blindness in one eye due to a shortage of blood reaching the retina. This could have been a symptom of serious medical problems, the result of stress and hypertension most easily claimed as a medical excuse, or the decision of his wife or her family to put the brakes on his spending. After finishing the classes to which he was committed to teach, he withdrew in the spring of 1854 from the Eclectic Medical Institute. (He also later said that, at this time, he left a position on the *Nonpareil,* which he never really seemed to have had.)[18]

Just as Bickley felt that respectability slipping from his grasp, the prospect of speculative state building loomed. In his *History of the Settlement and Indian Wars of Tazewell County,* he had asserted that "a slight glance at the maps of Virginia, Kentucky, Tennessee, and North Carolina will be sufficient to convince the most superficial, that in the course of things, a new state, at no very distant day, must be hewed out of the corners of the above states."[19] Perhaps a lack of interest in his 1852 proposal to dismember Virginia deflected his attentions to Mexico, Cuba, and Central America.

ENTREPRENEURIAL NATION BUILDING

As nation-states emerged, the contradictions innate in Mazzini's vision of cooperating and symbiotic patriotisms became increasingly and unavoidably apparent. Mexico's struggle for freedom from Spain recalled the War for Independence of the British colonies, with its Sons of Liberty. By 1846, however, these two young nationalisms had not undergone that Mazzinian experience of mutual recognition and respect. In the war that followed, the United States aspired to assimilate everything to its south as far as the Isthmus of Panama.[20]

Democratic journalist John L. O'Sullivan coined the term *Manifest Destiny*. He wrote, "That claim is by the right of our manifest destiny to overspread and to possess the whole of the continent which Providence has given us for the development of the great experiment of liberty and federated self-government entrusted to us." Midcentury orators of the Democratic cotton South specifically aspired to control "the golden circle," formed by extending the United States west and south into Mexico, then east along the Yucatán, and up through Cuba; Central America sometimes formed part of this plan as well. Interestingly, aside from the Mexican War of 1846–48, the U.S. government itself played little direct role in that expansion. In contrast, private organizations arranged a half-dozen incursions into Mexico.[21]

The Spanish-speaking provincial elites in the Yucatán had declared and sought to sustain independence from Mexico City in 1840–43 and again in 1845, on the eve of the American invasion. This conflict created an opening for the armed rising of the Mayan Indians there and what would be called the "Caste War" (1847–55). Private adventurers recruited nearly a thousand unpaid and ill-equipped American veterans for service of the Yucatán authorities in return for promises of pay and land. That conflict quickly killed or wounded more than a fifth of the Americans, who mostly moved on to other things by 1849, but more *Norteamericanos* would come.[22]

By 1848, Venezuelan-born Narcisco Lopez assumed the mantle of Cuban revolutionary aspirations. In September 1849, the U.S. authorities dissolved a concentration of nearly eight hundred armed men on Round Island near New Orleans, discouraging the arrival of more expected volunteers. In May

1850, Lopez took a small army of six hundred on the Cardenas Expedition, which landed and attacked that city before realizing that the occupying Spanish forces vastly outnumbered them and falling back to their boats. In August 1851, Lopez returned with more than four hundred volunteers in the ill-fated Bahia Honda Expedition, which the Spanish quickly overcame.[23]

John Henderson, a veteran of the Round Island fiasco, formulated the rituals and rites of the Order of the Lone Star, which began in the fall of 1851 at Lafayette, outside New Orleans. The name appealed to a tradition of conquest going back to the start of the nineteenth century. At that time, armed entrepreneurs from the United States seized West Florida and raised a blue flag with a single white star, a "lone star," which saw further use with the acquisition of Texas. The organization grew, naturally enough, from the Masonic associations of the Lopez movement and the Cuban *filibusteros*.

The *New York Times* thought it "a powerful secret organization, whose council rooms are to be encountered in every city along the Atlantic seaboard," and it claimed some notoriety when the Spanish authorities seized persons and documents in Cuba indicating a possible conspiracy. The order published its constitution and simultaneously asserted genuinely revolutionary credentials and middle-class respectability. One newspaper suggested that readers should "fancy a political organization, perfect in all its features, concealing its modes and times of action in impenetrable secrecy; and including strong and earnest men throughout the United States, all bent upon stretching our Southern frontier, until it takes in little less than all creation." With the perspective of distance, the *London Morning Chronicle* called it an "association of freebooters" that treated politics as "simply a speculation, which may or may not turn out to be profitable."[24]

The Order of the Lone Star claimed kinship with the European revolutionary societies. Know-Nothing congressman Lemuel D. Evans of Texas ascribed the most cynically Cuban motives to George N. Sanders, Pierre Soulé, and other Americans in encouraging exiled revolutionaries at London. These expansionists, he charged, urged a revolutionary strategy centered on Spain because it would likely spark a continental war that would both open the way for revolutions across Europe and permit the United States to liberate Cuba. Evans further implied that the conspirators had promised that, after the U.S. conquest, a Cuban plebiscite would decide whether to join the United States or take an independent course.[25]

As part of this strategy, Sanders and the Americans argued that radicals would further freedom on either side of Atlantic by agitating around slavery. Lajos Kossuth assured him that he "would never contribute anything to its internal division" among transatlantic republicans. English radicals bristled at Sander's use of republican rhetoric and newspapers to discountenance abolitionism. One wrote the *Leader* to complain that the paper published letters by characters such as Sanders: "To diffuse their pro-slavery poison through the land by means of your paper, the friends of freedom—the enemies of slavery—are refused the opportunity of administering an antidote through the same medium." Another suggested that "if they form an alliance with kidnappers and menhunters—with the framers of Fugitive Slave Laws and Nebraska Bills—in vain will be their professions of disinterestedness and philanthropy, their love of freedom and humanity. Their power to elevate and bless mankind will be at an end, and the masses of the oppressed and suffering will lose all faith in them for ever."[26]

John S. Ford of Texas described attempts by Americans to seize that island as "efforts to revolutionize Cuba." Its leaders in New York City included Sanders, whose defiance of convention in the interest of an open U.S. endorsement of European revolutionaries truncated his career as a diplomat in England. Another prominent figure in the order, Louis Schlessinger was a Jewish revolutionary "implicated in the Hungarian and German insurrections" before entering a business in liquor and cigars on Manhattan. An officer in the Lopez expedition, he gained a reputation for "the most dare-devil gallantry" before his capture and sentencing to life imprisonment at a Spanish fortress on the coast of Africa. After his escape, Schlessinger became involved with the Order of the Lone Star and the "Junta Central" in New York.[27]

The schemes of *Norteamericanos* advanced with the benign neglect of a succession of Democratic administrations. Earlier, the United States had tried to purchase Cuba as it had Florida, offering Spain $100 million. In 1853, Franklin Pierce captured the presidency with open plans to renew the bidding, and his inaugural address scoffed at "timid forebodings of evil from expansion." In 1854, Pierre Soulé, John Mason, and future president James Buchanan—respectively, the American ministers to Spain, France, and Britain—signed the "Ostend Manifesto." It declared Cuba "as necessary to the North American republic as any of its present members" and said it belonged to "that great family of states of which the Union is the Providential Nursery." They proposed offering Spain $130 million, the refusal of which "justified" a U.S. seizure of the island.[28] They then leaked the proposal to the press, which had the effect of allowing the United States to threaten Spain without having officially done so.

Elsewhere along "the golden circle," Americans made repeated efforts to seize more of Mexico. Several times, José Carvajal (or Carbajal) sought to establish the Republic of Sierra Madre in the states of Coahuila, Nuevo León, and Tamaulipas in northern Mexico; seeking allies in Texas, the insurrectionists suggested that such a republic might return the fugitive slaves fleeing into Mexico. In 1851, former quartermaster of California Joseph Morehead invaded Sonora. Arriving from California, a French nobleman named Gaston de Raousset de Boulbon brought hundreds of disappointed prospectors into Sonora, where they attempted a takeover in the fall of 1852.[29]

The greatest of all the *filibusteros*, William Walker, emerged from these attempts. In the fall of 1853, he led a handful of Americans into Lower California, surprising and overwhelming a Mexican garrison at La Paz. Born to a rigidly Calvinist family in Nashville, he earned a medical degree, toured Europe, and opened a practice in his hometown before moving on to New Orleans. There, he turned to law and to journalism as part owner of the *New Orleans Crescent*. Deciding to make a fresh start after the death of his fiancée, he went to California, became involved in the Democratic Party, and determined to secure the independence of Lower California. His successful invaders declared that independence on January 18, 1854, after which he announced that the new republic was annexing adjacent Sonora. In February, reinforcements increased his army to 150, but it faced a rising tide of resistance, not only from the Mexican officials but from the local population as well.[30] Driven back into the United States, Walker became even more ambitious, setting his sights on Central America.

Even the most well-planned and well-led efforts also failed. Count Gaston de Raousset de Boulbon made a second bid for territorial acquisition from April into August 1854. In 1855, Texas Ranger James Callahan took 111 other Rangers across the Rio Grande, allegedly chasing fugitive slaves, but, frustrated by what they perceived to be Mexican noncooperation, they torched Piedras Negras instead. In 1857, a former California state senator, Henry A. Crabb, took the Gasden Colonization Company into Mexico, where they warred with the authorities in Sonora, who captured and executed almost all of them by April, the rescue column of Granville Henderson Oury arriving far too late to save anybody.[31] Oury and others would return five years later under different circumstances.

Notwithstanding his failure in Mexico, Walker arrived in Nicaragua in May 1855 to pacify internal conflicts on behalf of the U.S. investors in Central American transit. U.S. support for the incursion had become increasingly sectionalized, as had the earlier interest in the Lopez project in Cuba. In June 1856, Walker had claimed the presidency and courted southern support within the United States by reintroducing slavery on September 22. Walker and some 1,200 Americans there on his behalf held on into April 1857 against the troops of Costa Rica, Guatemala, El Salvador, and Honduras, when Walker surrendered to the U.S. Navy and was repatriated.[32]

A probable cousin of Bickley's second wife, the former Rachel Kinney, made a bid of his own for power on the Nicaraguan coast. The Pennsylvania-born Henry Lawrence Kinney had fled his debtors in Illinois for the more promising terrain of Texas, where he appropriated the title "colonel," held office, founded Corpus Christi, and served in the Mexican War. In 1855, at the height of Walker's efforts in Nicaragua, Kinney steamed off to the Mosquito Coast of that country and tried to set himself up as governor of "the City and Territory of Greytown." Kinney's bid at Greytown collapsed with the defeat of Walker's government. Kinney, in turn, enjoyed some support from Sanders and other expansionists.[33]

Walker found considerable support back in the United States. Not only did Duff Green and William Marcy Tweed—of later "ring" fame—hold meetings for Walker, but the federal marshal who had him into custody was Capt. Isaiah Rynders, the spokesman of the Order of the Lone Star. Rynder's associates included Sanders, busily agitating for a "Red Republicanism" embracing the slaveholders' liberation of Cuba and a republicanism "for white men, and not for niggers in Europe." Rynders had sprung Walker from the custody of the U.S. Navy and personally took him to Washington, where Secretary of State Lewis Cass had Rynders release Walker, who immediately embarked on another Nicaraguan expedition.[34]

Nothing in Lippard's Brotherhood precluded the most ruthless expansionism. And if the process brought prominence to Kinney, Walker, Richardson Hardy, and John McCann—even as they failed—why not Bickley? On a more grand scale, if America was to be the Palestine of Redeemed Labor, how could the seizure of foreign territory by armed Americans be anything but an attempt to revolutionize and free it? How could conquest by American republicans be anything but liberation or even philanthropy?

KNIGHTS OF THE GOLDEN CIRCLE

The birth of Bickley's KGC is as confused as that of its founder, and for the same reason. Surely based on what Bickley told them, his coworkers at the Eclectic Medical Institute said that his founding of the KGC coincided with his editorship of the *West American Review*, which would have been as early as 1853. However, Bickley himself gave the year as 1854 and its goal as that of fostering American expansion, although newspapers like the *New Orleans Courier* and the *Vicksburg Star* later said that the goal had been more "to cultivate the martial spirit of our people, than anything else," the latter adding the specific information that the KGC started in Kentucky in the spring of that year. Yet while almost all of the secondary literature dates the KGC from 1854, not a single contemporary reference to the order goes back that far. The *Norfolk Day Book* offered, with the verisimilitude of detail, that five men started the KGC in 1857. In reality, there is no real indication that the KGC existed before 1858, the year given on the actual seal of the order.[35]

At times, Bickley actually denied founding the KGC at all. He told a fanciful tale of having been in Mexico—the timing and reasoning being left predictably unclear—where he encountered "an extensive order in that country known as 'Los Caballeros del Circulo de Oro,'" which dated from the earliest days of Mexico's struggle for independence, and had subsequently sought to achieve the independence of the Yucatán, Chiapas, Tabasco, and Oaxaca from Mexico City. After corresponding with the "Caballeros," he became the group's "agent" and, later, had merely presided at the founding meeting of a North American branch of the organization at Lexington, Kentucky.[36]

The one thing Bickley definitely learned was that the importance of any secret society turned largely on how it presented itself. Cincinnati had "an extensive organization of the Order of the Lone Star." Despite the rhetoric of military conquest, its activities remained strictly electoral, voting "almost unanimously" to endorse the 1852 Democratic presidential campaign, in hopes of getting a figure in the White House more friendly to its goals. Not long afterward, though, a New York paper reported that a Hungarian colonel had fifteen hundred volunteers at Cincinnati ready to move on Cuba. The *New York Times* traced the story to the mustering out of the émigré volunteers to fight with Louis Kossuth and declared the original story "framed to harmonize with current fables."[37] Such an ability to use smoke and mirrors to create the perception of scale certainly inspired Bickley's ambitions.

Then, too, the pins Bickley made for his organization displayed a lone star on one side and a Maltese cross on the other, reflecting the additional influence of the Sons of Malta. Applicants to that order paid an initiation of five dollars and were asked a legion of other sometimes personal questions. The list included whether they favored the acquisition of Cuba and anticipated when "the Stars and Stripes will float in pride over the Queen of the Antilles." After some ritualized roughhousing, blindfolded initiates got crowns and aprons before being brought together facing each other. At the third striking of a gong, initiates lost the blindfolds to confront each other wearing "a pair of ass's ears" and "a piece of untanned hide, with an imitation of the male organ of generation sticking out in front." In return for having been made asses, members enjoyed periodic banquets and expensive drinks, provided by the next collection of initiation money.[38] The later exposés of the Sons of Malta leave us a rare mental portrait of many of America's military and political leaders, but it certainly dramatized the standards of caveat emptor that informed Bickley's own creation.

Nevertheless, Bickley pursued prominence and success without succumbing to the lure of a secret society for some time. On January 15, 1855, "Prof. G. W. L. BICKLEY" took the platform at New York's Broadway Tabernacle for a series of lectures he called "Doomed Cities of Antiquity." His purpose was "throwing light upon questions of Biblical prophecy and interpretation" to urge a government-funded U.S. "expedition to Mesopotamia, Ancient Syria, Media, Asia Minor, &c." These lectures urging "the literal and exact fulfillment of prophecy" in the Bible garnered "but a slim attendance." Having failed to enlighten Godless Gotham, Bickley returned to Ohio, where he later claimed to have purchased and edited the *Daily Democratic Pennant* at Portsmouth; not surprisingly, the short-lived *Pennant* started in 1855 and folded in 1856, apparently without ever having been a daily.[39]

Then, too, Bickley's revolutionary activism seems limited to a May 1856 coup in the Eclectic Medical Institute. Deepening factionalism that dated from his own hiring erupted into a rebellion against the man who had hired him. Dr. Buchanan had become the dean and sought to promulgate a "free education" to expand the student body and enable the institute to support itself through book sales and supplementary revenue. Overcoming whatever personal loyalties he might have had, Bickley joined Buchanan's rivals, who "secured the key from the janitor's wife" and forced their way through the back.[40]

Bickley himself described the advance of Buchanan's "angry little army" against the "little Spartan band" of "some dozen or fifteen persons" who had occupied the building. As the two sides neared, those inside brandished "knives, pistols, chisels, bludgeons, blunderbusses, etc.," and Buchanan found his students "could not be persuaded, coaxed, nor driven upon those murderous weapons, which grinned solemn death from hand to pocket, and rendered terrific the bare thought of carrying the stairway by storm." Hours ticked by into the second night of occupation when another move on the building resulted in the defenders' producing a six-pound cannon "to sweep the passage if a rush should be made by the outsiders."[41] By then, even the city government responded, ending the most contentious faculty hire in the history of higher education in Cincinnati, and two rival colleges emerged.

That fall, Bickley returned to the Eclectic Medical Institute, minus Buchanan and the others. Under its new organization, he taught Physiology and Medical Jurisprudence, and his public lecture "Dynamic Physiology" became especially popular. Reflecting his respectability, the city directories listed him in 1858 as an "eclectic physician." Nevertheless, by early 1859, declining enrollment, particularly from the South, pushed the two rival colleges to unite.[42] The process left Bickley seeking his fortune elsewhere.

In the spring of 1858, while still on the medical faculty, he talked himself into a new career as the editor of the *Scientific Artisan*. The Patent Company at Cincinnati wanted a publication to rival *Scientific American,* and Bickley became its "original editor." By then, he had separated from his wife and boarded at the Gibson House. A coworker there later told Whitelaw J. Reid that the KGC had been "hatched in the *Artisan* office." He said that Bickley "had been sadly out of funds for some time, had borrowed of every one about the office till he could borrow no more, and was beginning to feel that he had about reached the end of his career in Cincinnati."[43]

The earliest credible mention of what became the KGC was Bickley's scheme to raise thirty-six thousand dollars "in a few months; and have a handsome regular income besides." In the wake of the Crimean War, Americans began organizing and supporting various military drill squads, particularly the color- fully dressed Zouaves, French units in colorful North African dress. Bickley decided to outdo them all by raising a company of sixty men who could travel through the country "giving exhibitions of the uniform and drill of the troops of all nations." Anyone wishing to join would pay a fee of six hundred dollars to the "treasurer, captain and general manager." When he advertised for "able- bodied persons who felt inclined to join a military company and secure steady employment," he found plenty of interested men, but few "with six hundred dollars to invest in this species of speculation." Based on his confidence in the prospects, though, Bickley rented a hall on credit and began organizing and drilling some of the more enthusiastic who replied to the advertisement.[44]

At some point—probably late in 1858—Bickley introduced two changes in the project. First, he transformed his "show company" into "a little fili- bustering exhibition." Although he asked his perplexed associates at work about "old California," his intentions settled on seizing "some part of Central America" as attempted by Walker or Kinney. It remains unclear how anyone could seriously imagine that a drill company of sixty *Norteamericanos* might succeed where Walker had failed with twelve hundred "immortals" and many reinforcements. He never seemed to wonder whether men signing up to perform a show might not see invading another country as a different matter entirely, which indicates that Bickley himself saw the primary importance of such a crusade as fund-raising.

In a related move, Bickley transformed the entire project into a secret society. He boasted that this would net "a very handsome income from the initiation fees." More important, an organization like the old Order of the Lone Star naturally concealed not only its military plans but also its numerical weakness from critics, potential investors, and actually par- ticipants. In the end, the reorganized body adopted a constitution, rituals, secret grips, and passwords that were, as one scholar described them, "pure Know-Nothingism."[45]

Bickley desperately needed money, particularly after the Kinneys cut him off. Coworkers later said that, throughout these months, he "had been borrowing money, right and left, and spending it freely." The Cincinnati businessman said that Bickley played "the regular 'confidence game' to secure a loan" with a skill worthy of "a veteran New York operator." Several creditors began pressing hard, including the assistant editor at the *Scientific Artisan,* whom he owed fifteen hundred dollars. Feigning disgust at their lack of vision, Bickley announced that he would collect several thousand dollars owed him in Memphis, where "his wife from whom he had separated"—the former Mrs. Dodson—resided with a daughter. Her relatives confirmed this, recalling that when Bickley turned up asking for money, she flatly refused.[46]

The *Scientific Artisan* office greeted Bickley when he returned emptyhanded. The creditors became "somewhat indignant; but he was astonished at their doubting the honor of a proud Southerner." He then declared that he would free himself of these "ill-bred" creditors by returning to Virginia and selling his estate with its "fifty or sixty negroes." The assistant editor reported that "the poor creditors (save one) saw him no more in the flesh." About the time Bickley left town, the owners of the military hall he had rented informed the *Artisan* that its editor had charged the cost to the publication. Shortly thereafter, his Cincinnati coworkers read with astonishment newspaper accounts identifying Bickley as a figure of immense importance as the head of a vast secret society.[47]

As an interesting aside, young Samuel L. Clemens turned up in Cincinnati during the formative years of Bickley's career. After finding a large bill in the streets of Keokuk (and failing to locate its owner), the young Missouri printer bought a ticket downriver, hoping it would be the first step toward fame and fortune south of the border. The year 1856 found him somewhat stranded in the narrow circles of the Cincinnati craft, where his interest in get-rich-quick schemes involving Latin America would likely acquainted him with Bickley.[48] In fact, one cannot help but wonder if the flamboyant founder of the KGC may have contributed something to Clemens's later creation of "the Duke" in his *Adventures of Huckleberry Finn.*

* * *

Some months after leaving Cincinnati—probably in 1859—Bickley quietly returned. The former assistant editor of the *Scientific Artisan,* who had become the editor when Bickley fled his creditors, happened to be at the Spencer House. In the register, both the initials and the handwriting of a "General G. W. Baez" stirred his curiosity. The hotel sent up a servant to see if the general was in, but he returned asking for the visitor's card. The editor complied, and the word came back that the general was out. In a bit, he sent up another message, using "the name of a low fellow who had been one of Bickley's original 'show company,' and had adhered to him through all his changes of plan," and found himself invited in to see General Baez. When he entered the room, Bickley was "not at all discomposed by the surprise" and explained that "some legal technicalities" had delayed the sale of the Virginia plantation, but he would soon send a check for the fifteen hundred dollars with interest.[49] That night "General Baez" predictably skipped town, taking Bickley with him.

The mythology of Bickley's KGC certainly served multiple purposes, some more straightforward than others. The *New York World* accurately described him as someone "less likely to bleed his enemies than his friends." "Great is his strategy in campaigns of peculation [*sic*], and wonderful his bravery in attacking the well-defended purses of his friends. Tremble when the General approaches, if you have a dollar unprotected by a cannon." Although he would prove "terrible as an army in making war upon your pocket, he is as harmless as a lamb in any other capacity."[50] Of course, those who could afford it found it a small price to pay for something that could engage in the kind of history that nothing but the KGC—or the idea of the KGC—might accomplish.

CHALLENGING
PART II
POWER

4. HIGHER LAWS

The Fulcrum of African American National Identity

Black Americans formed a variety of antebellum secret associations. One had three degrees of Captive, Redeemed, and Chosen, an initiate for which appeared blindfolded "in rough and ragged garments" with a chain about his neck. In the ritual, his request for "Deliverance" led to the question of how he expected to get it. "By his own efforts" came the reply. When a member passed to Redeemed, he lost the chain, but only by becoming Chosen would he learn "the full intention of the order," that "the general plan was freedom." Among the Chosen were still further degrees: Rulers, Judges, Princes, Chevaliers of Ethiopia, and Sterling Black Knights. Referring to the successful slave rebellion led by Toussaint L'Ouverture, the most secret revolutionary degree, Knight of St. Domingo, required mastery over "the principles of freedom and the authorities on revolution; revolt, rebellion, government—in short a digest of the best authorities."[1] The relatively few African Americans who enjoyed any real freedom under the law had little more than the Italian nationalists under the Austrians or French occupation, and they responded with similar associations.

Even as European revolutionaries applied the standards of fraternalism to national purposes, similar organizations contributed directly to shaping black identity in America. In fact, black orders bore far greater resemblance to the European societies than most of those among white Americans. Context made black associations more overtly more political and made one fundamental labor reform unavoidable for an African American leadership described as bound in "the triple chord of Masonry, Church fellowship and Anti-Slavery association."[2] Most important, repressive conditions in America drove active resistance to slavery underground, making particularly relevant

the accoutrements of fraternalism. As the explosive struggle over the extension of slavery into Kansas spurred radical activism among whites as well,
the secret society tradition in America tapped ever more deeply into the
experience of the African American—as well as European—associations.

AFRICAN AMERICAN SECRET SOCIETIES

No less than any other group in Western societies, those African Americans who engaged—and had the rare leisure to entertain that drive—made
Freemasonry a similarly ubiquitous model of organization. On the eve of
the American Revolution, English masons admitted Prince Hall, a mulatto
from the Indies, with fourteen other applicants of color. After American
independence, white masons declined fellowship with blacks, leaving Prince
Hall to secure in 1784 an English charter for his African Lodge. Although the
subsequent history remains obscure, the fact of exclusion became undeniable
among those African Americans who resumed efforts at building such associations in the 1820s. After a similar exclusion from the Odd Fellows, Peter
Ogden, a ship steward sailing between New York and Liverpool, persuaded
the black members to establish direct ties to England, bypassing the whites.
A succession of local benefit societies and mutual aid clubs formed among
blacks for precisely the same fraternal reasons they emerged among whites.[3]

The role of African American freemasonry depended upon time and place,
but its general significance can hardly be understated. Prince Hall provided
the black communities across the country with a more coherent leadership.
Martin R. Delany, William Wells Brown, Dr. James McCune Smith, and others
placed high store in their fraternal affiliation. One newcomer to New York
joined the order in his new hometown, at the same time he joined a church.
Amazingly, even in the South, the order offered a natural corollary of the
African Methodist Episcopal Church, both being independent black institutions. Despite escalating repression in the decade leading to war, New Orleans
blacks built five AME churches and three Prince Hall lodges.[4]

As among the clandestine nationalists in Europe, black fraternal orders
appealed primarily to the professionals and the "middle class," but that meant
something different than in the Old World. Although born to free parents in
New York, Dr. Smith had faced rejection by the Columbia College Medical
School and gone to Scotland for his medical training. Even after returning
a fully competent physician, the New York County Medical Society never
accepted him as a member. Treating patients of all races, he also took up
the pen as "Communipaw," the name echoing the legend of a multiracial
community of that name in New Jersey. On the other hand, Baptist minister

George Washington Dupee of Louisville spent years preaching while a slave and, after his manumission, actually earned his bread as a brick maker.[5] In short, the color bar itself created a scattering of black ministers, schoolteachers, and professionals, but—however legitimate the title—the extent to which they made a living from such pursuits and were "middle class" in a European sense varied.

So, too, laboring people constituted a much more prominent role in these fraternal societies, as in the antebellum black community generally. As the wider economy drew capital into new organizations of production, blacks occupied niches that used less capital and avoided direct competition with whites. Born in Virginia to free parents, George DeBaptiste became a barber and was particularly employable as a personal servant for wealthy gentlemen in their travels. He joined former general William Henry Harrison during the 1840 presidential campaign and even served as steward of the White House briefly, before Harrison's death. Afterward, he returned to Madison, Indiana—between Louisville and Cincinnati on the Ohio River—and began advising Kentucky slaves and using his trading business with Cincinnati to get them to safety. Convinced of his involvement in "nigger stealing," Kentucky authorities offered a reward for his arrest, but DeBaptiste continued his operations until 1849, when he moved to Detroit. As he had on the Ohio, DeBaptiste became involved in shipping, which created a direct route into Canada.[6]

Both ends of DeBaptiste's illustrious career underscore the plebeian nature of the underground network. Writers described his friend the tailor William Lambert as a "philanthropist," though his standing as an artisan would have made such a description peculiar among whites. At the other end, the steamboat traffic on the Ohio placed DeBaptiste in touch with a highly respected and relatively prosperous group of ship stewards, who needed fraternal associations as they traveled from one river town to another. Moreover, at the socially lower end of the membership, their associates extended beyond free blacks, and one scholar even referred to them at one point as "slave societies."[7]

The Ohio River provided not only a permeable barrier between states that accepted and rejected human slavery but a cordial environment for fraternal orders among blacks. Their work often moved them from one community to the other and required the mingling of free and slave with little suspicion. Encouraged by Prince Hall Masons at Cincinnati, some Louisville blacks were discussing whether to form a lodge as early as 1850. Methodist schoolteacher William H. Gibson had been initiated three years before at Baltimore and served with the majority of the group, which favored discretely locating the new Mount Moriah Lodge across the river at New Albany. For three years they crossed the river in skiffs at midnight and hiked the five miles to the city. In the end, they relocated their lodge to Louisville and remained quite active, even after the police raid of 1859, the result of the Harpers Ferry raid.[8] Although responsible for this state of affairs, white slaveholders had every reason to fear an organization that could regularly and repeatedly slip blacks back and forth across the Ohio in the middle of the night.

Though even less well documented than freemasonry, local variants on the order provided even more suggestive possibilities. Louisville's Benevolent Society—composed of slaves as well as free blacks—organized on the eve of the Civil War and came to be documented only because it later enlisted Gibson's help in its postwar reorganization as the "United Brothers of Friendship and Sisters of the Mysterious Ten."[9] Remarkably, fraternal organizations among slaves included Gibson, involved secretly crossing the Ohio at night.

In a similar border community, a St. Louis barber and AME minister headed the antebellum Knights of Liberty, upon which the postwar International Order of Twelve of the Knights and Daughters of Tabor grew. Born in Cincinnati to Virginia parents, Moses Dickson served an apprenticeship and attended school before heading south, where "he saw slavery in all its horrors; he witnessed such scenes of monstrous cruelty as caused his African blood to boil with suppressed indignation at the sight of the outrageous suffering of his people." He and some like-minded young men agreed to review plans for an antislavery association and to rendezvous after two years. In the course of his travels in Iowa, Illinois, and Wisconsin, Dickson apparently encountered various models of secret societies and persuaded the group to organize formally.[10] Like Gibson, Dickson demonstrates the connection between resistance to slavery and fraternal self-organization.

The underlying role of tradition and precedent remains as obscure among black secret societies as in European revolutionary circles. When blacks at Baltimore formed the Independent Order of St. Luke, they adopted the name of a degree in the Antient [sic] and Primitive Rite, ascribed to the earlier Brotherhood of Light, the Frates Lucis, which included mystic versions, such as Cagliostro, a founder of Egyptian-rite masonry. St. Luke was also the patron of Iatric freemasonry, that of the healers, indicating that the order may have foreshadowed Dr. Harvey Johnson's later Mutual United Brotherhood of Liberty.[11] Such suggestive associations took substance in the shadow of freemasonry.

Freemasonry offered its adherents and variants among black Americans a view of civilization directly emphasizing African origins. Albert L. Rawson, a multifaceted Orientalist, reminded students of the Bible that, in dim antiquity, "the descendants of Ham, in Egypt and Babylon, led the way as the pioneers in art, literature, and science. Mankind at the present day lies under infinite obligations to the genius and industry of those early ages, more especially for alphabetic writing, weaving cloth, architecture, astronomy, plastic art, sculpture, navigation and agriculture. The art of painting is also represented, and music indirectly, by drawings of instruments." Not surprisingly, Delany's 1853 tract was called *The Origin and Objects of Ancient Freemasonry: Its Introduction into the United States and Legitimacy among Colored Men.*[12] African Americans rooted their sense of identity in such arguments.

So, too, freemasonry offered the promise of reaching across the color bar, particularly in that the white society in the North tended to see the order as a means of self-improvement. William Cooper Nell, an African American printer who had learned the craft under William Lloyd Garrison at the *Liberator,* underscored the paradoxical willingness of white society to accept the idea of black fraternal orders and church membership while denying them civil rights:

> To make me a sectarian, Odd Fellow, Good Samaritan, Son of Temperance, or Free Mason, before you make me a man and a citizen, is to mock my heart and insult my head; liberty, first, names, societies and conventionalism afterwards. Of what advantage is the Church, State or any human Society or Institution to me, if I must purchase them at the price of chains, slavery and proscription? What, the glory of houses and lands if enjoyed upon sufferance? . . . Tell me I may walk in an Odd Fellow Society, and mob me for walking in a Temperance procession. Permit me to pass in a Free Mason procession, and club and stone me to death for being in an Anti-Slavery procession. Go when, where and with whom we please as servants or slaves—but denied place above or beneath ground—scarcely breathing air, or drinking water as gentlemen.

The dynamic of freemasonry, then, opened the door not only to a civic existence but to a more equal civic life that African Americans would largely shape themselves.[13]

Nor should we underestimate the importance of those exceptional white Masons who simply ignored the color bar. When Jacques Étienne Marconis de Négre personally arrived to introduce Egyptian freemasonry into the United States, he ignored the white Masonic taboos by attending to his business at the "United Grand Lodge of New York"—the Prince Hall Masons. Here, too, some accounts of this among black Masons describe this remarkable visitor himself as a black representative of the Grand Orient. Whatever the case, on November 9, 1856, Marconis brought to New York an order that at least some of the émigrés would have greeted with familiarity. One of them, Bernard Paul Ernest "Honeste" Saint-Gaudens, openly insisted "on associating with the negro Freemasons and presiding at their initiations." When other white

Freemasons blacklisted him for this, Saint-Gaudens thereafter "never attended any but negro lodge meetings, though he always explained to his children that Freemasonry was a sublime and impressive order."[14] Significantly, those hands across the color line came from those radical internationalist circles.

The emergence of such formations in any other distinct population in Western civilization would indicate clearly nationalist aspirations. Perhaps most whites find the concept of African American nationalism difficult to grasp, particularly at such a point when race relations remained defined first and foremost by the survival of African slavery. At the time, blacks regularly appealed to and sought the help of anyone capable of rendering such assistance. This did not preclude nationalist sentiment. Quite the contrary.

As the case of the Universal Democratic Republicans at New York well demonstrates, although paradoxical, Italian revolutionaries readily and systematically sought the cooperation and collaboration of French radicals. Neither that nor the fact that some French readily extended such assistance affected the existence, nature, or quality of nationalism among the Italians. So, too, the fact that blacks often elicited the help of whites in the United States is no argument against nationalist aspirations and sentiment among blacks.

Just as among Europeans, though, nationalists felt increasingly compelled to address the social conditions of their people. African Americans, free or slave and North or South, could not escape the realities of slavery. While other issues came up periodically, abolition largely subsumed every aspect of black labor reform.

BLACK LABOR REFORM

Circumstances forced upon African American secret societies one overriding labor reform: the resistance to the federal Fugitive Slave Law. This required not only careful and intricate planning and preparation, but doing so under as much scrutiny as any secret society among oppressed nations anywhere. They needed techniques ranging from the use of passwords and signs to safe means of ensuring the assistance of select whites.

Modern scholarship has largely demystified the "Underground Railroad," correctly pointing out that the legend of assisting runaway slaves almost always exaggerates the scale of organization, the importance of whites within it, and the role of that supporting network in the decision of individual slaves to flee to freedom. However, the deeper problem with the legend is the implication that one could generalize about the network, as though it were a formal national organization with regular meetings among a dues-paying membership with fixed abodes. Whether in the legendary view or the revisionist corrective, perhaps the greatest problem disallows the very great variations in escapes from slavery, depending on where and when they took place.

So, also, the actual numbers of those who gained freedom this way remain hotly debated, though some, on both sides of the slavery debate, have reasons to discern different numbers. A Virginia writer claimed that more than sixty-two thousand slaves had fled north between 1810 and 1850, and some thought it totaled one hundred thousand by the time of the Civil War. However, an abolitionist editor protested the estimate for 1850 as being at least ten times too high. Moreover, although unofficial estimates range from twenty-five to seventy-five thousand, the census numbers for blacks in western Canada officially numbered only eleven thousand in 1860.[15]

Nevertheless, we should not be overly dismissive of the larger estimates. Most of the escapes—and certainly the possibility of assistance—came in that last decade before the Civil War, after the abolitionist newspaperman cautioned against accepting higher numbers. Lambert offered very specific estimates that "nearly 40,000" gained freedom crossing "into Canada over Detroit and St. Clair rivers between the years 1829 and 1862," with a total of fifty thousand reaching Canada overall, with thousands more hiding in communities in the nonslaveholding states of the North.[16] Most runaways did not necessarily take up Canadian residence openly or indefinitely, and many thousands may well have gradually drifted back into the clustered population in the northern United States.

Black self-organization around this issue surely varied widely in size and effectiveness but reasonably became quite extensive at some times and places. Dickson's order in St. Louis later claimed to have aided runaway slaves. Interestingly, independent sources among the Prince Hall lodges at New Orleans confirmed contact with an AME minister from Missouri working on a steamboat. Further, an 1857 raid on a ceremony in New Orleans netted about thirty free blacks and slave members, indicating that in New Orleans, as in Louisville, the order admitted slaves as well as free blacks to their fellowship. That free blacks assumed a fraternal obligation to assist their enslaved brothers posed obvious implications, in terms of slavery.[17]

Much later, a newspaper reporter interviewed "philanthropist and tailor" William Lambert, the Detroit founder of the "African-American Mysteries; the Order of the Men of Oppression." The "son of a slave father and free mother; a man of education, wide reading, rare argumentative power," Lambert became not only a local spokesman for the black community but a widely known and respected associate of some of the greatest figures in the national agitation. From 1829 until the declaration of emancipation as a federal war goal, Lambert organized the spiriting of refugees into the safety of Canada, aided after 1849 by George DeBaptiste and his shipping operations into Canada.[18]

Lambert's organization made sure fugitives were "never left unprotected in their journeys, and the hardships they underwent to secure liberty were not only shared with them by their conductors, but repeated time after time by the hundred or so of men who cheerfully assumed this arduous duty." The operations, he recalled, had sufficient support to permit them to conceal the fugitives and wait "in barns and all sorts of retreats," if they were being watched. The order sheltered the fugitives until dark, after which they slipped to a home at the foot of Eighth Street belonging to a worker on the Michigan Central Railway. Using boats "concealed under the docks," they crossed the mile of water into Canada. "We never lost a man by capture at this point, so careful were we, and we took over as high as 1,600 in one year," declared Lambert.[19] Moving an average of four to five a day across the water to Canada does not sound nearly so strange for a network functioning at Detroit, where northbound routes out of the country converged, and during the 1850s, when slave flight peaked and disgust with slavery became commonplace in the North.

Nevertheless, the general membership claims of the organizers of these black secret societies about the scale of their work demand skepticism. With disarming specificity, Dickson described a national "army of true and trusty men" numbering more than forty-seven thousand by 1856, a figure for his Knights of Liberty said to include such local associations, such the original Order of Twelve at Galena. Lambert's interviewer reported his claim "that over 60,000 took the highest degree" in the African American Mysteries. Members of a secret society "composed almost exclusively of colored men" in wartime Richmond claimed branches "over the entire South."[20] To say the least, claims of forty-seven to sixty thousand members or of a regional scale of organization in different antislavery black fraternal orders seem excessive.

Yet other considerations caution against a blanket dismissal of these claims. The actual scale, coherence, and composition of the local resistance circles fluctuated wildly, depending mostly on how many runaways were passing through to freedom. Nevertheless, Dickson, Lambert in Detroit, and the unnamed brothers in the Confederate capital were likely discussing the same loose national network. As Dickson explicitly stated, the association to which he referred included local societies working under different names.

Certainly, antislavery militants cooperated locally, regardless of the name they used for their specific group. In that well-documented Boston movement, a Vigilance Committee formed in 1841, fell into disuse, and reorganized nine years later. Frederick Douglass addressed an August convention of former slaves at Cazenovia, New York, organizing for the same purposes.[21] Despite a dramatic and escalating series of confrontations and clashes with the authorities, most of their efforts avoided detection.

There were also some spectacular indications of a high level of cooperation among various local organizations. The largest, perhaps, in April 1848, sought to bring nearly eighty slaves out from under the institution at Washington, D.C., aboard the schooner *Pearl*. The scale alone terrorized slaveholders, particularly in such border areas, and demonstrated the extent of organization and planning among abolitionists.[22] Partly in response to this, Southern leaders insisted upon the inclusion of a much more demanding Fugitive Slave Act in the Compromise of 1850.

That loose "antislavery league" in the lower Midwest provided an example of an collaboration of these local groups. As a whole, the body consisted of "hundreds of men who were willing to engage in any enterprise which would defeat the swaggering negro hunter." It also had "a detective and spy system that was far superior to anything the slaveholder or the United States had." At times, they had "as many as fifty educated and intelligent young and middle-aged men" scouting along the length of the Ohio River for runaway slaves and ten engaged in regular work south of the river.[23] Those regularly involved in such activities at any given point may have numbered only in the hundreds—or even dozens—but those ready and willing to violate the federal Fugitive Slave Laws over the years might well have run into the thousands.

However limited and later exaggerated, white allies played a key role, and an increasing one through the 1850s. Lewis Hayden, a prominent Boston Freemason, formed a pillar of black respectability in that community, but had escaped slavery from his native Kentucky into Ohio, then to Detroit, before moving on to Boston. He contributed to shaping a resistance to the Fugitive Slave Law that involved a division of labor between blacks and whites, such as James N. Buffum and John C. Cluer, who performed roles denied African Americans at the time. Both associated with the land-reform radicals involved in the Brotherhood of the Union. They challenged the return of runaways in the courts, while Hayden or Nell mobilized a menacing black street presence to pressure the courts. Later, as resistance stiffened, actions by essentially black crowds to secure the release of a runaway came to include whites such as Cluer and Richard Hinton.[24]

Most of all, those who left any record of aid accorded runaway slaves mentioned passwords, signs, and accoutrements of secret societies, necessary to avoid the authorities and the law. Approaching the next stop, one of the hunted could use something like "Cross over" as a password when delivered in a dialogue; an applicant asked "Cross?" to which the reply was "Over." A seemingly meaningless exchange about travel ended by mentioning "a place called Safety." "Have you a brother there? I think I know him," said one. "I know you now. You traveled on the road." As well, the fugitive could inquire with a sign, "pulling the knuckle of the right forefinger over the knuckle of the same finger on the left hand. The answer was to reverse the fingers as described."[25] Those claiming forty-seven to sixty thousand members were echoing the numbers of fugitives assumed rescued by the Underground Railroad and presumably sharing the secret signs that defined "membership."

Also like their European contemporaries, American blacks embraced labor reforms that went beyond the question of slavery. Several participated in the land-reform movement alongside members of the Brotherhood of the Union. On the fringes of the movement was Peter Humphries Clark, the Ohio schoolteacher who became the most prominent black socialist in postwar America. The 1851 National Industrial Congress seated "a colored gentleman from Philadelphia," John C. Bowers, who had been involved in the self-organization of black coachmen and other black workers for decades and then represented what was variously called the "Philadelphia Land Association" and the "Truth Association," described as a "Building Society of colored men."[26]

On their own, antebellum blacks began taking up such questions. The July 1853 "National Colored Convention" at Rochester not only included Clark but also placed on its National Council Day Nell, Dr. Smith, Frederick Douglass, and William C. Munroe of Detroit. It endorsed the national organization of "a Protective Union for the purchase and sale of articles of domestic consumption, and shall unite and aid in the formation of branches auxiliary to their own."[27]

In January 1854, a Massachusetts state convention discussed protective unions. Already, Henry O. Remington and presumably other participants had worked alongside white Fourierists in such cooperative ventures. He, Lewis Hayden, and others urged the measure. In the end, it resolved to form "a State Protective Union Association, with branches in the different parts of the State, under the control of the colored people" as "a source of wealth—economy being the poor man's revenue—as well as a means of promoting our union and elevation."[28] As among whites or Europeans, small numbers initially took up these questions for the benefit of the many and in hopes that the many would follow.

In this context, practical labor reform meant direct action to assist runaway slaves. Some—perhaps only a few—in any African American community would take action to assist a runaway, even if they were going to be acting virtually alone, and this meant they would not end alone. Since the local black population generally would suffer the consequences if they were caught, community leaders acted to ensure that those engaged in aiding runaways not be caught. Over time, a network to cover such activities coalesced, becoming more coherent depending on the numbers being moved. Taking runaways through areas where there were few blacks in a position to help, sympathetic whites might be enlisted, as needed, to make the process work. In this sense, antislavery work typified how determined action by a relatively small number of former runaways and freedmen could galvanize relatively large responses by much wider antislavery constituencies.

These, in turn, increasingly refocused the amorphous antislavery concerns among whites in revolutionary and radical societies about a universal democratic republicanism on issues of liberty closer to home. Through the 1850s, black intransigence on this question ultimately got the issue of aiding runaway slaves discussed on the floor of the National Industrial Congresses. In the context of Kansas, John Brown and others elaborated assisting slave escapes into a national abolitionist strategy.

THE INTERRACIAL PREHISTORY
OF RADICAL REPUBLICANISM

African Americans had repeatedly demonstrated their preference for freedom and their general willingness to risk all to secure it. Just as the black community generally could not stand aside as fugitives were pursued—or as some in the community aided them—white abolitionists could not have stood aside as blacks took immediate and direct action for emancipation. In the course of the struggle over Kansas, they not only combined to resist the return of fugitive slaves but also began crossing over into slaveholding Missouri to liberate groups of slaves. The authorities—federal or territorial— were unable to stop this dynamic either, and all the efforts of the proslavery forces to force the question popularized and spread a spectrum of antislavery sentiment in the North. Congressional passage of the Kansas-Nebraska Act in February 1854 marked the final blow to the political coalitions that had dominated politics nationally for a generation.

The actual events in Kansas fueled the rapid growth and success of the Republican insurgency. Both friend and foe ascribed the most active efforts to impose a proslavery territorial government there to "Border Ruffians" functioning under the protection and direction of well-organized associations, called Southern Rights' Clubs or the Sons of the South. Most often, they were referred to as the three-degree "blue lodge" masons, which seemed to have served as feeders for the Southern jurisdiction of Scottish-rite free-masonry. Rooted in Charleston, the jurisdiction experienced tremendous western growth at this time under the leadership of Albert Pike, then living in Arkansas.[29]

Suspicions of Pike's "blue lodges" generally represented little more than an after-the-fact suspicion of conspiracy based on violence that was certainly real enough. In all likelihood, any KGCs likely came by way of Texas. For example, a large group of self-described "Texas Rangers" moved into the Fort Scott area, got attacked, and "never stopped till they got back to Red River." Northern sources referred to the proslavery convention that organized the territorial government at Lecompton as "the K.G.C. Convention."[30]

The free-state movement that resisted these groups and the proslavery "bogus legislature" included number of familiar figures. Augustus and John Otis Wattles of Cincinnati's Truth Brotherhood and the community at Utopia had long and deep associations with the effort to build black schools and the organization of Carthagena. Prominent free staters, such as Erastus D. Ladd, Edward Lynde, and William Vanzandt Barr, had been members of the Brotherhood of the Union back East, as had likely been William Addison Phillips. The Wattles and Phillips rode with John Brown, who had been in Europe in the wake of the 1848–49 revolution. Émigrés fighting alongside them included August Bondi, a Jewish student active in the Vienna risings; Charles W. Lenhardt, a Polish printer who had fought in Germany and Hungary; and the former Chartist Hinton. Brown criticized not only slavery but "our forms of social and political life" as well and "thought society ought to be organized on a less selfish basis; for, while material interests gained something by the deification of pure selfishness, men and women lost much by it."[31]

Back East, their kindred spirits clustered about the Radical Abolitionist Party. Among those at the edges of the party were Frederick Douglass, Susan B. Anthony, and William Lloyd Garrison, as well as Clark, visiting from Ohio. In 1856, the Radical Abolitionists waged state campaigns in New York, Pennsylvania, Ohio, and Illinois and nominated Gerrit Smith for president, remaining unconcerned when the *Times* scoffed that "private candidates, cast their votes indirectly but no less serviceably for the Polks, and Pierces of Pro-Slavery choice." Dr. James McCune Smith astutely observed that "Human Freedom, that is Human Brotherhood, is not periled in Kansas. The question has not even been raised; the fight there is about freedom of opinion, not of person; it is behind the age, altogether." Nevertheless, Radical Abolitionists realized that the character of the struggle over Kansas had changed everything. Their candidate complained that people "are looking after ballots when their eyes should be fixed on bayonets—they are counting votes when they should be mustering armed men—they are looking after civil rulers when they should be searching after military ones."[32]

The radicals of the Ouvrier Circle and their comrades had continued to drift toward antislavery politics. Their annual National Industrial Congresses admitted the first blacks requesting participation in 1851 and had Free Democratic congressman Charles Durkee chair that of 1852. In 1854, members of the Ouvrier Donald C. Henderson and David Marsh blunted an attempt to hold a session in the South, citing the degradation of labor there and the need of the congress to "give expression to its feelings against slavery." Proposals recommended that adherents support no candidate for office unless he "pledged his sacred honor to resist the aggression of the Southern Slave power." Another recommended that they "hail with joy and welcome the fugitive freeman, whom we swear to protect by the rights of our States and the strength of our arms." That same year, Alvan E. Bovay, a New York transplant and possible former member, chaired protest meetings at the former Fourierist community at Ripon, Wisconsin, that called for a new Republican Party.[33]

Members of the Brotherhood of the Union virtually dominated the 1855 National Industrial Congress at Cleveland. Ohioan John Hancock Klippart called the body to order, and the individuals present from the East—George Henry Evans from New Jersey, Gerrit Smith from New York, and John Sheddon of Pennsylvania—did nothing to distract from that dynamic. All of them had already become identified with the new Republicans, if not the Radical Abolitionist Party. Openly defying the bipartisan assumptions on slavery and race, the Industrial Congress selected as one of its two secretaries the local black newspaper editor, William H. Day.[34]

The following year, the organizers felt no need for any gathering independent of the abolitionists. Evans, the founding land reformer and longstanding antislavery editor, died in February 1856, leaving the agitation in the hands of three from the Ourvrier—John Commerford, Joshua K. Ingalls, and national secretary Ben Price. A few weeks later, they and other members and associates of the circle—John Windt, William Arbuthnot, and Keyes Arthur Bailey—changed the upcoming Industrial Congress into a "National Land Reform Convention." This would meet on the Fourth of July at Albany, coinciding with that of the Radical Abolitionists, itself timed to coincide with the Republican convention. A few Democratically inclined diehards from Pennsylvania and Delaware ignored this change and tried to hold their own National Industrial Congress, but the first session ended in chaos, and only eight people attended the second, including several who showed up to insist upon its adjournment sine die.[35] Such lopsided numbers make it correspondingly difficult to see this as a division in the ranks of the antebellum movement.

Nevertheless, a "Workingmen's Provisional Committee" that the Ouvrier sought to establish for the fall 1855 elections "split into fragments and factions." Henderson, Arbuthnot, and William West headed groups seeking local alliances with, respectively, Republican, Democratic, and Whig or Know-Nothings. The reputed Democratic affinities for the European revolutions proved a factor. One observer charged national Democratic leaders such as James Buchanan with plans to encourage coordinated risings against the old order in Europe and an American challenge to Spain's control of Cuba. Among the radicals, Ira B. Davis could not overlook Buchanan's posturing as a friend of the European revolution and even claimed that Buchanan had personally "assured him that he had always been and always would be, in favor of the dominant principles of the Homestead Bill." As late as 1856, Davis organized a workingmen's meeting for Buchanan that Commerford chaired.[36]

However, the Republican organization proved more dynamic. Leaders of the new party, such as 1856 candidate John C. Frémont, clung to that forlorn illusion that voters would resolve these issues in a generally peaceful, lawful, and reasoned way and pledged only to keep slavery out of the western territories. Still, no less a radical than John Brown's comrade Dick Hinton became an ardent supporter, a "friendly acquaintance" with him and his wife for years thereafter. In August, Frémont's campaign inspired "the largest political meeting of our German fellow citizens which ever assembled in this country." Among the officers were such prominent members of the Kommunist Klub as Friedrich Kapp and Friedrich or Fritz Jacobi, as well as Adolph Douai, the Texas editor and socialist. While in the city, Frémont told a committee of "workingmen" of his personal sympathies for land and labor reform. By the fall, some of the most prominent radicals embraced the party. Veteran agitator Lewis Ryckman ran on its ticket for the state assembly from the Lower East Side, and the skeptical Thomas A. Devyr weighed Horace Greeley's proposal to edit a Republican campaign sheet to be called the *Land Reformer*. Still skeptical, Radical Abolitionist Goodell predicted that the party would fold the following year rather than hold firm in opposition to the *Dred Scott* decision, which threatened to make slavery a national institution.[37]

Far more durably, Henderson's committee formed the "Mechanics and Workingmen's Central Republican Union" in September. It urged the organization of "all workingmen favorable to the cause of Free Labor, Free Soil and Fremont and Dayton." The group included Fourierist Charles A. Dana of the *Tribune*, as well as members and likely members of the Ouvrier Circle, such as Bailey, Ingalls, Windt, John H. Keyser, William Rowe, Henry Beeny, and John A. Smith. It supported a glee club and opened "reading rooms" to working-class voters. They took notice when South Carolina officials warned white workers to leave the state because, as *"foreigners, having no sympathy with our peculiar social organization, . . . they entertain and have expressed publicly opinions hostile to the institution of Slavery,* and dangerous to the peace and good order of this community." One of them challenged a prominent Southern politician to a debate, noting that he would "hardly consent to come down to the level of a *'mere* mechanic.' The 'fustest families' of Virginia have peculiar notions of dignity on this subject. They *own* their working men, and do not permit them to enter into any discussions whatever." This body of Ouvrier Circle Republicans grew strong enough to survive the elections.[38]

The association found itself part of a broader, if more moderate, working-class Republicanism. William Oland Bourne, a schoolteacher associated with the Five Point Mission, wrote poetry and lectured at literary societies before finding enough support to launch his *American Brotherhood*. The paper, with its Lippardian name, advocated cheap money, easy loans on low interest, and hostility to "speculators and money-dealers, whose business, instead of exchange, is debased into a money-trade." By 1856, he claimed to speak for a small group of like-minded "Iron Platform" Democrats and cooperated with Robert B. Minturn, Robert M. Poer, and others who shared an interest in mild reforms such as temperance and higher tariffs. They blew hot and cold over Kansas and espoused antislavery as something that would be beneficial to the whites.[39] However, they poured their efforts unsparingly into mobilizing working-class voters against the slaveholders.

The concerns over the "Slave Power Conspiracy" that united these currents represented no mere "paranoid style," but reflected the classical interests of the veteran land reformers. As was the case in antiquity, imperial ambitions had serious repercussions for life at home. Having established "Republican" political associations for a generation, they saw themselves in conflict with antirepublican standards drawing America "rapidly the way of ancient Rome." Representative government, they warned, could not survive the unchecked drive to cheapen labor, which would stratify Americans into being the "brokers in human flesh" or slaves of one sort or another.[40] Many of the thousands who had signed land-reform petitions over the previous decade traced many social ills back to a slaveholding land monopoly.

Then, too, what they encountered around them reinforced these fears. In Kansas, proslavery gangs gathered in places like Fort Titus, named for its proprietor, Pennsylvania-born "pirate" Harry Titus, who eventually lent his name to Titusville, Florida. In addition to Kansas, "Gallant Harry" participated in the Lopez fiasco in Cuba and the Walker campaign in Central America.[41]

Those eager to impose a government of their own choosing on people abroad did not need to hesitate to do so on people in their own country.

In the wake of the 1856 elections, Hugh Forbes of the old Universal Democratic Republicans sought to reclaim the language of radical republicanism. Determined to give voice to the émigrés, he launched the *European,* a weekly that pledged to "show the actual condition—moral, physical and mental—of all classes of the people of the various States of this Confederation, whether natives or emigrants, freemen or slaves," and "to sustain the cause of Republicanism against those who would sacrifice it to preserve the domination over the freemen of the North by the slave-owning aristocracy of the South." He declared, "So that slavery be abolished I care not what may accomplish that destruction." Furthermore, "Had any plan of giving liberty to slaves been decided upon, based on common sense and common honesty," he later wrote, "I should certainly have approved and probably have participated in it." William Lloyd Garrison found the *European* "thoroughly imbued with the spirit of impartial freedom, and makes no compromise with the slave oligarchy in our land—taking the only tenable ground, that between Liberty and Slavery, no union can possibly exist." In March or early April 1857, Joshua Leavitt of the *New York Independent* sent John Brown to Forbes.[42]

By that point, the antislavery experience in Kansas had moved Brown to a scheme worthy of any European revolutionist: a scheduled dash into slaveholding states in an attempt to encourage a mass flight to freedom. Back East, Brown consulted not only Forbes but also Gerrit Smith and Thaddeus Hyatt, whose partner in the electrical lighting business was Ingalls of the Ouvrier Circle. As well, though, they met with William H. Day, James McCune Smith, and other black leaders.[43]

In May 1858, Brown arranged for a largely black convention at Chatham, Canada, to authorize him as the commander in chief of a paramilitary venture. Martin Delany presided, and participants included adherents of the African American Mysteries, such as Lambert and probably Monroe. The heavy contingent of Prince Hall Masons included Osborn P. Anderson, who elected personally to participate in the raid. While the convention deliberated, Luke Parsons encountered information on the "African Mysteries" or "African American Mysteries," and told the other white abolitionists with Brown that blacks had their own secret society to take direct action against slavery. Regrettably, we know this only because one of the white abolitionists recorded the report in order to dismiss it as "some such confounded humbug." Nevertheless, Forbes's loose coalition of various nationalities—each sharing a sense that only self-emancipation could attain their freedom—included at the edges a circle of African Americans.[44] Such concerns about national self-emancipation remained central to the politics of Forbes abroad and in the United States.

Hinton discussed Forbes's connection with that "small coterie of clever colored men in New York City, revolving around a well-known physician of that race," surely Dr. James McCune Smith. Hinton complained that those circles cultivated "a counter race contempt, antagonism, and rage" against whites, but Smith articulated the same kinds of social radicalism as Forbes or Hinton. Urging the pursuit of a nobler ideal in the nineteenth century, he surveyed the material preoccupations of the society and concluded that "money is not that nobler idea; but liberty, equality, human brotherhood, in a word—manhood—is that nobler ideal." Indeed, as early as 1852, Smith wrote that it was "quite too late in the day to get up an association for the propagation of the pure African, or Irish, or any other breed."[45] Among these African American protonationalists, as surely as among the European groups, events seemed to demand internationalist concerns.

* * *

Much of the African American contribution to the secret society traditions involved what could certainly be viewed as protonationalist thinking. Charles L. Redmond "was very sorry that so many colored people had suffered themselves to be led by white men, after all. He wanted to see black men stand up for and by themselves." Referring to the land reformers, who had been organized as "Young America," he "wanted to see a black Young America marching together, boldly and bravely." Yet Redmond "wouldn't hear of such a thing as liberty in Canada; he must have liberty in America, for he would be satisfied with nothing qualified."[46] Such sentiment suited a revolutionary nationalism, in which the fight for justice neither precluded nor required the support and cooperation of the wider humanity.

The African American experience in America actually validated the model of the European revolutionary secret society better than any of its limited successes in the Old World. A small group of blacks determined to resist slavery created a dynamic that pulled virtually the entire community with them, which inspired and brought along all the white support necessary to construct an initial mechanism for challenging slavery, though it still remained insufficient for its actual overthrow. This determination ran deeper than slavery's expansion, and the violence in Kansas took it far beyond electoral politics. They even raised aspirations for armed rebellions that would have warmed the heart of any Blanquist.

5. DECISIVE MEANS

Political Violence and National Self-Definition

From 1859 into 1860, U.S. Army colonel Robert E. Lee found that being a virtual paragon of orderly respectability was no insurance against being up to his neck in armed conspiracies. He took leave from his command in Texas and returned to Virginia just in time to be sent to deal with the seizure of the U.S. Arsenal at Harpers Ferry by armed abolitionists. Lee returned to rumors that Juan Cortina's La Raza Unida had about six hundred "Indians, negroes and Mexicans" ready to invade the United States. Ever ready to face enemies unseen, George W. L. Bickley announced that his secret Knights of the Golden Circle and its allies in the Texas Rangers would invade Mexico first, a plan said to have driven "the negroes on the river to join Cortinas, for most of them are fugitives from Texas." Lee explained that he did not have the authority either to federalize the trigger-happy Texans or to lead them into Mexico and asked everybody to go home.[1] Mere resistance to the law seemed now to have conjured a rash of armed men with public threats and secret plots.

Political violence challenged the old Enlightenment faith that reason and right would guide the new nation-states, but the nation-states themselves had been subverting that faith for almost a century. Events in Europe continued to confirm the disaffection of the Ourvrier Circle and its allies among the Universal Democratic Republicans in America. Armed conflict in the Kansas Territory had already forcibly refocused their Brotherhood of the Union whose agrarian, socialist, and abolitionist visions had relied so heavily on reasoned moral discourse. On the other hand, groups such as the Knights of the Golden Circle had always equated progress with the violent subjugation of the more primitive.

TYRANNICIDE

In 1857 the remnants of the Ouvrier Circle moved into a broader transatlantic alliance. Two years earlier, Polish, French, German, Italian, and Hungarian émigré associations in London formed a short-lived "International Committee" to celebrate the February revolution. The effort to extend this group into a permanent organization included such figures as French socialist Louis Blanc, Russian revolutionary Alexander Herzen, cooperationist George J. Holyoake, Chartist land reformer Bronterre O'Brien, English Garibaldian Hugh Forbes, and German Communists with Karl Marx and Friedrich Engels. In June 1857, they sent copies of their resolutions to their peers in New York City.²

Other issues preoccupied Forbes when the circular arrived from London. His *Manual for the Patriotic Volunteer* and other writings impressed American abolitionists, and the *Independent* praised it as "preparation of the oppressed peoples of Europe," adding that "a few copies have gone to Kansas." Between the lecture circuit and the newspaper, Forbes made enough to send something to his wife and children back in Paris, but he remained particularly interested in Kansas, though scornful of the antislavery efforts to make merely a "Kansas for white people."³

On this basis, the eastern abolitionist backers of John Brown sent him to recruit Forbes as a military adviser. Expecting to find a small army to train in Iowa, Forbes found only an irregularly armed dozen or so veterans of the Kansas conflict, with vague notions of using "some twenty-five to fifty (colored and white mixed), well armed and bringing a quantity of spare arms, to beat up a slave quarter in Virginia." Forbes challenged Brown's plan in "as temperate as language could express," but their arguments eventually "grew more heated." Forbes questioned sending a hopelessly small strike force in the hopes it would immediately recruit militarily viable numbers, particularly with "no preparatory notice having been given to the slaves." If Brown's gamble failed to get immediate success, the raid would be suicidal. Moreover, if it did spark a slave rebellion, it would be "sweeping like a prairie fire from Mason and Dixon's line to the Gulf of Mexico" in such a spontaneous and disorganized fashion that it would be "easily subdued" on a local level.⁴

As an alternative, Forbes proposed a series of small armed bands along the border with slave states to make regular crippling strikes against the institution, subverting the value of slavery, which would roll back the borders in which the institution could function. Later, Lysander Spooner—often cited as a founder of American anarchism—and William Ellaby Lincoln, a black student at Oberlin, made very similar arguments. Without any apparent connection to Forbes, Lincoln offered particularly sage advice that Brown engage in "an armed diversion a la Garibaldi."[5] Once overruled, Forbes returned east, where he haunted antislavery leaders with dire but entirely accurate forebodings of an impending disaster.

Fearful that these plans would become public and implicate them, those back East closest to the Brown plan began an escalating series of attacks on Forbes to discredit him. A "letter from Paris" exaggerating his prison time and describing him as having been long active in the Kansas struggle appeared in the *New York Herald,* which prompted a letter to the *New York Times* to appear, correcting rumors and claims about Forbes's career.[6]

As this dispute smoldered behind the scenes, Felice Orsini, back in Paris, acted. On January 14, 1858, he led an attack on Napoleon III as the emperor made his way to the opera. The authorities in Paris quickly seized Orsini, and those in London arrested Simon Bernard, a member of the Philadelphes who had helped Orsini prepare the explosives. English radicals and the émigré community there rallied to defend both. Aided by attorneys such as Charles Bradlaugh, the radical freethinker, Bernard turned his hearing into an indictment of the French monarchy, and the British jury took only fifteen minutes to acquit him unanimously.[7]

In America, émigré radicals sponsored a public rally on April 22, 1858, to honor Orsini and his comrades. "*Revolutionists of all the Nationalities*" to the number of five thousand marched through the streets with four times as many viewing their demonstration. The German banner displayed "the Goddess of Reason—embracing a white man and a negro, under the auspices of the Universal Republic." The principal American speaker, John Allen, had argued, ten years before, that "the cause of labor was one. The time had come when the laborers of the North must make common cause with the laborers of the South; and the prejudices of color be done away with." The Orsini defense meeting called for "a Permanent Revolutionary Committee" of one hundred "for the spread of true liberty throughout the world."[8] The previous summer's London proposal for an International Committee came to fruition.

Similar, if smaller, demonstrations took place elsewhere. A military unit led Chicago's "Red Republican demonstration." Long a nonresistant opponent of violence, William Lloyd Garrison paraphrased Benjamin Franklin's adage that "our country is the world; our countrymen are all mankind." Furthermore, "In every country where political and social rights can be attained by the normal exercise of peaceful liberty we are pacific reformers," wrote Garrison. He added, "In every country where the use of the sword is necessary to get rid of a deadening tyranny, previous to any reform, we are revolutionists."[9]

The organization behind the rallies in New York took up the International Association. "The leading cities of the Union followed the example of New

York; the watchword of our time is fraternization of nations." On May 26, about fifty participants, mostly Germans, "intermingled with several Frenchmen," braved some "very bad weather" to gather at Steuben House and arrange translating the statutes of the Société Internationale into German and English. The International Association hit a responsive chord with the article: "We recognize no predilections for nationality or race, for caste or condition, for complexion or sex; our aim is nothing less than the conciliation of all human interests, the freedom and happiness of all mankind, and the achievement and perpetuation of the *Universal Republic*." That summer, affiliates formed at New York, Boston, Cincinnati, and Chicago with their own Central Committee.[10]

On June 23, the Germans hosted their mass meeting of some twelve hundred. Friedrich Albert Sorge—a violinist and the founder of organizational Marxism in the United States—spoke in German, French, and English. There, a French tailor urged "the proletarians" not to leave the fate of the movement in the hands of the bourgeois gentlemen but to look to their own leadership and interests. Setting aside the press allegations that he called repeatedly for a bloodbath, the American speaker, Lyman Whiting Case, agreed that "the only point at issue between the tyrants and the people, was the simple question between capital and labor" and that "the aristocracy of capital was the only aristocracy with which the people had to content, and that aristocracy erected its thrones on Fifth-avenue as in the capitals of Europe; both must be met by physical force."[11] The membership and activities of the International Association indicate that it largely just extended the functioning of the earlier Universal Democratic Republicans.

The French secret society tradition in America has gotten less attention, partly because of the presence of Marxists among the Germans and partly because most of the French themselves returned to Europe in the next few years. Indeed, it served as an umbrella for various groups to celebrate together the revolutionary anniversaries of French history in February, June, and September. French sections of the International Association formed not only in New York and Boston but in St. Louis and New Orleans as well, with some cothinkers as far away as San Francisco. Their spokesmen included such luminaries as Claude Pelletier, a Lyon libertarian socialist, and Gustave Dime, a fugitive from hard labor in France who provided much of the leadership. A Proudhonist of sorts, Frederick Tufferd, one of the editors of *Le Socialiste* in New York, also edited the *Bulletin de l'Union Républicaine* and later wrote on the American movement for French publications.[12]

Most striking, perhaps, was the brilliant, if erratic, Parisian-born paperhanger and house painter Joseph Déjacque. After a nominal education, he went to sea, learned his trade, and joined the radical Christian group that directed the L'Atelier (the Workshop). During the uprisings of 1848, he participated in the most radical, working-class wing, which seized and held about half of the city from June 22 to June 25. In restoring order, the army killed several thousand, while wounding and arresting many more, including Déjacque. After several incarcerations, he wrote *Lazareenes, fables et poesies sociales* in 1851, which landed him in trouble again, after which he left for Belgium, then England, and finally America in the spring of 1854. He took what work he could but aspired to editing a paper, launching *Le Libertaire* after coming to New York City. One account described Déjacque's speech as "thoroughly socialist, and advocated the reversement of the present order of married relations, and all institutions—a splendid specimen of a free lover."[13]

Déjacque's *Libertaire* pushed the same direction as had Forbes's *European.* Both spoke about not only "the peculiar institution" in the South but also racial prejudice and *Negrophobie,* as well as the ongoing U.S. war against the Native peoples in the West. They blasted the hypocrisy of American pretensions to freedom evident in what Forbes denounced as "the spirit of filibusterism"; he rarely published an issue of his *European* without an article on Kansas or Nicaragua or both.[14]

The Germans entertained unrealistically higher ambitions for themselves. The *Allgemeine Arbeiterbund* initiated an International Association gathering on January 14, 1859, the anniversary of Orsini's attack. The French, Italian, and Polish societies joined them. Friederich Kapp of the Kommunist Klub spoke on Orsini and Pierri, while Déjacque scoffed at moderates and urged a greater role for working-class leaders. In the wake of this demonstration, on January 17, the German group sponsored a national convention "composed of delegates from various socialistic organizations throughout the country." These included Philadelphia, Cleveland, Chicago, Boston, and Louisville as well as New York and Williamsburg. "The delegates say they labor to elect a President of the United States pledged to carry out its principles."[15]

Events moved the masses of English-speaking Americans and confirmed the radicalism of the émigré coalition. Massive layoffs in the building trades and other crafts had marked the beginnings of "hard times" in the mid-1850s. When the panic of 1857 began bringing down parts of the economic infrastructure, hopes of a rapid recovery faded. Many who had participated in the large labor movements earlier in the decade held mass protest meetings even as they pounded the pavements or, if lucky enough to keep their jobs, suffered a 15 percent to 20 percent reduction in real wages. Against this backdrop of urgency, the Republican advocacy of a protective tariff promised immediate relief and seemed to supplement the land-reform demands as a means of eradicating social injustice.[16]

The new party in Congress took every advantage of this shifting sentiment, making good on their promises for a Homestead Act. In the House, Galusha Grow did call the measure to a vote in February 1858, noting that it had been "discussed for eight years or more." In a largely sectional vote, the House passed the bill 120 to 76. About two weeks later, Benjamin F. Wade, Andrew Johnson, Henry Wilson, James Shields, and William H. Seward got the measure to the floor of the Senate, where Southern officeholders asserted the priority of a discussion of Cuba. Wade quipped with some bitterness, "The question is shall we give land to the landless or niggers to the niggerless." The Senate cast a generally sectional vote in favor of the bill, but President James Buchanan vetoed the Homestead Act. At that point, even the most loyal Jacksonian labor figures—such as Thomas Ainge Devyr and John Commerford—turned their backs on the party, the latter running for the assembly himself in 1859 as a Republican.[17] Hemorrhaging its working-class constituencies, the Democratic Party veered toward the abyss, taking the entire second-party system with it.

Commerford, like his Ourvrier Circle brother Albert Brisbane, had begun to think about applying land-reform principles with a cooperative "unitary household" colonization of the West. A critic asserted that they hoped to mingle "socialism, spiritualism, free loveism and Mormonism all together, in one grand orgie." However, Case's remarks to the International Association rally demonstrated just how far beyond the old communitarianism the movement had come. As "an American born" descendant of Presidents John Adams and John Quincy Adams, Case declared that, in the absence of feudalism and monarchy, the struggle in the United States would have to be directly against capitalism; he urged all his comrades to "fight this battle peaceably if they could but forcibly if necessary."[18] Such were the sentiments characteristic of the "red republicanism" on both sides of the Atlantic.

The International Association, however, began crumbling in short order. It survived to hold memorial activities in April 1859 for Dr. Louis Szpaczek, "an ardent Socialist" and Polish physician to Kossuth; Turners; the Social Reformers Society; the Allgemeine Arbeiterbund; and the International Society, with eulogies by Kapp in German and Julian Allen in English. In London, though, differences over Giuseppe Mazzini's nationalism and over the presence of women in the leadership began causing problems; the French émigrés in the Order of Memphis tried to transcend this by extending membership to Mazzini, Charles Bradlaugh, and Garibaldi, but the Polish Revolutionary

Commune withdrew in January 1859. In New York, though, the émigrés celebrated their armed revolts in the Old World with what Joseph Déjacque called "the devoted habit" in June 1859 and managed to hold together for one final anniversary commemoration on June 25, 1860.[19]

TAKING UP ARMS, 1859–60

Democratic planters relied heavily on violence and the threat of violence to maintain mastery not only over African slaves but also over those whites who did not own slaves or share this obsession. Periodically, the authorities had rumors of slave revolts to justify the imposition of particularly severe measures. In the wake of Harpers Ferry, the Southern elite faced a national insurgency that threatened to topple the two-party arrangements that had allowed it to exercise power since the days of Andrew Jackson.

Events south of the border saved Bickley and his KGC from complete obscurity. The War of the Reform in Mexico pitted Benito Juárez and his Liberalistas against the conservatives and shattered the already marginalized administration in the outlying parts of Mexico. Meanwhile, vague rumors circulated about "a secret association . . . having for its object the conquest of Mexico," and the press reprinted Bickley's enigmatic instructions for the presumably vast KGC to "pursue their ordinary business till November." Horace Greeley wrote later that Bickley had "for months been traversing the Slave States, organizing lodges and enlisting recruits for a grand foray on Mexico, with intent to 'regenerate' her, after the Walker pattern."[20]

Events permitted the KGC to promise a very tangible version of Lippard's hazy visions, but almost everything in the press on the subject merited the most severe skepticism, unless independently confirmed. Its self-appointed generalissimo managed knowledge of the order and of himself not by keeping it secret but by the regular dissemination of contradictory information. As the earlier Order of the Lone Star knew, a self-planted item in any newspaper would likely be reprinted nationally. As with Bickley's own birth, predating the origins of the KGC allowed for creating a mythical history of the order's earlier secret existence, which made plausible its rumored association with William Walker and the Nicaraguan effort, the excursions on the Mexican border, and the Cuban filibustering.[21]

A handful of Bickley's social betters across the Ohio River in Kentucky made all of this seem plausible. George Nicholas Sanders provided an outstanding example of one of these figures with whom Bickley may well have collaborated but certainly hoped to emulate. Born in Kentucky only a few days after Abraham Lincoln, Sanders belonged to a prominent family of transplanted Virginians and had first come to public attention over the effort to make Texas a national issue. Through the 1850s, Sander had sought to harness mid-nineteenth-century nationalism and the republicanism of Orsini to Southern sectionalist aspirations toward nationhood based on white supremacism.[22] Bickley never had anything like those advantages in life, but he had the temerity to act as though he did in a period of time when the Southern elite desperately needed such things done.

Duff Green also saw some of these possibilities. He once ran a store in partnership with Ben Helm, later brother-in-law of Abraham Lincoln, and Lincoln's stepmother had been a regular customer there. However, Green went on to edit the *United States Telegraph* as an organ of President Andrew Jackson before ostentatiously siding with John C. Calhoun—one of whose sons had married Green's daughter—and he published Nathaniel Beverley Tucker's 1836 novel, *The Partisan Leader,* with its prophecy of a Southern rebellion. He likely used child labor to print the book, having had a notorious clash over the question with the Columbia Typographical Union. After a stint in Europe in 1841–43, Green returned to serve as President James K. Polk's man in Texas. His interest in organizing a transcontinental railroad by the southern route from New Orleans explained much of his interest in "our American Italy—Mexico," and proposed destroying the Mississippi Delta.[23] Unlike Bickley, however, Green had impressive connections to the highest level of the Democratic hierarchy.

Bickley's Nativist connections and later activities in that area would have involved him with Louisville's secessionist mastermind, Blanton Duncan. A Nashville paper later described Duncan as a "writer of circulars for the Know Nothing Lodge of Kentucky, and latterly grand fabricator of Confederate rigmaroles." The son of a Whig congressman, Duncan owned real estate from Indiana to Texas, including plantation land in Bolivar and Washington counties, Mississippi, which made enjoying the good life in Louisville possible. In 1855, he won a bet over a shooting match for two thousand dollars.[24] Like Green and unlike Bickley, Duncan had money and connections, and he regularly traveled abroad and would have been an important ally for Bickley.

While the planters and their spokesmen produced an ample supply of hard-drinking, hot-tempered, blustering jingoists, the gentlemen balked at the activities in which a more plebeian leader could engage. Bickley called them together for the KGC's first national convention in August 1859 at White Sulphur Springs, Virginia. Reportedly "attended by about one hundred men, the doors being guarded by men in uniform," the pro-Democratic and rabidly anti-Catholic order claimed to "interfere with no man's politics or his religion." Members overseas belonged to the Foreign Legion, which promised each recruit fourteen dollars monthly with "arms, ammunition, uniforms, etc., to be furnished by the board of war before leaving American soil" and pledged sixty-four hundred acres of land. It took a dollar to join and "a weekly tax of ten cents." Recruitment and fund-raising would be the "chief business" of "all the subordinate officers" of the American Legion (over which Bickley was to be "president"), headquartered at Baltimore.[25]

Some sources describe a KGC of significance there. The local press reported a local castle with "nearly one thousand men, mostly young, and many from some very respectable families." Reportedly, they met at the armory to be drilled daily by U.S. officers, and members reportedly included local officials and William Byrne, a wealthy businessman also organizing "national volunteers" on behalf of the Southern Rights presidential campaign of John C. Breckenridge. Other likely members included the memorable Cipriano Ferrandini, a barber and "captain" in the KGC who used the names "Ruscelli" and "Orsini," as well as Michael O'Laughlen, a boyhood friend of John Wilkes Booth, and perhaps Booth himself.[26]

The meaning of references to the KGC is questionable. There seems little doubt whether Breckenridge Democrats functioned beyond the election or formed military companies. It may even be that some of those participants signed up for the KGC at one of Bickley's meetings, but the order seemed to have provided nothing but a generic label for what secessionists were doing in Baltimore with or without the label. Indeed, family papers in the Maryland State Archives indicate that Ferrandini held his commission as a "captain" in the militia, not the KGC, and the very little documentary information we have about Bickley's order mandates the exclusion of Catholics, such as Ferrandini.[27] Upon closer inspection, most after-the-fact accounts implying a substantive KGC functioning as part of Bickley's organization dissipate in this way.

In the wake of the convention, Bickley resumed his tour with "one or two 'military men' from the South." Passing the hat, he presented himself as "the Commander-in-Chief in the Crimea, where he had rapidly risen in the ranks of the Russian Army to the position of General, and had been decorated with the Cross of Honor by the Czar; of what the Czar, in conversation, had said to him, and of the particular inquiries afterwards propounded to him by Napoleon III, in person, concerning the reasons that had induced him to join the Russian forces instead of lending his mighty sword and military abilities to the allies; of what he had done when he was an officer of the American Army in Mexico." Bickley assured a Montgomery audience that the KGC had been "originally intended to advance and subserve the interests of the Southern States," while claiming its goal as Mexico before New Yorkers. There he made his cousin "the

Treasurer of the 'Castle,'" got the "Colonel of a celebrated New-York regiment" to take charge of "the hundred men, more or less, who had signed the roll," and skipped town without paying rent for the meeting hall in the Bowery.[28]

It was not Bickley's largely spectral KGC but Juan Cortina's La Raza Unida that crossed the Rio Grande. On September 28, while residents of Brownsville were attending a fiesta across the border in Matamoros, the nationalist caudillo and his men raided the Brownsville jail, freeing a prisoner accused of shooting a white lawman. Before leaving, Cortina issued a proclamation asserting the rights of Mexican Texans, rallying the support of the poorer Mexicans on both sides of the river. As Texas Ranger John Salmon "Rip" Ford illegally scrambled back and forth across the international frontier with Mexico, the terrified local Anglo elites found the KGC a useful presence. Rather perceptively, some contemporaries thought Bickley "a mere tool," for the order, "under shrewder manipulation of concealed hands, became an organization of some significance."[29]

Whatever the mechanics of the process, the KGC came to life in Texas. Bickley and his "philanthropic filibusters" mastered the art of getting favorable press coverage. The *New Orleans Courier* compared his ambitions in Mexico to those of the foreigners who had aided the American Revolution, willfully ignoring his plan to play the role of Washington and the Continental Congress as well. Rumor identified with the order Governor Sam Houston and his lieutenant, Eber Worthington Cave, also a correspondent of the late George Lippard. Less questionably, Ford, Alfred M. Hobby, George Cupples, John B. Lubbock, and Benjamin McCulloch joined, with Elkhanah Bracken Greer and Trevanion Theodore Teel becoming public spokesmen for the Texas KGC. In short order, it claimed thirty-two local "castles," covering not only such places as Houston, Galveston, Austin, and San Antonio but also small towns such as La Grange, where its sixty members included "the most respectable and enterprising of our citizens" and steady growth. Stories also circulated of ten thousand armed KGCs along the border, but these rumors likely originated with the order itself.[30]

Based strictly on the bits and pieces of more reliable data, there is no reason to believe KGC membership was more than one or two thousand in Texas with no more than another thousand or so scattered elsewhere in the South. This may include their large numbers said to be engaged in military drill, the kind of activities that would be widely reported and available. For this reason, it seems that, in most cases, KGC membership amounted to little more than paying an initiation fee. In the end, the U.S. military command under Col. Robert E. Lee would have documented any signs of such a large operation along the border.

However, other conspiracies preoccupied Lee, who was back East on leave to settle his father-in-law's estate when he received news on October 17 that a small force of abolitionists had seized the federal arsenal at Harpers Ferry. Brown had planned the raid earlier at Detroit with George DeBaptiste, William Lambert, Frederick Douglass, and others. At least in part, they said, "the expedition was armed here and started from here, and there are still living in Detroit several colored men who helped arrange the plan, and are familiar with it from its first inception." Setting aside the misgivings of Forbes and others, Brown led his little band of men into Harper's Ferry.[31] The townsmen there seized arms of their own and pinned the raiders in the engine house until Lee arrived with federal troops, who took the survivors to nearby Charles Town with plans to try them for treason.

Among the Virginia militia coming by train from Richmond was the actor John Wilkes Booth. Several accounts indicate that he managed to talk his way into the unit due to some secret society connection. Two of Booth's fellow actors, George Wren and Samuel K. Chester, recalled he had joined a "society" there; although it may have been no more than a secessionist-dominated Masonic lodge, Wren explicitly identified it as the KGC.[32]

Almost as soon as the surviving raiders fell into the hands of the authorities, Dick Hinton began recruiting volunteers for a rescue mission. Participants ranged from Augustus Wattles and others in Kansas to Forbes's New York comrades in that city's Kommunist Klub. Independently, Charles Lenhardt left Cincinnati Law School, where he had gone after Kansas, and used the Masonic passwords and secret signs he had learned from the Border Ruffians in Kansas to join the armed guards around John Brown and wait for the escape attempt. Matters got as far as scouting the jail and escape routes but failed because Brown declined to cooperate for fear that it would cause more bloodshed. The authorities believed they had uncovered "a conspiracy of formidable extent, in name and numbers."[33] On December 2, Virginia authorities hanged Brown for "treason" to their state.

Meanwhile, Congress launched an investigation. Forbes left the country, but the New York Herald bribed his former landlord and seized a trunk with documents by other of Brown's association, such as William A. Phillips, Richard J. Hinton, and James Redpath. Official investigations followed, implicating also Edward Daniels of Wisconsin and Augustus Wattles, "an obscure abolition scamp."[34]

The spirit of John Brown touched with fire the antislavery radicals, not the least of whom were those long involved with Hugh Forbes. Déjacque praised Brown in Le Libertaire, and the speaker at a Polish event in the city "made some very lengthy remarks about John Brown and Harpers Ferry, eulogizing Brown as a hero of the first order, whom he regarded as a victim of the slave power. Slavery he denounced as a crime equal to assassination." When the German Jewish secularist Max Langenschwartz turned up at a spiritualist meeting, it was to declare history "but the record of a perpetual struggle for social equality," adding that "talking is of no use. His remedy for social wrongs is *revolution*. . . . His model Reformer is John Brown. He would make every despot a head shorter."[35]

After the judicial killings of Brown and his men, what had been essentially a black agenda—to resist slavery by any and all means—became that of the entire antislavery movement. Those engaged in the rescue plans for Brown's men established a new "John Brown League." Members took "a binding oath to devote our lives to the destruction of American Slavery: to engage in no occupation that could prevent our marching at an hour's notice, and to obey an order to march without question." Although it had officers, grips, signs, and obligations like a fraternal order, it was paramilitary secret society, comparable to that of the Carbonari or the Blanquists on the Continent. An Ohio participant later said that it "numbered 25,000 members, scattered through Kansas, Iowa, Northern Ohio, New York and Canada."[36] Although obscure, likely exaggerated, and short-lived, it represented a considerable step toward the professionalization of revolutionary politics in America.

Texas authorities cited rumors of a multiracial army of Corinistas amassing on the border to justify the concentration of a reported two thousand gunmen along the Rio Grande. Soon, the *Vicksburg Star* spoke of "a military body of ten thousand men, fully equipped for war." The *Charleston Mercury* described "about 5,000, picked men, and with what party they are in league with, is still a mystery." It closed by asking, "Is old San Jacinto at the head of the Knights of the Golden Circle? *Quien sabe!*" The stories served the purpose of warning that Cortina would face a KGC army possibly commanded by Sam Houston himself. Of course, the fear of an invasion of Mexico inspired "the negroes on the river to join Cortinas, for most of them are fugitives from Texas." Lee not only declined to federalize the trigger-happy state troops or lead them across the border but insisted that they disband as well. While the KGC provided a cover for those who remained, it provided none of the numbers needed for a serious campaign.[37]

In short order, the New Orleans Castle of the KGC, which claimed fifteen hundred members, investigated Bickley and expelled him on April 6, 1860. Bickley's General Order No. 564 responded by calling a national convention at Raleigh in May. Proclaiming values "dear to every Southern heart," Bickley invited the interest of "Southern gentlemen, with evidences of social position," presumably demonstrable through contributions. "Sir Charles Bickley" also clarified the new emphasis on "gentlemen of character and respectability," rather than the "rowdies, gamblers, and other disreputable elements" of New Orleans, adding that the convention would "purge the order of all unworthy members; and that hereafter it will only consist of 'Southern gentlemen, by birth, education and practice—men capable of building up a high grade of civilization in the country towards which their energies are directed." The convention selected a "permanent Commander-in-Chief," a "permanent President," and "a board of advisement" before adjourning.[38] Given the record, one might well be tempted to regard Bickley and the entire KGC as a little more than a confidence scam.

The ease of the May 1860 KGC reorganization hints that there was actually very little of it to reorganize. Bickley's report doubled as "an *open letter* for the great Southern public" and asserted the fiction that, for six years, the KGC had "braved the slurs of Abolitionists and rivals," as well as "rowdyism." The order established the Knights of the Iron Hand as a preliminary military degree, a second degree for finance, and the Knights of the Columbian Star as a governing degree, with a military Foreign Council and a strictly advisory Home Council. Following the precedent of the Order of the Lone Star, the KGC couched its goal "to occupy and annex Mexico a la Texas" as revolutionary and progressive, a fit American application of European republicanism.[39]

KGC practices told more than its rhetoric. Time and space forbid—and our purposes do not require—a thorough exploration of the contradictions in Bickley's public statements. His shortsighted desire to solicit funds probably inspired his public announcement that he had secret letters of invitation from both Juárez and conservative general Miguel Gregorio de la Luz Atenógenes Miramón y Tarelo, which domestic consideration in Mexico forbade his making public—which, of course, he was doing. In July 1860, the counsel of the Juaristas at New Orleans declared his claims "false in every respect," after which the KGC declared that it would enter Mexico to aid Miramón. (The *New York Times* also plausibly blamed the KGC for the New Orleans disinformation, widely circulated in the American press, that the Juárez government had collapsed.) Even sympathizers of the scheme acknowledged that any KGC incursion would "meet with resistance from all classes." In particular, "the masses and peons are determined, priest-ridden centralists, and exhibit the most bitter hatred for Americans."[40]

Throughout, Bickley claimed that the KGC invasion of Mexico would not be filibustering, because such a campaign would be "only a decent way of getting hold of the country, by some kind of conquest, and the bringing it into the United States, or else adding it to the Southern Confederacy." The

Southern Intelligencer acknowledged the disclaimer to be "more ornamental than practical. And the denial of Filibusterism was as little convincing as the denial that the thing is being used as a political engine."[41] Easily lost in the Bickleyisms was the fact that the KGC had redefined its territorial ambitions as strictly sectional in terms of the South—or, more accurately, it had refined national ambitions for expansion to those of "the Southern Confederacy" rather than the United States.

FALL 1860: THE NATIONAL CRISIS

The apparent planning for a KGC expedition continued. Bickley promised that the order would "cross at the earliest possible moment, and I only ask our friends and the press to give us that assistance which we ought to expect of them." He acknowledged that "many of the most prominent men in the organization believe that no attempt should be made until the first of December," but he believed that, by then, "we may be more needed at home than abroad." In the end, he called for the order to concentrate in Encinal (presently western Webb) County, along the Rio Grande, by September 15, 1860, with the intention of crossing the Rio Grande into Mexico by October 1. The *Norfolk Day Book* cheered them on, writing, "These men were scattered through the country from the mountains of Virginia to the Gulf of Mexico, and for some time have been awaiting orders to concentrate at some point convenient to the scene of their future operations." It added that "the movement of these men toward the Rio Grande is pregnant with much importance to the South, and is the commencement of a grand programme that has been preparing for several years." The press nowhere near the border reported about two thousand KGC under Bickley and Greer "quartered on the Rio Grande, prepared at any moment to pour into Mexico," to join the Liberals. [42]

Reports of what actually happened on the border differed greatly, with the *Corpus Christi Ranchero* documenting what it called Bickley's "mismanagement." Capt. Patrick H. Thorpe led a "detachment" through the town on its way to an expected rendezvous near Brownsville, where it "expected to meet a large force" to occupy Matamoros, "while the main force marched and occupied Monterey, as a place for head-quarters." A week later, it noted "another small detachment" that also found "no one, ten, or fifty thousand concentrated at any point in this section." Into late October, the *Ranchero* reported the piecemeal appearance of small bands "of gallant knights" who arrived only to be "disappointed in the number of braves . . . at the lowest calculation one thousand men." In the end, the thousands reported by a compliant national press hardly amounted to a few hundred adventurers.

The *Ranchero* warned that Mexicans "from all parties" would resist any such "quixotic and desperate expeditions of this kind." Still, well beyond the November election, the Associated Press reported that "the army of the Knights of the Golden Circle is on the eve of leaving for Mexico."[43] For the second time, the KGC's "invasion" fizzled ingloriously.

Bickley did not go to the border himself before leaving Galveston for Austin. He faced what threatened to become a public relations disaster. Having created a situation in which he had only a body of four or five hundred men—by his new estimate—he claimed his hands were tied because they "would face disaster should he lead them into Mexico." He blamed the media for the confusion in South Texas, although it seems to have only repeated what he told them. He also cited the logistical problems of mounting an invasion and even repeated the very specific earlier charge of the Order of the Lone Star that George Law's U.S. Mail Steamship Company had failed the project. Bickley also noted the failure of the U.S. authorities to support William Walker's third and final filibustering expedition to Central America, one that left him stranded in Belize and facing a Honduran firing squad in September. Finally, the approaching presidential elections complicated everything.[44]

Whatever the realities, the KGC emerged posturing as a sectional power across the South. The first duty Bickley had assumed with KGC's reorganization was the appointment of subordinate officers charged with fund-raising in a dozen states: Alabama, Florida, Georgia, Kentucky, Maryland, Mississippi, North Carolina, South Carolina, Tennessee, and Virginia, as well as Louisiana and Texas. There were also hints that the order existed on one level or another in the Indian Territory, at least among the Southern Democratic functionaries of the U.S. government there. This certainly fitted Bickley's claim that the KGC was "originally intended to advance and subserve the interests of the Southern States." Moreover, the press-inflated "invasion" of Mexico contributed something to unraveling the Jacksonian coalition across the North. It raised the political price for Northern leaders willing to compromise over slavery and created yet another irresistible incentive for the unification of the Ourvrier and the abolitionists.[45]

However, Bickley simultaneously presented himself as a figure fostering progress through national unity. He had Benjamin Urner, the old Cincinnati Fourierist, print not only *Rules, Regulations & Principles of the KGC* for Southern readers but *Address of the National Executive Committee of the Union League, to the Citizens of the United States* for Northern readers. Although two officers of the Union League signed the latter, the style, language, and argument were Bickley's. Although there is no further record of anything done or written by this antebellum "Union League," it promised to save the

Union by preventing the aggressive criticisms of slavery by abolitionists or, indeed, Republicans. It even offered its own strange parody of the Declaration of Independence.[46]

Meanwhile, International Association activities continued in New York City. In June 1860, radicals met at the Steuben House to recall the repression of the workers. Déjacque recalled how "the proletarian giant, fell bathed into its blood under the blows from God Reaction." It had, however, won a "moral victory, by the idea which was spread of its wounds, like a revolutionary plague, on the old world, and infested it with a virus of death."[47]

Members of the old Ouvrier Circle often pursued their older preoccupations, some in conjunction with the Europeans and others attempting to rebuild the large movement of which they had glimmers in the past. Through the summer, Ira B. Davis—an exception who never went over to the Republicans—took the call for radical self-organization into the spiritualist movement, and Ouvrier Circle's local *Herald of Progress* reported meetings to discuss the abolition of capitalism. On October 7, 1860, the Infidel Association of America held its annual meeting in New York's City Assembly Rooms on Broadway. By then, Ben Price had become the national secretary of the National Land Reform Association, which continued to attempt agitation for years.[48]

By then, whatever influence the Republicans had in the working-class quarters of Lower Manhattan, they owed the Ourvrier Circle. They and their supporters dominated the Republican convention in the overwhelmingly Democratic Fourth Congressional District—including the Fourth, Sixth, Tenth, and Fourteenth wards on the Lower East Side—nominating "Honest John" Commerford for Congress. Accounts of the meetings mention familiar names, such as William West, Henry Beeny, and Benjamin Price. The effort had the help of German radicals, such as Friedrich Jacobi, a Baden émigré among the leaders of the local Kommunist Klub, and Commerford spent the night before the election with the Garibaldi Wide-Awakes.[49]

On the evening of October 19, members of the Ourvrier Circle organized no fewer than three campaign events on the Lower East Side. This included a Tenth Ward torchlight march to an open-air rally, where speakers reminded them that the workingmen in the Sons of Liberty had moved through the same streets. A victory in 1860, however, would prove more involved. In the end, Commerford's shoestring workingmen's campaign got 3,324 votes, or 26.7 percent of the total. The honesty of the vote could be seriously questioned in the machine-dominated Sixth Ward, which officially reported fewer votes for Commerford than Lincoln.[50]

Two weeks later, veterans of the campaign rejoined Davis and others for one last antebellum Industrial Congress. They invited "associations of Mechanics,

Laborers, Land-reformers, Protective Unions, Progressives and Humanitarians" to send representatives to the Metropolitan Hall on Tuesday and Wednesday, November 20 and 21. The published summary of their resolutions read:

> That the present system of commerce is false—that the laborer should receive the full net product of his labor—that all intermediates between producers and consumers are non-essential; they should exchange with each other the products of their own labor—that the legal recognition of paper currency should cease—that land monopoly is an evil—that the public lands should be given to actual settlers—that a homestead exemption law should be passed— that women are entitled to an equal voice with men in the administration of government, and to the same freedom of industrial pursuits, and the same compensation enjoyed by men.

The resolutions restated the old antebellum concerns but within the inclusive resolutions of the International Association: "We recognize no predilections for nationality or race, for caste or condition, for complexion or sex; our aim is nothing less than the conciliation of all human interests, the freedom and happiness of all mankind, and the achievement and perpetuation of the *Universal Republic.*"[51]

In contrast, the few Republicans in places like Virginia briefly tried to organize themselves, and supporters of both the old Whigs and the regular Democrats sought to cool the frenzy of the Southern Rights faction, but they found plots everywhere. Under torture, slaves willingly affirmed virtually any rumors. The panic assumed greater proportions as vigilance committees found ever-wider plots, on the basis of which they sought even more sweeping powers. They seized, whipped, and murdered whites as well as blacks with the sanction of the society's masters. Newspapers in the Deep South urged "a thorough expurgation" of the hidden abolitionists in their midst: "Now the time has come for wiping these creatures out." The *Clayton Banner* insisted that anyone was "liable to a *just suspicion,* it is their own fault or misfortune, and our *safety demands* that *all such be rendered incapable of prowling about and putting into execution their apparent designs.*"[52] In short, the KGC provided a label for vigilantes ready, willing, and able to go beyond the law.

Across the South, the violence and threats of violence that characterized the election reappeared with renewed vigor. Local groups vied over who could negate the impact of the election first. The *Clayton Banner* declared explicitly, "It must be by *coup d'etat,* or it will fall through and fail." The "ordinary Legislature" should declare secession rather than a state convention, and the measure should be coupled to "an act, denouncing as traitors, and putting out of legal protection, whoever may gainsay the measure." Self-declared Minute Men took to the roads in Mississippi and Alabama. This round, the focus of the threats and violence expanded even further, making a particular target of Northern-born whites in the region.[53]

Nevertheless, by the time the visionary proposals of the NIC for the future of the nation saw print, the secession of South Carolina challenged any future at all for the United States. The election had tested the loyalty of its losers and found it wanting, as the wealthiest, most powerful, and most autocratic forces in that society chose to demolish the political mechanisms essential to social reform in order to ensure the legality of human slavery in places where it did not yet exist.

* * *

On the brink of most devastating conflict in American history, the Ourvrier Circle had extended the secret society tradition into many channels. The fascination with Orsini's dramatic attempt to murder Napoleon III reflected their openness to the value of selective acts of political violence. However, violence—like secrecy itself—was the means to a social end, defined by antislavery associations and its militant advocacy of women's rights as a more inclusive and democratic republic.

On the other hand, the KGC had taken the secret society tradition into very different channels. Although few of the ardent sectionalists to whom Bickley appealed found Orsini's example hopeful, some did. Through the 1850s, white supremacist George N. Sanders watched the vast population and power of the nonslaveholding states stirring to action against the South and justified Southern resistance up to the point of violence and tyrannicide. Despite its entrepreneurial roots in a con man's posturing, the KGC contributed toward the justification of violence to establish a more exclusive and hierarchical civilization.

PART III
ENDS

6. THE COUNTERFEIT NATION

The KGC, Secession, and the Confederate Experience

The horsemen of George W. L. Bickley's Apocalypse rode beneath a "dark blue flag with a lone white star bordered with red in the center." The flag of the old Republic of West Florida had become the symbol of filibustering ambitions to tear single independent state from neighboring foreign provinces. It became woven into the Lone Star Flag of Texas, and, in Kansas, became identified with the "blue lodges." In January 1861, Mississippi raised the old flag under which part of it gained independence from Spain, and it become the "Bonnie Blue Flag" of secessionist fame.[1] *In hoc signo,* Bickley promised conquest.

Secession transformed the KGC from a political confidence game into a multipurpose tool for a nation-building enterprise. That is, the KGC eased the effort of the Southern elite to build a nation by secession from a country it could no longer control and acquire the new territory they believed they could. Over time, Bickley fine-tuned his flattery of the Southern elite, shaping for them a tool that appealed to popular prejudices against republican ideology. In response, the masters of the new Confederate nation found the KGC most useful as an all-purpose label for its enforcement arm at the defining margins of the new Confederate States of America.

THE IDEOLOGICAL CONTRIBUTION OF THE KGC

Bickley was no ideologue or thinker but a salesman of rhetoric with a good eye for what the market wanted. He tried to serve those who could best reward him by articulating an ideological justification for a new American nation, in which white supremacy formed the cornerstone. As Bickley wrote in a letter, "God seems to have chosen, by preference, the Anglo-American race to control and direct the ultimatums of these mutations. We have been blessed with extraordinary privileges and advantages, and we are morally bound to faithfully discharge the high trust which the Almighty has conferred on us as a people."[2]

The KGC banned from membership "any confirmed drunkard, professional gambler, rowdy, convict, felon, abolitionist, negro, Indian, minor, idiot or foreigner." Beyond this, the order hoped within the wider society to "place the power in the hands of the most educated and moral, and oppose the recognition of any Negro, Mulatto, Indian, or mixed blood to citizenship." Indeed, it required of members a pledge to "do all I can" to keep "Negro, Mulatto, Indian, or mixed blood" people from obtaining citizenship and "to prevent any Roman Catholic" from taking public office.[3]

The *Houston Telegraph* described Bickley's order as growing from "the deep and settled hatred of the General to the Abolitionists and any mistaken philanthropist who could desire the freedom of the negro." In reality, Bickley seems to have been personally more ambiguous about his real views on race. He once persuaded his Cincinnati creditors to let him return to Virginia to sell his estate with "fifty or sixty negroes," but there is no evidence that he ever actually owned a single slave, much less an estate, and his most articulate defense of slavery was, bizarrely, that it represented the democratic will of blacks, who, he wrote, were "acquainted with the leading movements in the political world, are moral, and many read; few write, and their reading is mostly confined to the bible." In his *Adalaska,* a Negro servant named Bolivar defends the small community hidden in the caverns of Genreva, and part of the culmination of the story is when a character from the white elite becomes "no longer ashamed to acknowledge old Bolivar as his equal."[4] Bickley's ambivalence never stood in the way of his advocating what seemed the most marketable for the KGC.

Bickley placed Indians under a similar proscription. He believed "the day is coming when the western wilds must be converted into happy homes, and if the red-man who now occupies them is not first taught to fill the injunction laid upon Adam, he must go the way of his ancestors and be no more known among the nations of the earth." He confidently asserted that they had become "but little more advanced than they were centuries ago." Nevertheless, sources, friendly and hostile, indicate that the KGC had a small and select following among prowhite, pro-Southern factions in the so-called Five Civilized Nations of the Indian Territory.[5]

It seemed evident that all "knights" would be male. Bickley "would make woman my equal and restore to her, her natural rights" only in that she would "share, in common with man, the business transactions of life, and thus afford her fields of labor in which to develop her god-like faculties." These faculties made her "eminently qualified to instill Christianity in the plastic minds of children." He thought that "to see a feminine, soft-handed clerk measuring lace, while a rosy-cheeked girl is chopping wood to make him a fire, induces me to think man has forgotten from whence he sprung." Notwithstanding that he was himself medically uneducated and entirely unqualified, Bickley acted as an administrator at the Eclectic Medical Institute during 1856–57 to ban female students, on the grounds that professional training would "unsex the woman physician in a perverse and dehumanizing way." He favored neither woman suffrage nor "petticoat government."[6]

Bickley espoused what later Protestants would call Fundamentalism. The KGC required prospective members to share this view of religion, formally requiring their positive answers to the questions "Do you believe in the religion of Jesus Christ?" and "Are you willing to help in spreading it?" Society would be based upon "the broad declaration that the Old and New Testaments—the Holy Bible—is the revealed will of God." The order hoped to impose such an understanding of Christianity on the wider society, taking the position that "the Bible shall be adopted for use in all public schools." The purpose of his 1855 lecture, "Doomed Cities of Antiquity," had been "to demonstrate the truth of the Bible by the literal and exact fulfillment of prophecy." In the KGC's world, "innovations on the written word of God ought to be discountenanced by all men."[7]

The KGC espoused a particularly venomous version of an Anglo-American "muscular Christianity." Bickley boasted of the unprecedented level of "civilized and Christian progression as is exhibited by this young and vigorous nation." He also argued that "Republicanism, founded on Christianity, first rose in the new world, and hence we claim this continent as the sacred home of Liberty." This required his contemporaries to "be men—Christian and consistent men—energetic Anglo-Americans."[8]

By the time of the 1860 elections, Bickley saw the kind of German free-thinkers allied to the Brotherhood of the Union at New York or Philadelphia as the antithesis of the order he had built in Cincinnati. He indicted the immigrants before an Austin crowd: "The great West was being rapidly settled by Europeans who arrived in our country with deep rooted prejudices against slavery, until the anti-slavery party was no longer confined to the manufacturing districts of New England, but like some fatal epidemic, it has spread over the whole North and West."[9]

As with other critics of European immigration, Bickley tended to muddle the issue with Catholicism. As one Kansas paper declared:

A leading feature of this infamous association is the proscription of foreigners and Catholics. This is in perfect harmony with the spirit of aristocracy and intolerance prevalent among the leaders of the chivalry, and shows that they aim at the destruction of every liberal principle in our form of government. Such doctrines will increase the abhorrence in which they are held by the people of the loyal States. For, we rejoice to say, that the patriotic devotion of the foreign-born citizens to their adopted land, as exhibited by their recent brave services in its defence, has swept from the North the last vestige of Know Nothing bigotry and prejudice.

As early as his 1852 organization of the Wayne Circle of the Brotherhood of the Union, he wanted an organization that would exclude "all worshippers of the Pope." Indeed, the order proposed to seize "the enormous wealth of the Romish Church in Mexico" with "*the confiscation of three hundred millions of dollars to the use of the K.G.C.!*"[10]

The first goal of the KGC had been "to Anglicize the fairest portion of the Western Continent" by seizing Mexico and the rest of "the golden circle." This would "introduce Anglo-Saxon energy and American prudence among a people who have heretofore been incapable of self-government, and who are actually inviting them to come and teach them how to live and be happy." The KGC aspired "to Americanize and Africanize Mexico; that is to say, that Americans shall take Mexico, and establish Slavery there, and open the slave trade." Because the growing infusion of white blood into the existing slave population supposedly threatened its necessary manageability, the KGC advocated the resumption of the slave trade and a direct infusion of African blood.[11]

South of the border, the KGC would "reduce the Peon system to Perpetual Slavery." It would then divide the enslaved people "to have and hold forever" among the KGC members. Members of the third, second, and first degree of the KGC would get, respectively, a sixth, a third, and half of the slaves. In short, the KGC urged driving out the free blacks from the slaveholding states, particularly pushing those from Texas into Mexico, after which the order would impose Anglo-Saxon order on that country and reenslave them. With the benefit of an outsider's perspective, the *London Spectator* thought it "rather like a dream of some mad slaveholder than a grave and definite project, which, nevertheless, we believe it to be." The English publication asked readers to contemplate "the awful increase of human misery" implicit in the KGC's project.[12]

Such a solution required a strong state, and Bickley's recognition of "Limited Monarchy as the best form of Government for the purpose in view, since it can be made strong and effective." However, in clarifying the "limited" nature of this power, Bickley defined his goal as "a great military Government in Mexico, of which he should be emperor." In the KGC's proposal for "a monarchial government in the territory they propose to seize," a Kansas newspaper found "another evidence that the public sentiment of the South is gradually becoming hostile to republican institutions. Thus slavery and political despotism go hand in hand."[13] In truth, if such a government suited the establishment and security of slavery in Mexico, it would be all the more necessary in the United States, where slavery was under attack.

As "the only military circle of Americanism," the KGC proposed to exterminate those heresies rooted in an "unguarded liberty—liberty freed from the trammels of the Bible and the Constitution—leads only to political heresy, to civil commotion and discord, to irreverence, arrogance, and final misery; and all who have made deadly threats at Americanism, have denounced the Constitution of our fathers and the bible of their faith." Moreover, "those who set up visionary codes of human systems in opposition to the Eternal Word of the living God," declared Bickley, "took exceptions to the Constitution which permitted the Southern States to hold Africans and their descendants in perpetual bondage." In the North, "Millerism and Spiritualism, every Utopian idea has numerous advocates," creating a "democracy unrestrained by domestic slavery" that "debases the mechanic." Initiates to the KGC pledged to "labor not only for the existence of Domestic Slavery" but "a government strong enough to protect and perpetuate it."[14]

Sectional hostility became central to the KGC message. Bickley warned that "Northern men have been called to edit our papers and Northern women to educate and train our daughters. The one propagates abolitionism by insidious clippings of abolition arguments, and weak comments thereof; the other, while their conduct is, so far as we have observed in the main, irreproachable, by constantly reminding the child of our duty to be kind and affable, and that we are all the work of the Creator, and of one race, so impress the child's mind that by the time it arrives at maturity it is already abolitionized." He warned that "the Republican or Northern party is abolitionized—the Southern party is going rapidly to secession."[15]

In short, the efforts of "Christian and consistent men—energetic Anglo-Americans" would be in sectional interests, because "the destiny of our Slave States and Mexico is now in our hands." The alternative, leaving power to shift north, would reduce the South "to vassalage." "There are now but two parties—a Northern and a Southern party; the one with manufacturing, the other with agricultural interests—and that their variance is so great that a reconciliation is almost an impossibility." Taking Mexico would make the South equal to the North within the Union or "a Southern Confederacy." He stated, "We shall have in our own hands the cotton, tobacco, sugar, coffee, rice, corn and tea lands of the continent, and the world's great store-house of mineral wealth."[16]

Bickley insisted that power could be securely vested only in the hands of the dominant class of landholders and slaveholders, of which he had never been a member but to which he sought to pander shamelessly. "Who ever knew a practical shoemaker, or a maker of pinheads, to have a man's ambition? They own neither land or property, and have no tie to then institutions of the country." So it was that Bickley sketched his hopes for "a great Democratic monarchy . . . which shall vie in grandeur with the Old Roman Empire." And he asked, "Are we not justified, then, in trying to build up and preserve such a 'People's Empire' as this would be?"[17] Beneath the rhetoric of states' rights and liberty lurked a government of unprecedented centralized authority capable of sustaining slavery.

The KGC sought to build a nation of which the cornerstone would be "the natural conservative element of all Democracies—domestic slavery." It explicitly stated that, when it conquered Mexico, the acceptance of slavery would be a requirement of citizenship, but this also formed an essential feature of "Americanism." Not only would this be taught in the schools and preached from the pulpit, but "he who refuses assent to them ought to be ruled out of society, and thus guard the great body against attractive heresies under captivating forms, whose adoption could lead to anarchy, infidelity and public enslavement."[18]

Bickley's blend of Christianity, racism, and sectional mistrust aimed at a marketable self-justification for the Southern white elite. However, its implementation required the recruitment of the ambitious who were less constrained by constitutional and legal scruples. He did not share—and never did—the belief of many of his former comrades in the Brotherhood of the Union through class conflict, the expropriation and democratization of property, and the elimination of property in slaves. Instead, he sought a society in which all whites benefited through an expansion of national wealth, particularly from expansion, and a sharing of what expansion would make available there. His "original pet idea of slave stealing" remained "the substratum upon which their mud-sills were laid."[19]

The proposal required a jackbooted direct action to deal with abolitionists and others the KGC sought to purge from society. The author of *An Authentic Exposition of the "K.G.C."* saw abolitionism as "the pretext, during the past few years, for every species of secession scoundrelism." Members promised their "best exertions to find out any and every Abolitionist whether man, woman or child, and forward the name of such to General Bickley or his lawful successor." They investigated "any smuggler or traveler trading with negroes or doing any unlawful act," dealing with them "in any way the 'Guards' may see proper." However, they were not only supposed to inform their superiors in the KGC but also supposed to take "proper steps" unconstrained by due process. That is, they "may barrel him up and throw him in a river, tar and feather him, and send him North, shoot, hang, or deal with him otherwise, as their 'judgments' may dictate."[20] It was an approach that could be expanded to any targets deemed subversive of the order.

The KGC suppression of differences would not really restrict freedom, explained Bickley, but would be necessary to ensure it. Unrestrained by civil liberties, the security of slavery justified the imposition of ethnic and ideological with claims of its own victimhood and the necessity of freeing itself from further victimization. The KGC justified silencing abolitionists without discussion or even the sanction of law because those it targeted sought a world that would not permit any disputation of the idea that "the negro will be equal to the white man." For this reason, Bickley insisted that "our people must present an unbroken front—no division should now be tolerated. The old party issues should be forgotten, and we should have but one Electoral Ticket in the South," which, he insisted, would be the only way to elect "a representative man" as president in 1860.[21]

Nevertheless, Bickley never seemed to lose sight of his real goals. This involved not formulating ideas but selling a product. At one point, he insisted that, in the KGC, "there is no opportunity for individual speculation in the organization. We are Americans, united for certain laudable ends, in the accomplishment of which every man in Christendom is interested, and those in the United States peculiarly so." In the midst of all these grand political plans, Bickley overheard other travelers at Napoleon, Arkansas, discussing the state's debt. He suggested that "the parties combining would buy State indebtedness at low figures," then "buy, on time, an interest in every paper in the State," which would then agitate for payment of the debt on face value, realizing millions on the operation.[22]

SECESSION'S ENFORCERS

Secessionists saw a unitary "South" victimized by unmerited conspiratorial intrigues that made the United States uninhabitable for them. They certainly seized upon stories, such as that in the *Continental Monthly* that the slaves had some kind of "Masonic league, the object of which is insurrection, and an overthrow of the whites." The press also treated the Republican campaign organization, the "Wide Awakes," as a paramilitary group "to enforce Black

Republican misrule upon the South—to subjugate resisting Southern States."
On the basis of these imagined and intangible dangers, those advocating the
dissolution of the Constitution could see themselves as "constitutionalists,
and when the provisions of that instrument are violated, then our people are
secessionists."[23] Bickley and the KGC played their most visible role on the
borders of the South, where many balked at secession.

The KGC's biggest role would be in Texas, where its living founding father, Governor Sam Houston, remained an ardent Unionist. In November,
Bickley gave a political address at Austin as the president of the American
Legion.[24] Although Elkhanah B. Greer attended the Democratic convention
at Charleston as a Southern Rights delegate, Bickley "began by denying all
political objects and purposes; and he patriotically advised the election of
Breckinridge, Douglas or Bell, if either could defeat Lincoln.—He disavowed
disunion objects—and yet he insisted that there are but two parties—a Northern and Southern party." He also "regarded it as a foregone conclusion, that
if Lincoln was elected, resistance would surely follow," and offered the KGC
as "the rallying army for the Southern disunionist." He warned, "Put off this
crisis another term and we are lost. The border States are slipping from our
grasp, and unless the people are aroused to a full sense of their danger, the
Southern Confederacy will embrace only the cotton States." As is so often
the case, the two failures of the KGC to seize Mexican territory turned out
to have been for the best, because, said Bickley, success in bringing new territory into the United States would have been "a dangerous experiment, and
not to be countenanced for one moment."

James P. Newcomb's *Alamo Express* at San Antonio and George Washington
Paschal's *Southern Intelligencer* of Austin reported the dramatic exchange
when the latter rose from the audience. The Georgia-born Paschal noted that
the KGC deployed members "as spies upon travelers, and even marks baggage,
and that baggage has come marked to this city as suspicious," calling it "a secret
police . . . as dangerous to the innocent as the guilty." Bickley said that the
order would "obey Southern Governors and . . . raise the standard of rebellion,
if they are not satisfied with the 'Presidential election.'" But, Paschal insisted,
"Revolutions must be the work of the people. We elect governors to see that
the laws are executed; not to inaugurate revolution. . . . Evils exist, dangers
threaten, but to the people belong the questions of life, liberty, property and
honor." The *Alamo Express* added its editorial appeal that Texans resort to "no
political secret conclaves—no reign of terror—but let all political subjects be
openly and boldly discussed."

In the end, the Texas state convention voted to secede on February 1, making it the seventh state to do so. However, it became the first to place the issue

before the voters in a referendum scheduled for February 23, and secessionist leaders worried that the KGC's penchant for vigilantism had created something of a backlash. When Bickley, Virginius Despeaux Groner, and other knights toured the state, the usually sympathetic *Marshall* (Texas) *Republican* covered it "without endorsing or being understood as endorsing them."[25] As in the border troubles, the KGC provided elites a cover for extralegal measures while distancing itself when such things became controversial.

Notwithstanding the ambivalence of the elite about an open alliance with KGC, the order provided a ready cover for action by the Texas authorities against the federal government without waiting for the vote of the people. After using the weight of the U.S. government to push beyond the border Juan Nepomuceno Cortina and his demand that Texas acknowledge the legal rights of Mexican residents, secessionists readily turned the same method on other Texans. When the Alamo Rifles voted not to replace the Stars and Stripes with the Lone Star Flag until people voted, the KGC's City Guards sent a representative to urge a combined response in the face of the continued presence of federal forces in the state. On February 16, six nearby castles of the KGC provided a portion of the state forces that demanded the surrender of the federal arsenal at San Antonio. U.S. colonel David Emanuel Twiggs, the seventy-one-year-old Georgian in command there, turned over his 160 soldiers and property worth $1.3 million in San Antonio. As Ben McCulloch's men celebrated the surrender, Col. Robert E. Lee returned from a trip to the Mexican border, expressed his shock at the surrender, and privately said that he would never have capitulated to the secessionists had he been in charge.[26]

The KGC's own state convention at San Antonio on February 22 marked something of its high-water mark as a real organization. The day before, Bickley Castle condemned the *Alamo Express* for having "used its columns for the purpose of injuring the K.G.C., an order devoted to the protection of southern interests and preservation of southern institutions." Although the order claimed "approximately 8000 members" at one point, the state convention enumerated the KGC military force "in the amount of 929 horse, and 139 foot," and tendered the services of the Order to the authorities of Texas. The convention declared any attempt by "any non-slaveholding government, power or people" to "be hostile to the rights and interests of the South and the K.G.C." and a "just cause of war."[27]

The next day, the referendum ratified secession by a vote of 46,153 to 14,747, amid pervasive charges of voter intimidation and fraud, which were worse in some places than others. San Antonio had "two secession newspapers thundering away for the last three months—the court house clique . . . embracing all the State and County and some of the city officials" forming "strong combinations arrayed against the Union party." Despite this, San Antonio voters actually rejected secession 827 to 709, and there were even pockets of Unionism in the state. Nevertheless, the vote was a signal for secessionists—under the rubric of the KGC—to bully into silence the newspapers, officeholders, and voters who had opposed them. Indeed, the KGC at Mobile unfurled a Confederate flag "with fifteen stars instead of seven."[28] For Bickley, secession represented not only a state mandate to be imposed universally upon reluctant voters but also a sectional mandate to be imposed upon reluctant states in the name of the entire South.

At noon on March 2, the anniversary of Texas independence, the secession ordinance took effect, and the authorities—under the useful guise of the KGC—replaced the flags and seized federal installations. The KGC nominally took Fort Davis and the chain of outposts west from San Antonio toward El Paso. The *New York Times* accepted the identification on face value and wondered "how many forts have been given up to the Texas Knights of the Golden Circle, and to what regiments belong the brave and loyal men who have been thus sacrificed to the sordid passions and craven abjectness of their commands."[29]

By then, Bickley claimed the purpose of KGC had always been "the dismemberment of the Union." As secession unfolded, the order adopted, as an emblem, "a simple triangular white card, something resembling the Knights' spear" with 7, 3, and 5 in the corners with 61 and a capital R in the center, symbolically implying a secret plan for fifteen slave states to enter into "revolution" in 1861. So, too, it became quite plausible to claim that the secessionist leaders were, in fact, in the KGC. The names mentioned as members mingled those like Ben McCulloch, who had some relation to the KGC, with those who had definitely opposed it like Sam Houston, and we should not forget the earlier claims about Winfield Scott. For these reasons, skepticism is the proper response to references implying the membership of John C. Breckenridge, Howell Cobb, Jefferson Davis, John B. Floyd, Pryor Lea, John A. Quitman, Robert A. Toombs, Louis T. Wigfall, and William L. Yancey.[30]

Surely, Bickley's decision to allow the KGC—or its name—to be used to such purposes is inseparable from his soliciting of slaveholders to secure the future of the institution through the KGC. He had early suggested that each slaveholder send one dollar "per head for each slave" to raise $4 million for the conquest "to enable him to supply all deficiencies and launch his Knights upon Mexico in overwhelming—that is regenerating force." The security for slavery would increase the value of slaves $100 per head. Horace Greeley quipped wryly that he expected Bickley to "fall considerably short of his $4,000,000," but the resourceful fund-raiser sought to inspire this by claiming that Texas had already raised $498,000 "and appeals to her sister Southern States for contributions."[31]

The credulous Northern press accepted at face value Bickley's claims to have been "traversing the Slave States, organizing lodges and enlisting recruits for a grand foray on Mexico, with intent to 'regenerate' her, after the Walker pattern." The abolitionist *National Era* reported that the object of the KGC was to Americanize, Southernize, and Africanize Mexico, which would "establish Slavery there, and open the slave trade." Bickley was "a fire-eater, disunionist, and one of the many thousand restless spirits who desire to live without labor, to be a hero of some kind, and a *ruler* by the grace of powder, and not by the voice of the people, though professing to be a *Democrat*." One thought Bickley's contempt for the law in the North would merit "a half contemptuous dismissal to the penitentiary," though it might attain "some real influence and position" under "the more favorable skies of the sunny South."[32] Without engineering secession, the KGC did make secession easier by providing a cover for the extralegal strong-arming of opponents by the dominant faction of the Democratic Party.

The one place beyond Texas that the KGC had some genuine organization and strength may have been along the Mexican border. Blanton Duncan allegedly became "the first man in Kentucky . . . to make a secession speech after the election of Lincoln," having supported Bell or Stephen A. Douglas for president—he apparently claimed both later. Duncan raised the First Kentucky as "a battalion," in which unit KGC captain Patrick H. Thorpe served. There, the KGC was described as "a valuable auxiliary to the secession movement, and has been the chief instrument in precipitating the people of the South into rebellion and revolution."[33] One could raise troops and give speeches, while remaining a gentleman, but secession required less honorable tactics best done under the aegis of a secret society.

In January 1861, the *Louisville Journal* reported that the KGC included "scores, if not hundreds of young, reckless, impulsive spirits," some from the families of "the wealthiest and most patriotic citizens of Kentucky," estimating four to five hundred in the city by March. During meetings in preparation for a state convention, the KGC left notes on the doors of Unionists threatening "Death to the Submissionists! Down with the left wing of the Lincoln Party!" The order "threatened to knock down and drag out every Union man" and hoped to "purify Louisville, 'the most rotten spot in Kentucky.'" Yet when it called a meeting of the "Southern Rights" men, more Unionists showed up. The KGC made secession in Louisville "the very quintessence of mobocracy . . . striving directly or indirectly, openly or covertly, to inaugurate mob rule and a reign of terror and of anarchy in Kentucky."[34] Kentuckians did not respond well to the threats, which had an effect opposite that intended.

The *Journal* published a remarkable exposé of the KGC, with the editor's giving "our solemn assurance as an editor and as a man" as to the authenticity of the documents. Bickley had "induced a gentleman of respectability, then residing in Kentucky, to cash a check for a few hundred dollars on a bank in which he had no funds," after which he skipped town, leaving behind the documents. The source for this story was almost certainly Kentucky's Col. Benjamin M. Harney, later an officer in the Union army, who became the only one of Bickley's handpicked representatives to so defect. The *Frankfort Commonwealth* assured any of "these valiant Knights" hoping to take the state capital that "every Union man, woman and child in Franklin county will welcome them 'with bloody hands to hospitable graves.'"[35]

The order may have played some role elsewhere. Secessionist vigilantism in Missouri seems to have often claimed to act under the rubric of the KGC, and unionists tended to attribute it to the order as well, so it is difficult to gauge what substance may have been there. It was said that there, and in Kentucky, the KGC acted through the State Guards and militias behind the claim of acting on behalf of the state. If so, the approach eventually permitted the Confederacy to add, on paper at least, the twelfth and thirteenth of the fifteen slave states the KGC had promised.[36]

Having an extralegal association to accomplish goals without the sanction of law did not really require an extensive and genuinely autonomous order. The *Vicksburg Sun* thought, "The past history and present aspects of our political affairs seemed to demand that an organization such as the K.G.C., fully armed and equipped and officered, was absolutely necessary." Even before the election, the KGC accosted strangers passing through their communities. "We now need men who will step boldly out and declare themselves either for or against us," declared Bickley. "The disposition to 'shirk' the question and issue is ill-adapted to the dangers which now threaten us." Efforts to suppress the "yet a few" remaining Southern voices against secession in Maryland, Virginia, Missouri, and Arkansas were ascribed to the KGC. In Tennessee, it reportedly grilled strangers and tarred and feathered a Nashville music teacher caught with old copies of the *New York Tribune* in his possession.[37] Where such places did not have an actual society equipped, officered, and ready for action, the disembodied idea of an association "such as the KGC" sufficed to define the Confederacy by its margins.

Bickley chose to be flexible. He declared this or that pronouncement likely remained as flexible as the KGC's rituals, and "nearly every castle" had modified its ritual, described as being "by no means as permanent or unalterable as that of other secret orders."[38] None of this, of course, mitigates the fact that such views had any appeal, and deceptiveness in the interest of marketability seems somehow an appropriate foundation for the origins of ideas capable of unmaking American civilization.

"Several Virginia gentlemen"—Bickley likely among them—visited Harrodsburg in mid-June. That night, noises from "the old shooting gallery" at the "Spring Grounds" drew the Town Guard there. The Guard heard voices as they approached and then stumbled onto "an assembly of Knights of the Golden Circle *in masks!*" One of the guards knocked off the disguise of one KGC, "and a lawyer and secessionist stood forth." Because some of the guards sympathized with the secessionists, they chose not to pursue their investigation, but a Unionist reported the encounter to the *Louisville Journal.*[39]

CONFEDERATE MARGINALIZATION OF THE KGC

References to an autonomous KGC, as it demonstrably existed, seemed to fade quickly once secession got beyond the need for strong-arming and began to exercise state power through the usual channels. Put another way, the KGC faded as "the poetry of the revolution is passing away." The order's responses varied, but all were fairly ineffective. In May 1861, Texas KGC leader C. A. Russell charged the membership to meet its military destiny. "Arouse the military spirit of your neighbors, organize them into companies and teach them military tactics and science." He urged them to "sow the seed that shall bring forth fruits of blessing to our country and glory to our Order." Charles A. Russell also noted that "when the pending storm shall have passed, should other work demand our attention, the K.G.C. will be prepared for action."[40]

A few KGC units are mentioned among those Texas Confederates engaged in what might be regarded as filibustering. R. H. Williams and other local KGCs, including a company under Trevanon T. Teel, again gathered in San Antonio's Alamo Plaza in late October 1861 to join the expedition assembling at Fort Bliss near El Paso that December for an invasion of the New Mexico Territory (including the present states of New Mexico and Arizona). Teel got command of Battery B of the First Texas Light Artillery with four six-pounders, and Lt. Col. John R. Baylor, a KGC leader, became the Confederate governor of the "Arizona" territory, that is, the Messilla Valley of southern New Mexico, and veteran filibuster Granville H. Oury, who had failed to rescue the Gasden Colonization Company five years before, went to represent the territory in the Confederate Congress.[41]

Planners envisioned this campaign as a conquest. Years before, Texas had actually sent a judge to New Mexico, on the grounds that people there were incapable of self-government. When the locals disputed his authority, the jurist replied scornfully that the territory's population was a quarter Pueblo Indians and three-quarters mere peons "not worthy to be trusted in any way." After accounting for a quarter and three-quarters of the population, the somewhat mathematically challenged judge added that "the remainder, to say the least of them, are Mexicans." Beyond U.S. territory, though, Teel still thought it "an easy thing to take those States, and the Mexican President would be glad to get rid of them, and at the same time improve his exchequer."[42]

By mid-March 1862, Governor Baylor announced a chillingly modern pacification policy along the border. He told his subordinates that "the Congress of the Confederate States has passed a law declaring extermination to all hostile Indians. You will therefore use all means to persuade the Apaches or any tribe to come in for the purpose of making peace, and when you get them together kill all the grown Indians and take the children prisoners and sell them to defray the expense of killing the adult Indians. Buy whiskey and such other goods as may be necessary for the Indians and I will order vouchers given to cover the amount expended." Therefore, as he sent them against those Native peoples within reach, he advised them to say nothing of their orders to anyone who might object and said, "Leave nothing undone to insure success, and have a sufficient number of men around to allow no Indian to escape."[43]

The specter of the KGC stomped heavily along the border. Two Texas Unionists, Edmund J. Davis and William W. Montgomery, had enlisted a regiment among the refugees in Mexico and were in the process of transporting them to the United States for mustering. Being in Mexico, they took pains to remain within the bounds of that country's laws, but KGC leader George W. Chilton raised a volunteer force that assaulted the guards on the Mexican border and crossed into the sovereign republic, where they kidnapped the two "traitors" and removed them to Texas, where they murdered Montgomery.[44] With a logic worthy of Bickley himself, Chilton's Confederate superiors disclaimed responsibility for this act of war against Mexico and the murder of prisoners while simultaneously praising his conduct.

Logistically doomed from the onset, the Confederate filibuster into New Mexico collapsed into a great disaster. Despite some initial successes, Federal columns from Colorado and California, bolstered by New Mexican volunteers, defeated the Confederates outside Sante Fe in March and destroyed their supply wagons. In early April 1862, as the hungry Texans fled, Teel supervised the burial of the Confederate artillery at Albuquerque.[45] With them was interred the distinctive, but clearly limited, military history of the KGC.

Stories of the KGC in the West may have became as pervasive as the expansionist impulse, but members, former members, or active sympathizers may well have played a major role in the rather marginal history of secession in the region. Confederates hoped to find support among the Mormons in Utah and the large numbers of transplanted Southerners in Colorado. Contemporary rumor and local folklore made much of the fact that disgruntled Southerners gathered in Denver at the Criterion Saloon of Charley Harrison, a gunslinger and bully who had earlier killed a black man in cold blood. So, too, talk of an entire Colorado regiment emerged when some Southerners determined to leave the territory and join the Confederacy assembled at Mace's Hole, near the present Beulah.[46]

Later stories of a delegation of Confederate officers sent to lead an uprising in 1863 grew from Harrison's return with a handful of other guerrillas from Capt. William C. Quantrill's band. On May 22, 1863, while on their way across Kansas, they opened fire on some Osage Indians when passing through their domains, ending in the massacre of all but two of the self-appointed officers.[47] What was recalled as an official delegation from the Confederate army dissolves into an interesting little conspiracy that itself is read into the evidence for little more than an ill-advised venture by freebooters hoping to prey upon a commerce less picked over than that in Missouri.

California Unionists had little doubt that the KGC planned a rising at the start. The Southern Rights faction would "seize the reins of Government, the Mint, Custom-house, the Forts and Government property, and declare for a Pacific Republic, to take in upper and Lower California, Oregon, Arizona and New Mexico—in case of secession of the Slave States." They thought it "composed of the numerous class of office-holders, office-seekers and adventurers who are thrown out of office by the change of Administration, having nothing to lose and everything to gain by such a movement."[48]

Still, secessionism on the West Coast fizzled pretty quickly. David S. Terry had earlier killed U.S. Senator David C. Broderick in a duel, and Assemblyman Daniel Showalter of Mariposa County has dispatched Assemblyman Charles W. Piercy of San Bernardino in a similar encounter, using rifles. After Terry fled the state for Texas, the Federal military seized all boats and ferries on the Colorado River and required a permit to pass beyond, with garrisons along the stagecoach route through San Diego County eastbound on the road toward Tucson. On November 22, 1861, a detachment of the First California Cavalry intercepted Assemblyman Showalter with eighteen armed secessionists. The rebels took oaths of allegiance and regained their freedom, after which Showalter made a successful second attempt to reach Texas, this time by way of Mexico. He later became a lieutenant colonel in the Fourth

Texas Cavalry Battalion in the Arizona Brigade.[49] Whatever reality existed of a KGC in the West, its largest organized activity seems to been the flight of fewer than two dozen men to Texas.

In the end, not only does a distinctive KGC contribution to the Confederate military remain elusive, but it seems doubtful on almost any level. McCulloch, Ford, Chilton, and others who had used the KGC for their own purposes or, at least, did not publicly refute their rumored association are perhaps the poorest measure of the order's real importance. Of Bickley's sixteen handpicked fund-raisers, only a dozen left a record of any Confederate service, that service rarely approaching their KGC military title. Two of Bickley's officers enlisted as colonels, and Greer eventually attained a rank of brigadier general. The list included two Confederate captains, while a KGC "colonel" and a "major" served as sergeants, and military service records note a half-dozen other KGC officers as enlisted men.[50]

Tales and rumors aside, as war revealed a KGC of limited scale and use, the Confederate authorities shuttled Bickley quickly to the rear. It was claimed— by Bickley, to be sure—that Richmond commissioned him as a brigadier general with orders to raise a brigade in southwestern Virginia, but there is no record of the commission or any such arrangement. While he may (or may not) have returned to that corner of the state to recruit, his lack of success did not prevent him from claiming the rank. There does exist a record of his commission as a surgeon, inspiring the fondest hope that, given his complete lack of medical training, his service remained honorific and brief. Other sources say he left after a year or so and spent "the remainder of the war period with his relations in Virginia."[51]

By the summer of 1863, though, Bickley lived in eastern Tennessee, where he claimed to have moved the headquarters of what remained of the KGC. However, he seems to have decided, at some point, to put the order into mothballs. In July 1863, he and his third wife headed for Indiana to see his relatives, and—bizarrely traveling under his own name—he found himself almost immediately under arrest for spying.[52]

Befitting Bickley's confirmed lack of any strong political sentiments whatsoever, he immediately threw himself on the mercy of the Federal government. On December 18, 1863, he wrote President Lincoln from his confinement "in a cell seven by three and a half feet, which contains besides myself, a bed, a stool and water and urinal buckets, so that when everything is put up compactly I have left me for ever—a space of six feet by eighteen inches, about the size of a common coffin." After an 1865 hearing, the judicial authorities denied any power to order his dismissal from Fort Lafayette.[53] So realities continued to circumscribe Bickley's dream of empire for some time.

Other entrepreneurial secessionists came to similarly lackluster ends. After a similarly brief and highly publicized military service, Blanton Duncan opened an operation for printing treasury bills in Richmond, displaying a management style that helped inspire a Richmond Typographical Society strong enough to prevail against him. Duncan solicited the help of Baltimore secret society man and detective John H. Winder against the hired hands, in return for which he put Winder on the $1,000 Confederate bill. By May 1862, Duncan left Richmond to the union and moved his operation to Columbus, South Carolina, this time sending abroad for printers. However, his high-handed use of government power against his competitors ended in April 1863 when South Carolina state officials used their influence to deny him any further contracts.[54]

Certainly more wealthy, if just as eccentric, the septuagenarian Duff Green envisaged a new America. The father-in-law of the late John C. Calhoun, he envisioned the Confederacy as "an Elysium on earth, which should be the forerunner of the coming millennium." He lobbied Richmond to establish a centralized banking system and foster industry within a slaveholding capitalist civilization, in which there would be "no strikes, no bread riots, and no constant war between labor and capital." With his own wealth diversified across the South from woolen mills in Virginia to factories in Georgia, to a Mississippi plantation and beyond, Green had much to gain from such a course personally.[55] Never impressed with such schemes, the Confederate authorities had less time for them as the concerns of war pressed upon them.

George N. Sanders—the admirer of Felice Orsini—who had aspired to be Green's successor in London, turned up in Canada. He soon established himself in Montreal alongside Patrick Charles Martin, Jacob Thompson, and others as a kind of quasi-official Confederate Secret Service. Thompson and Clement C. Clay had arrived in Montreal with a million in gold from Jefferson Davis early in 1864. They planned various missions to demoralize Unionist sentiment in the North in hopes of discouraging Lincoln's reelection. As the Federals successfully pushed the Confederate army back to Richmond, the latter's efforts turned increasingly toward blockade running, smuggling, and other operations with plenty of opportunity for personal profit. This increasingly involved self-recruited characters such as Alexander "Sandy" Keith, a hereditary Freemason from Halifax embarking on a diversified criminal career, including planting bombs on passenger ships for the insurance.[56]

* * *

The KGC's embrace of a distinctive Confederate nationalism should not obscure the features it shared with other national currents. The KGC amounted to very little more than most of them, and its impact, too, came mostly in the fear it engendered among its enemies. Federal misunderstanding of the KGC permitted smaller real threats to come closer to fruition than they should have. However, this does not tell us that the KGC was unimportant but rather clarifies how the spectral hand of the KGC helped to write the closing chapters of the Civil War and pointed the course of the postwar Reconstruction of the South.

More substantively, perhaps, the KGC accurately expressed secessionist arrogance in its most pristine form. To the extent to which Bickley or others actually believed it, they appealed to a small elite by arguing that it could and should shape the common future of the human race. While this created a paradox for republican secret societies struggling against ancient elites, it caused little problem for the KGC in courting the benevolence of a new one. Its nemesis, the antislavery secret societies, addressed this paradox directly.

7. THE REPUBLIC SAVED

Secret Societies and the Survival of the Union

The outbreak of war in Mexico coincided with the conflict in the United States. In May 1861, Confederates drove the small band of Juan Nepomuceno Cortina's La Raza from Zapata County, Texas, killing seven and capturing eleven others they subsequently hanged or shot. French imperial intervention south of the border precluded the easy resumption of that abbreviated "Second Cortina War." The original Cinco del Mayo in 1862 found Cortina at the successful defense of San Lorenzo at Puebla, after which he engaged in a series of political somersaults to secure his place as an independent and powerful caudillo. After briefly cooperating with the imperialists, he proclaimed himself governor of Tamaulipas and served President Benito Juárez as a general. He responded to developments in Texas by undermining his old KGC enemies and doing everything he could to assist the Union forces when they landed at the coast.[1] As among African and Native Americans, secret societies among Cortina's people saw the American Civil War as an opportunity to transform the nature of American life and their place within it.

The American Civil War moved into radical, even revolutionary channels with the involvement of broader layers of the population. In part, this reflected the Unionist fear of a hidden and indeterminate power in the hands of the KGC. In response, Unionists in the South turned to secret societies followed by their admirers and supporters in the North. Veterans of the Ouvrier Circle and Free Democrats participated fully in this war effort.

UNIONIST PANIC AND KGC REALITIES

The most important impact of the KGC came, paradoxically, where it seems to have hardly ever existed. By common consent, the KGC became a useful generic veil to cover all sorts of activities. Proponents and opponents of what it advocated used it to magnify or denigrate the influence of its goals or the cleverness of its organizers.

This not to say that there were not apparently real conspiracies aplenty. Some evidence exists indicating that George N. Sanders stalked Lincoln from Cincinnati to Washington on the February 1861 trip to the inauguration. A plot to murder Lincoln in Baltimore involved such colorful figures as Cypriano Ferrandini, a southernized Italian admirer of Felice Orsini. In addition to this man—"the Orsini who undertook to slay President Lincoln"—those implicated included friends and acquaintances of the actor John Wilkes Booth and, it has been suggested, Booth himself.[2] Yet whatever actual historical truth there is to such accounts is viewed through layers of the yellowed veneer of systemic exaggerations and fictionalizations that suited some on both sides.

At the war's onset, Harry J. Seymour—a leader of the Northern jurisdiction of the Scottish Rite Masons and head of the Order of Memphis—staged a play at New York called *Knights of the Golden Circle*. Hardly less creative were the fictions of the Federal agent who penned *An Authentic Exposition of the "K.G.C."*[3] Despite these discussions, nobody directly addressed the key questions about the actual nature of the KGC, its membership, or its relationship to the Democratic Party or to any real Confederate secret service operations.

The government informant combined some of the hard numbers he actually counted with wildly exaggerated estimates based on rumors. Marion County (Indianapolis) reportedly had a disturbing thousand men ready to rise in armed revolt, though the hard numbers on membership make this impossible. He ascribed ten members to Washington County, while writing that it had thirty thousand voters who "will never compromise with Black Republicanism" and "at least ten thousand who will shoulder their muskets in defense of the rights of their Southern brethren." So, too, in Sullivan County, he counted only "from fifteen to twenty Jeff Davis subjects" in Carlisle, with "about" thirty members countywide, but accepted on face value their boast of having "at the best calculation, two thousand fighting men, who will, at a moment's warning, in case of need, march to the standard of Southern Rights." Madison, with eighteen members, allegedly had a thousand ready to rise in rebellion. The agent estimated only fifteen members at Evansville, but reported it could mobilize "a couple of regiments, armed and equipped." In the end, he wrote that we might "safely estimate" "at least 10,000" members in Indiana.[4]

The same exaggerations characterized such estimates across the North. The author acknowledged that there were "many traitors in the North" not in the KGC but believed they functioned as "the disciples of one or more who live in the neighborhood." Even if there were three hundred members of a secret society at Cairo with "from 100 to 200 in neighboring towns," it is unclear whether that would support an extrapolation of numbers statewide to "safely estimate" five thousand for Illinois. In a similar way, the author estimated the same number for each of Ohio, Michigan, and Iowa, and "at least 15,000" for Pennsylvania. New York was said to have "about 50,000" and supporting a brigade of five thousand. Overall, his totals suggested one hundred thousand from the North.[5] A KGC in those states probably never had a hundredth of such a number and probably could not have maintained a thousandth of it for long.

Democratic papers ascribed the myth to government fabrications. The *Brooklyn Daily Eagle,* for example, asserted that the KGC had been "conjured up out of the imagination of the administration agents," a position echoed by historian Frank Klement's *Dark Lanterns,* which dismissed virtually everything on the subject as politically motivated frauds and forgeries. The most obvious explanation for the bizarre exaggerations, of course, seems to be the public statements of George W. L. Bickley and the KGC, which had long predated any Federal investigations or prosecutions.[6] Since virtually everybody involved had every reason to fuel the exaggerations, the KGC became largely a victim of its own self-promotion.

This is not to say that the Federal authorities did not take full advantage of these exaggerations. There were arrests and trials of American citizens for their alleged involvement in the KGC in early 1862 through mid-1863. Recalling "the revolutionary lessons of the past," the Federal informant advised that "it is never a good policy to undervalue the strength and the chances of a foe, if one would be sure of victory. On the other hand, it is far better to overestimate them."[7] In short, it seemed safest to assume Bickley's version of the KGC to be accurate rather than to risk not acting against it.

Those predisposed to do so saw plenty of indications of a pervasive KGC conspiracy. The lack of any real evidence indicated not the lack of a conspiracy but its insidious cleverness. Those unwilling to acknowledge the innate unpopularity of conscription found the easiest explanation of any draft resistance, including the riots from Charleston, Illinois, to those in New York and Boston, as the work of a hidden enemy. Any Democratic organization—particularly any with fraternal features—could look very much like one's expectations of the KGC, if those expectations were property trained.[8] The KGC provided a kind of shorthand for such things, and its actual role or even its existence did not enter into the equation.

For their part, the Confederate authorities in Richmond realized by the spring of 1862 that any KGC that had existed behind Federal lines had become unreliable, disorganized, or "moribund." Secessionist sympathizers, as well as antiwar Northern Democrats—the "Copperheads"—tried attempts to form local secret societies, under the name of the Mutual Protection Society, the Circle of Honor, or the Circle or Knights of the Mighty Host. Kentucky and Tennessee had a Night-Hawk Association.[9] The Confederate government itself made one singular bid to make real the shadow of the KGC when Jefferson Davis dispatched Emile Longuemare to contact key Democrats in the northern and western states.

The shadowy Longuemare chose obscurity as surely as Bickley had sought notoriety. He allegedly "belonged to an aristocratic old French family of St. Louis, Southern sympathizers, who had cast in their entire fortune with the Confederacy and were thus brought into reduced circumstances." His uncle and aunt were said to have personally equipped the First Missouri in which their son, Emile's cousin, became a captain. "A romantic incident of Winston Churchill's novel *The Crisis,* where a young Southern officer breaks his sword at Camp Jackson rather than yield it to an enemy, was recognized in St. Louis as an actual occurrence in the career of Captain Charles Longuemare, Jr." While his family was actually neither that old in the area nor aristocratic, Longuemare seemed to have had a relative living near Davis Bend in Mississippi, Eugene Longuemare, who crossed into Arkansas to serve in the Helena Light Artillery and may have been the means through which Emile gained the ear of the Confederate president.[10]

When Longuemare returned to St. Louis, the Federal authorities stepped up their queries about him and his relatives, but seem not to have directly interfered with his activities. He organized a meeting in the city at Fifth and Market, founding the Order of American Knights under Phineas C. Wright, a New Orleans lawyer controlling an inner circle called Sons of Liberty, which may be the same association identified with the Copperheads. Projected as an organization to rebuild the Democratic Party as a disunionist movement, the OAK also planned to function as a fifth column, arming itself and engaging in acts of sabotage. Beneath Wright operated the state heads: H. H. Dodd in Indiana, Charles Lucas Hunt in Missouri, and James Alphonsus McMasters in New York, with Justice Joshua Bullitt of the court of appeals heading the Kentucky organization. Meanwhile, Professor Joseph W. Snow, a graduate of Genesee College, took charge of the Rome Academy in the autumn of 1863 and added the Confederate agent to the faculty, a position from which Longuemare continued his activities.[11]

The presence of McMasters, perhaps the most prominent lay voice of Catholicism in the country, would have been particularly chilling. The son of a

New York Presbyterian minister, McMasters became one of the most prominent American converts. After studying for the priesthood in Belgium, he acquired the *New York Freeman's Journal* and transformed it into an independent,
feisty Catholic voice hostile to abolitionism and radicalism of any sort. Like
Wright, McMasters would frequently be described as a mere critic who was
repressed because of his "views," but evidence for his overtly pro-Confederate
activities more than justified his periodic arrests and investigation.[12]

Hunt had watched the 1848–49 revolutions from the perspective of his
Jesuit friends in Belgium. Upon returning to St. Louis, his family became
integral to the development of Roman Catholicism in the archdiocese. There,
the sympathies of the slaveholding archbishop, Peter Richard Kenrick, were
such that William Henry Seward tried to get Archbishop John Hughes of
New York to persuade the Vatican to remove Kenrick. Hunt's mother and
uncle provided Archbishop Kenrick the land for building new churches to
reach the expanding German population in his jurisdiction.[13]

Hunt, then the Belgian consul at St. Louis, provided the OAK with another
layer of cover. It functioned there alternately as the Southern League or Le
Corps de Belgique. One is tempted to see this as the work of McMasters, who
had, no doubt, retained some friends in the church and civic hierarchy there.
By the summer of 1864, the Unionist officials in Missouri seized Hunt and dissolved the Belgian order.[14] The involvement of McMasters, the Longuemares,
and Belgian diplomats hints at a curious American presence of the kind of
ultramontane reactionary Catholicism familiar to any member of the Italian
or French revolutionary secret societies of the mid–nineteenth century.

Incidentally, the Belgian connection not only provided the Confederacy
with Hunt and McMasters but also King Leopold's kinsman Duke Ernst II
of Saxe-Gotha and Coburg. That tiny country had only become independent
from the Netherlands in 1830, and its moderate constitutional monarchy
found the Catholic Church and alliance with Napoleon III of France a bul-
wark against further revolution. Duke Ernst II actually appointed as consul
to the Confederacy Ernst Raven, who had been the duke's bookbinder before
moving to America and settling in Austin in 1848. There, Raven served as a
city alderman and did contract work for the state government. His diplomatic
assignment moved him to Galveston, the state's largest port, from which he
could maintain close ties to Napoleon's 1862 venture into Mexico.

The OAK seems to have attempted to liaise between Confederate sympathizers among the Democrats and various freelance operations also loosely
associated with Richmond. Jacob Thompson, Patrick Martin, and George N.
Sanders pursued a succession of schemes out of Montreal. Aided by escaped
Confederate prisoners of war, they also enlisted the help of local adventur-

ers, such as Alexander "Sandy" Keith, a hereditary freemason, conspirator, and con artist from Halifax.[15] Their plans included bank robberies, blockade running, and insurance fraud, as well as prison escapes, piracy, arson, kidnapping, assassinations, and infecting the East Coast with smallpox.

THE EMERGENCE OF UNIONIST SECRET SOCIETIES

Secret societies among Unionists emerged directly from the exclusionist and repressive ideology of the secessionists. The KGC followed the Nativist model in requiring members to give priority in voting to its own third-degree members running for office, but it did not see electoral victory as a requirement for legitimacy. Elections provided a manageable means of getting control of the government. Just to make sure, the KGC planned to get members into position to do the vote counting as well. It also recommended the old techniques of importing voters from adjoining states, which had been employed in Kansas, and then intimidating perceived opponents. However, the KGC never accepted the legitimacy of any election that did not mandate its course and explicitly declared, after secession, its stand that uncooperative Unionists were "to be driven out." In response, Southern Unionists had to look to their own resources.[16]

Opponents of secession in the South organized in the teeth of repression and the threat of repression. Reactions to the KGC or general secessionist strong-arming under that rubric inspired Union Clubs at St. Louis as early as January 1861, in Louisville in May, and in Maryland and along the Ohio River in the early months of the war. Even more secretive "Union Leagues" appeared in Tennessee among those Unionists who "sought refuge in inaccessible places and caves in the mountains of their State," where they gathered around "improvised altars, covered with 'Old Glory,' on which lay the open Bible," and formulated rituals similar to those of the old Brotherhood of the Union, which had several circles in the state before the war.[17]

Virginia Unionists organized as well. In the western mountain counties, William Erskine Stevenson, a Pittsburgh cabinetmaker—an ally, if not a member of, the Brotherhood of the Union—and a defiant Republican, led the localized revolt against the secessionist government in Richmond, laying the foundation for what became the new state of West Virginia. To the east, in Richmond itself, the once and future labor reformer William Emmette Coleman likely participated in the espionage and sabotage of the Confederacy, possibly through service in its Quartermasters Corps.[18]

In North Carolina, where Coleman spent part of the war, Unionists created the "Heroes of America." Secret peace societies also developed in Mississippi and Alabama, as did the Peace and Constitutional Society in northwestern Arkansas. These organizations generally assisted Federal spies, Unionist fugitives, and Confederate prisoners. They established and maintained some coordination with the Federal authorities, and members of the Heroes recognized each other, as had the antislavery organizations in territorial Kansas, by wearing a red string on their lapels. Growing with the unpopularity of the war, they penetrated the Confederate army, planned mutinies, and periodically helped elect antiwar candidates. The authorities conducted investigations and held trials.[19]

Organized resistance to secession took place alongside the KGC in Texas. A "gentleman from Western Texas" reported twenty-five thousand Germans there with fifteen thousand elsewhere in the state remaining steadfastly loyal. They faced "the tyranny of the organized band of marauders, known as the Knights of the Golden Circle, whose object is Slavery extension, and territorial acquisition." An "informant" who "traveled extensively in Mexico" found many Germans there ready to resist any invasion across the Rio Grande. Two shiploads already set off from Texas. "A decided majority of the Texans are in favor of the Union, but the reign of terror established by the Knights of the Golden Circle has suppressed nearly all opposition to their brutal tyranny."[20]

Blacks in the South had their own tradition of organizing in secret that had even deeper roots. One must consider the account in the *Continental Monthly,* asserting "positively that the negroes throughout the South have a similar, or sort of a Masonic league, the object of which is insurrection, and an overthrow of the whites. The writer tells some remarkable stories concerning a certain slave whom he calls Scipio, who acknowledges the existence of the league, a fact which, while not positively known, is suspected by many of the slave-holders, the more moderate of whom are disposed to ward off the blow by a system of gradual emancipation." The extent to which this represented exaggeration can never been known with certainty.[21]

Early in the war, John Scobell, a black Federal agent at Richmond, located an underground "Loyal League" in the heart of the Confederate capital. A "conductor" took him and a white agent into a large, dark room and whistled, and they answered that they were "Friends of Uncle Abe!" seeking "Light and Liberty!" A trapdoor opened overhead, allowing dim light into the room as a rope ladder was dropped to them. Climbing up, they found themselves in a room "surrounded by a body of negroes, numbering about forty," and the presiding officer, "a tall, well-formed negro, about thirty-five years of age," sitting at a barrel with the American flag draped over it, who took charge of the information. The agents wrote a quick explanation of their dilemma and helped sew the information they hoped to convey in the president's coat, after which he left to deliver the information safely to Washington.[22] That such a level of organization, intermeshed into a broader network, existed in the repressive climate of the wartime capital makes it likely to have existed in some form in earlier, less repressive conditions.

Many Southern members of unauthorized secret societies became actively engaged in espionage and sabotage on behalf of the Union. Romantic nationalists from abroad found themselves easily drawn to such assumptions. Many of these ventures, on both sides, seem to have been freelance and fostered more by adventurers than agents of their respective governments. The destruction of the Confederate records and those essential to Federal clandestine operations leaves us dependent on unverified private memoirs. Given this void, it is often tempting to take what may have been intended as fiction as history, even with very little attempt to verify the essential facts.[23]

Southern refugees brought this tradition north, where Republican organizations embraced the leagues, which provided an organized political base unprecedented in American history. Twelve individuals, one a refugee from Tennessee, formed the first northern lodge of the Union League of America at Pekin, Illinois, on June 25, 1862. Agents of the Pekin council organized other groups at Peoria, Bloomington, Kingston, Decatur, and Chicago, holding a statewide convention in September. By the spring of 1863, Union Leagues spread across Indiana, Ohio, Wisconsin, Michigan, Minnesota, and Iowa; shortly thereafter, a new San Francisco league began organizing new chapters across the Far West. As in the South, paramilitary organization sometimes accompanied these local leagues.[24]

In the large cities, the urban elites adopted the organizations, eclipsing the activities of these plebeian Union Leagues. After the initial appearance of the leagues at Washington, groups formed at Philadelphia by late 1862, New York City in January 1863, and Boston the following month. At such places, the leagues remained aloof from the national organization and generally evolved into select clubs for the local elite, as did the Chicago Union League.[25]

Unionist sentiment and organization surfaced with Federal occupation. Reflecting a more radical interpretation, New York's Workingmen's Democratic-Republican Association took on "the duty of this association to make every practical effort to reach the workingmen of the South with our appeal for union and brotherhood among the workingmen of the country, in all places where it is possible to reach them."[26]

Kindred spirits emerged in places like New Orleans. Although the same age as Joseph Déjacque—who had lived in the Crescent City before coming to New York—Jean-Charles Houzeau had the benefits of birth to an aristocratic but enlightened Belgian family and a scientific education that landed him a position as an astronomer. He also sought to apply the ideas of Claude Henri Saint-Simon, the socialist, to the problems of the Industrial Revolution. He also became a member of the underground revolutionary circles and found himself in a kind of voluntary exile by October 1857, when he landed at New Orleans.[27] Like Déjacque, Houzeau turned to journalism, but, unlike Déjacque, Houzeau persisted.

THE FATE OF THE ÉMIGRÉ FREE DEMOCRATS

Even as the U.S. Congress investigated Harpers Ferry, the most active leader of the antebellum émigrés pursued his fate elsewhere. In April 1860, rebellions in Messina and Palermo against the Kingdom of the Two Sicilies revived Hugh Forbes's hopes. Nearly eleven years after the Roman Republic, he rejoined Giuseppe Garibaldi as the royalist citadel at Messina fell into revolutionary hands. On July 25, Garibaldi approved Forbes's proposal to raise an English Legion, and, over the next few days, Forbes gathered together some of the English serving in existing units and issued a formal invitation to English sympathizers.[28]

Soon, Garibaldi announced plans for an International Legion to aid the Italian cause. Others planned to raise units of volunteers from France, Poland, Switzerland, Germany, and elsewhere, after which, Garibaldi argued, veterans of these legions would return to liberate their homelands. At least one American, William de Rohan—a wounded American veteran of the Mexican War—served with them in Sicily, and Edwin A. Stevens, a native of Yorkshire who would eventually cross the Atlantic to serve in the Union army, also joined Garibaldi's army. Recruiters left for England at the start of August.[29]

Events, however, moved quickly past Forbes. An "injury on the foot" took him from the field on September 24, and when he limped back into action, Garibaldi had replaced him with John Peard, now slated for fame as "Garibaldi's Englishman." As the war moved on, Forbes found himself in charge of the Messina garrison, complaining that he, a trained soldier, had been passed over in favor of Peard, a lawyer who simply happened to be touring Italy at the time the revolution began. The *Times* reported that Peard's legion had fallen in number to about 550, but Garibaldi's purposes in launching the "English Legion" had always been less military than diplomatic. On October 30, Garibaldi sent Forbes to organize all "idle volunteers" at Naples into a cavalry unit. The movement also issued a translation of Forbes's *Compendio del Volontario Patriotico*.[30]

Tensions persisted between Forbes, the old revolutionary, and younger officers who had fought in Crimea while he had been agitated against American slavery. Nevertheless, the foreigners at Naples did well in the face of the enemy. Reports told of their turning back a Neapolitan force five times their number.[31] As in prior ventures, though, pragmatic politics would trump Garibaldian military flamboyance.

A month later, on November 28, Forbes felt so excluded that he sent a report to the London Garibaldi Committee in which his alienation had him alternating between the third and first persons. A month later, he forwarded the report to Lord John Russell through an old friend, George Villiers, the fourth earl of Clarendon, who had run the Foreign Office before Lord Russell took charge. In his cover letter, Forbes reminded the British government that none of his activities had disserved the interest of England, which stood to gain from an independent and united Italy, with weakened continental powers. As one historian noted, Forbes had "professed the faith ten years too soon for prudence and respectability, and so earned nothing but detraction, besides an excellent chance of being set up against a wall and shot."[32]

Peard, meanwhile, deflected criticism onto his rival. He told the English public that a court of inquiry had ascribed the problems of the expedition to "the malicious interference of persons unconnected with the brigade," particularly Forbes. Seventeen officers, said Peard, had asked Forbes to resign. The recriminations lingered past the campaign and into 1861.[33]

Garibaldi wisely seems to have resolved the matter by using Forbes to foster his own idea of international solidarity. In 1861, the old warrior arrived "on the Polish scene of action with a sort of commission from Garibaldi." By the time Russian conscription sparked a Polish rebellion in January 1863, Forbes had enough to lay Poland's nationalist claims before the English public in *Poland, and the Interests and Duties of Western Civilization*. Later that year, though, a correspondent of Horace Greeley's *New York Tribune* reported Forbes was "now in Paris."[34]

The following year, Forbes hit on a scheme to improve the functioning of steam power in water, focusing the energy into a tube. He and his partners got patents, and when Garibaldi visited London in April 1864, he attended a demonstration of the new invention at the Serpentine, near the site of the international exposition.[35]

Nevertheless, the old Carbonari seems to have continued to comment on events back in America as "Carbon," a European correspondent of William Lloyd Garrison's *Liberator*. "I am poor and have some leisure," he declared at one point, implicitly offering his services to the cause of progress. Warning against the imperial ambitions of Napoleon III in Cochinchina and Mexico, he urged the U.S. government "to arm all the colored people" and grant them land, something for which they would live and fight. Elsewhere, he argued that landownership should "be vested in the nation for the benefit of the whole people" and that the proper "use of government" would be "to clothe the naked, to feed the hungry, to shelter the houseless" and generally "to restrain evil, and create good."[36]

Back in the United States, the outbreak of war delivered the final blow to the members and organizations of the old Universal Democratic Republicans. With many of the Italians and French back in Europe, the Germans pressed onward, gaining a certain national notoriety with a mass meeting on July 24, 1861. Two thousand of them rallied on Hester Street to demand that the mayor launch a public works program to secure the employment of the unemployed to support those, especially, with relations in the military. The press widely reprinted the story, mostly to denounce it bitterly. A correspondent of the *Philadelphia Inquirer* blamed everything on "a little clique of German Socialists in this city" who embraced "these imported and mischievous 'isms.'" Less interested in alienating the immigrants by an attack, the Democratic *New York Herald* blamed the land reformers and other working-class radicals who had been around for longer; the proposal, it wrote, began "less with the workingmen, as a class, than with a small knot of restless and unprincipled agitators, who for the last twenty years have been endeavoring to make use of them as a stepping stone to political notoriety and influence."[37] Nevertheless, within weeks, Gen. John C. Frémont established a new rallying point by attempting to expand the Union war goals to include emancipation.

Another old Garibaldian, Gustave Paul Cluseret had served with Frémont and sought to reconstitute the remnants of Forbes's old organization. Born near Paris, he had become an officer in the Garde Mobile during 1848 and had helped suppress the revolt, but experience in Algeria apparently soured him on imperial ventures. In 1860, he had joined Garibaldi and Forbes in the Italian campaign, though he left to join the American war effort. He served under both Frémont and conservative general George B. McClellan, but he left the army as a brigadier general for journalism and political agitation. Cluseret's widely reprinted "American Military Sketches" excoriated McClellan and the narrowness of his antiemancipationist politics.[38]

Like Forbes, Cluseret advocated an "Ultimate Reconstruction," on which he elaborated in the *New Nation,* for the same readership as had Forbes's *European.* "We desire the creation of a nation in the place of a confederation," he insisted, with "national education and national institutions." He hoped to see the army reorganized so as not to be a nursery for politicians, "a diminution of the powers of the Executive, and that Cabinet ministers be made in a greater degree responsible to Congress."[39]

The *New Nation* provided a platform, however short-lived, for discussion of the "social question." A veteran of the French societies, Claude Pelletier described the strike wave in the spring of 1864 as "the preliminary skirmishes of the future war which the abolition of the wages system must infallibly bring about; a war that will be much more serious and gigantic than that which the abolition of slavery has rendered necessary." Pelletier expected the confrontation when "slavery, direct and brutal, will no longer exist." The émigré paper also published materials by and about American radicals such as Albert Brisbane, Thomas J. Durant, and Stephen Pearl Andrews.[40]

However, the focus of Cluseret's radicalism remained the "absolute and complete liberty, without distinction of race or color, and not at a future period more or less remote, but radically and at once." While others talked of emancipation, Cluseret's paper assailed Democratic papers such as the *World* for racial comments about the march of black soldiers to the front, denounced atrocities against them in the field, and asserted their rights to equality within the army, including to commission as officers. The *New Nation* essentially assailed racism in its many forms. Well over a century before white scholars discovered the importance of "whiteness," Cluseret warned about "the White Side of the Black Question," rooting racism in the chosen racial identity of Euro-Americans.[41]

Initially, Cluseret hoped to mobilize émigré radicals and abolitionists discontented with Lincoln's gradualism in the interests of Frémont's 1864 presidential bid. In the end, though, the émigrés remained more consistently interested in unseating Lincoln than were the more pragmatic American radicals.[42] By the time Frémont himself abandoned the idea, Cluseret and other émigrés had already broken with the project and turned to reelect Abraham Lincoln.

THE OURVRIER CIRCLE

Forbes's comrades of the old Ouvrier Circle responded to events with notable speed and coherence. On April 20, news of the war at New York City inspired "the largest meeting, without exception, that was ever held on this continent, and the most enthusiastic." Some one hundred thousand gathered around multiple stands of speakers in Union Square. In the full flush of crisis, the city fathers put forward an unusually representative collection of speakers, including John Commerford, Friedrich Kapp of the Kommunist Klub, abolitionists such as Theodore Tilton, and reform Democrats such as John Cochrane. With quiet dignity, Ira B. Davis acknowledged that he had voted against Lincoln, "but, so help him God, he would do all in his power to support him while he lawfully held the seat of power. Whoever exercised the right of suffrage was bound to support the party that succeeded." He added, "The traitors of the South had underrated the honesty and patriotism of New-York."[43] At New York City, the remnants of the Ouvrier Circle and the Arbeiterbund had struggled for a place within this broad Unionist coalition.

By the fall of 1861, the Ouvrier Circle itself had reorganized as the Patriotic Union League. In October, they sent a delegation to the Taxpayers Union Party to urge a common Union ticket, but found themselves "excluded from the meeting" by the old Whig leadership of the local Republicans. A few weeks later, Commerford reported the exclusion to the meeting at Union Hall, No. 187 Bowery. The group had organizations in eight wards, the German Union League had agreed to joint action, and "delegates from several Trades Unions would be present at the next meeting." Years later, Joshua K. Ingalls of the National Land Reform Association recalled how their Brotherhood of the Union "was absorbed during the war by the Union League."[44]

Such Union League and related Loyal Leagues in New York drew together men with a broad range of views. These included Peter Cooper, the old Locofoco and future Greenback presidential candidate, former Fourierist Parke Godwin, and the Kommunist Klub's Freidrich Kapp, and other radicals, such as William Oland Bourne and Robert M. Poer—new voices of the Republican "workingman"—regularly shared the platform. So did the visiting radicals, including John P. Hale and other old Free Democrats.[45]

Bourne's old "Iron Platform" Democrats reemerged as a "Democratic Republican Party" based upon its own "Democratic League." Their antislavery politics and their eagerness to encourage Southern white insurgents against planter politics recalled the old Free Democratic League. It also had a "Workingmen's Democratic-Republican Association," though it "does not at present hold *public meetings*" in order to function "in a far more effective and economical manner by correspondence with other Associations and the circulation of documents." Through it, Bourne regularly cautioned against "a crude and ill-advised radicalism," insisting that "the interests of Labor and Capital are mutual."[46] The success of the enterprise rested on the politics of class identity cultivated by a generation of working-class radicals.

A high proportion of those radicals who were young enough to do so entered the army, and the losses were noteworthy. Fritz Jacobi of the Kommunist Klub had been killed in action at Fredericksburg, and Ben Price, the carpenter Ouvrier, died at the head of one wing of his regiment in a rear-guard action after the Gettysburg campaign. In November and December 1863, such luminaries as Cooper, William Marcy Tweed, Daniel Sickles, and John Jacob Astor Jr. formed a committee to raise volunteers. It, too, brought together Fourierists, German Communists, and American veterans of the Ouvrier Circle, including Ingalls and Henry Beeny.[47]

The following March, the Workingmen's Democratic-Republican Association informed President Lincoln that he had been elected an honorary member. The president replied by citing an earlier message to Congress on the dignity of labor and added, "The most notable feature of the disturbance in your City last Summer was the hanging of some working people by other working people. It should never be so. The strongest bond of human sympathy, outside of the family relation, should be one uniting all working people of all nations, tongues, and kindreds; nor should this lead to a war on property or owners of property." The association responded that "it is the general desire of the workingmen of the United States that the next President of the United [States] shall be from Springfield, Ill., and that his name be Abraham Lincoln."[48]

In September 1864, workers participated in the broader mobilization over the issue of municipal reform. A meeting at the Cooper Institute was "filled with the workingmen of New-York who came forward to express their dissat-isfaction with the present management of our City Government, and to take management of our City Government, and to take action which would secure a reform." They "unanimously elected president" H. C. Wittenberg, an ally, if not member, of the Ouvrier, with Poer as the secretary. Other participants included Peter Baker of the Typographical Union. The Citizens Association coalition explicitly denied being "antagonistic to Trades' Unions, . . . saying that it desires no interference, direct or indirect, with the Trades' Unions, or with any of their regulations for the promotion of trade interests." It appealed "to the working classes, simply as citizens," declaring that "members of the various trades can participate freely and earnestly, as citizens without in the least compromising their position in their trade relations." Still, it boasted that its state nominations included "the strongest array of practical, hard-working men of the people that has ever been presented by a State convention." Among the usual suspects present through these meetings were Davis, Beeny, and Commerford, who ran for councilman from the Fourth District.[49]

The Brotherhood of the Union played out a bit differently in Lippard's own Philadelphia. By 1860, the editors of the *United States Mechanics' Own* and other radicals began to urge its revival, but what was left of it clearly came to be identified closely with the efforts of the old Arbeiterbund in the local needle trades. The war increased that distress and revived activity in that craft. The particular cooperative model of the Rochdale Society of Equitable Pioneers became especially popular. Against this backdrop, in 1862, Uriah Smith Stephens and others started the Garment Cutters' Association of Philadelphia and its successor, the Knights of Labor.[50] The importance of this reached far beyond one trade in one city.

Elsewhere, associations such as the Union League reached across racial lines. Essential to organizing refugees and raising troops were black leaders such as Martin R. Delany and James McCune Smith at New York, George DeBaptiste and William Lambert at Detroit, Peter Humphries Clark at Cincinnati, and others. These men had long-standing connections with Masonic lodges, the Radical Abolitionists, the Chatham convention, and the Ourvrier Circle and Brotherhood of the Union. In the spring of 1862, the "Contraband Relief Association" formed at Cincinnati, later growing into the Western Freedman's Aid Commission. In the fall of 1863, Chicago organized the "Northwestern Freeman's Aid Commission." Under these auspices, they gathered runaways into camps, built barracks, and secured access to land for them.[51]

Under the protection of the Federal authorities and white Unionists such as Jean-Charles Houzeau, blacks themselves began making a bid for greater power. The son of a black Creole and a Swiss immigrant, J. Clovis Laizer was "admitted without the least suspicion" to employment as a white and held membership in the New Orleans Typographical Union. Thomas J. Durant, the long-isolated Fourierist, came to the fore as a leader of the local Unionists and a primary advocate of black suffrage, cheered by New Orleans blacks at their January 1865 convention. Arriving to assist them was the black spiritualist Pascal Beverly Randolph, then claiming to resurrect—actually inventing and introducing—his own mystical version of "Rosicrucianism" in the United States.[52] With the wartime arrival of the Federal forces, radicals like Durant, Houzeau, Laizer, Randolph, and others would eventually enjoy the revolutionary opportunity to reshape their society.

* * *

The strategies of the Confederate underground focused increasingly on the plans to drive the uncompromising Unionism of Lincoln from power. In the summer of 1864, the OAK of Longuemare tried to coax participants in the Democratic National Convention at Chicago into a "Northwest conspiracy," funding Democratic campaigns in hopes of sparking armed rebellions behind Federal lines and a breakout of prisoners at Camp Douglas, just south of Chicago.[53] The plans failed due to the lack of serious interest in treason among the Copperheads.

With Lincoln's reelection in November, Longuemare and McMasters met agents of Sanders and Thompson in New York City to plan nothing less than the destruction of the city. McMasters backed out of the plot and Longuemare left town, but a half-dozen arsonists made the attempt on the night of November 25, doing considerable damage and providing yet another chapter in a dismally handcrafted nineteenth-century conflict pursued with modern ferocity.[54]

EPILOGUE: LONG SHADOWS

Lineages of the Secret Society Tradition in America

The secret society traditions of the Old World not only helped to shape the course of the Civil War but also influenced the nation's processing of that experience into memory. Perhaps the oddest thing about how historical memory has treated secret societies in Civil War America is that it virtually ignores those that actually existed while making so much out of a largely paper organization invented by a confidence man. Deep predispositions shaped a history that would accord more substance to the shadow of the KGC than it would willingly cede to the substance of genuinely radical associations or European émigrés, black nationalists, or American radicals of any sort.

The lineages of the mid-nineteenth-century American secret societies persisted through the rest of the century and beyond. Certainly, such secret societies—or the idea of them—haunted the closing events of the conflict from Washington to the Rio Grande. Workers and radicals built upon the legacy of groups like the Ourvrier Circle of the Brotherhood of the Union, though they began abandoning secrecy within a generation of the Civil War. Nevertheless, secret societies and conspiracies became an essential feature of the carefully constructed postwar perception that an underlying order had somehow survived the chaos of war.

THE LAST RITES

The kind of political and military shorthand that ends the history of Civil War at Appomattox minimizes those later events that recall the importance of the secret society tradition. Two of these noteworthy later events concern us here: the murder of Abraham Lincoln and the Confederate decision to fight one last battle that could not possibly influence the outcome of the war.

A loose network of Confederate patriots and entrepreneurs acted from their faith in the power of secretly organizing a small group of protagonists and in its silencing of opponents. Actor John Wilkes Booth began as a smuggler of such necessary items as quinine. After meeting with Confederate sympathizers in Boston, he began recruiting people for a plan to kidnap President Lincoln, who then regularly rode the three miles alone from the White House to the Old Soldiers' Home. By the first week of August 1864, Booth met Samuel Arnold and Michael O'Laughlin in Baltimore's City Hotel.[1]

Booth's scheme coincided with—and was probably a part of—official Confederate plans to kidnap the president that summer. Washington had ended the prisoner-of-war exchanges when the Confederacy refused to parole black soldiers as well as whites, and the Confederates hoped that seizing the president would force the Federals to resume bartering. Capt. Thomas Nelson Conrad, a chaplain and native of Fairfax County, organized an effort to kidnap the president with a mad mounted dash into the city and back into Virginia. Conrad abandoned this plan when a regular cavalry escort began to accompany Lincoln.[2]

Later in the year, Booth planned a variant of the kidnapping scheme that would spirit Lincoln far east into Maryland before crossing the Potomac into Virginia. On October 18–27, he visited Montreal, staying at the unofficial headquarters of the Confederate operatives, St. Lawrence Hall, and was seen meeting Patrick Martin and George Nicholas Sanders. Booth returned to the States with letters of introduction to Drs. William Queen and Samuel Mudd near Bryantown in Maryland, and Mudd introduced him to a Confederate agent named Thomas Harbin, who joined the kidnapping plot.[3]

In Washington, Booth's operation expanded.[4] The Surratts entered into the plans two days before Christmas, when Mudd visited Washington to take Booth over to the boardinghouse on H Street. John Harrison Surratt had ventured out of Washington after an 1851 fire, establishing the Surratt House and Tavern at a rural crossroads. Even though he became the postmaster there, he bought and kept the H Street house back in the capital. After he died, his widow, Mary Elizabeth Jenkins Surratt, moved back to Washington, and their son, John H. Surratt Jr., became a courier for the local secessionist underground.

By early 1865, they brought others on board. Booth, Mudd, and the young Surratt took Louis Wiechmann to Booth's room at the National Hotel, where they discussed the kidnapping operation. Booth may have met David E.

Herold in his earlier quinine-smuggling activities, but Herold's knowledge of southern Maryland made him a valuable asset to the plan. Hearing that they needed a boatman, Harbin recruited the Prussian-born George A. Atzerodt, who had begun to assist in ferrying Confederates over the Potomac.

About this time, Lewis T. Powell (alias Lewis Payne or Paine) probably entered into the plot, though a later story had Booth meeting him in Richmond. Wounded at Gettysburg, the Florida Confederate had escaped from prison in Baltimore and joined Col. John Singleton Mosby's partisan rangers in northern Virginia. In mid-January 1865, Powell took an oath of allegiance, which allowed him to return to Baltimore, where he became closely associated with the Confederate underground. He turned up at Surratt's in February, and Booth is said to have taken him "under his wing."[5]

The associations with Mosby's raiders are particularly suggestive. A year earlier, Mosby's men had carried off one of the slickest operations of the war, capturing a Union general out of his Fairfax County headquarters, next door to Captain Conrad's house. Conrad's plans for seizing Lincoln would have surely left Mosby's men responsible for covering the planned escape. Thereafter, Mosby operated in the Washington area, providing a liaison between Richmond and the remaining Confederate underground in the Federal capital.[6]

The group continued to debate how best to kidnap the president. On March 15, Booth met Surratt, Arnold, Atzerodt, Herold, O'Laughlin, and Powell at a restaurant on Pennsylvania Avenue. They agreed to make the attempt in two days, when Lincoln attended a play at the Campbell Hospital, just outside the capital, but the president's last-minute decision not to go forced an indefinite postponement. Toward the end of the month, they discussed the president's visit to Ford Theatre, deciding that O'Laughlen could put the gas lights out while others seized Lincoln in the dark, but they could not figure how to remove him. On March 28, Arnold wrote Booth, urging him to abandon the project as hopeless, but Booth sent provisions and liquor to Mudd's house anyway.[7]

At the start of April, Booth told Atzerodt of plans to decapitate the U.S. government by blowing up the White House, a plan that coincided with the Confederate government's sending of Sgt. Thomas F. "Frank" Harney with special ordnance. A former lieutenant in the Sixth Missouri, he had been wounded and held prisoner before returning to the war primarily as an explosives expert. The Confederate authorities tapped him for this dangerous, clandestine operation in the enemy capital.[8] This strange Confederate version of a Guy Fawkes plot came to an end on April 4.

On that day, Union troops occupied Richmond. Visiting nearby City Point at the time, President Lincoln hurried up the James River to see the fallen capital. While there, Duff Green turned up at the barge to berate him. A wave of demoralization swept through the ranks of secessionists everywhere.

Meanwhile, Federal authorities actually learned about the plan to blow up the White House from one of the Confederate enlisted men in Richmond. Fearful that it might take place after it was too late to affect the war's outcome, he warned Union officials in hopes of preventing it. Lincoln himself dismissed the danger, but six days later, a detachment of Illinois cavalry blundered into about 150 of Mosby's command under Capt. George B. Baylor at Burke's Station in Fairfax County, only about fifteen miles from Washington. Dispersing this force made futile any hope of using explosives.[9]

By then, though, Gen. Robert E. Lee had surrendered the Army of Northern Virginia at Appomattox. There remained a Confederate government on the run and several large, if comparatively lackluster, armies in the field. The loss of the capital and Lee's army took the heart out of the Confederacy.

On April 14, Booth called another meeting. He assigned Herald to guide Powell to kill Secretary of State William H. Seward, then recovering from a carriage accident. Atzerodt would also attack Vice President Andrew Johnson. These events would take place at about 10:15 p.m., timed to coordinate with Booth's own attack on Lincoln at John Ford's Theatre.

What happened that night is well known. Atzerrodt and Powell failed miserably. The former took a rented room at the Kirkwood House above Johnson, but made no attempt on his life. Powell, on the other hand, barged into Seward's house, injuring a total of five people, including Seward, whom he cut deeply across the lower face. Herald had already fled by the time Powell emerged, leaving the would-be assassin to shelter in a wooded lot about a mile from Navy Yard Bridge, eventually spending some three days there. John Wilkes Booth, however, accomplished what Felice Orsini had not.[10] It took little time after the president's murder for it to become obvious that even that loss could not long postpone the implosion of what remained of the Confederacy.

Still, as the magnitude of the disaster unraveled, the government brought in figures on whom it could rely to investigate and unravel the conspiracy. Prominent among them was the spiritualist and future theosophist Henry S. Olcott, who had himself worked undercover to report on John Brown's hanging for the *Tribune*. Another was Britton A. Hill, the St. Louis lawyer and future Greenback-Laborite, urging the unity of the Grange and labor organizations.[11]

Almost a month later and a thousand miles away, another John Ford set the stage for yet another final apparition of the KGC's specter. Juan N. Cortina had steered his own course along the Confederacy's troubled border with

Mexico, then torn by its own civil war. The Federals held at Brazos Santiago on the Texas coast near the mouth of the Rio Grande, but a tacit alliance between Cortina and the Unionists emerged, as did an informal truce with the secessionist forces under John S. Ford.[12]

A Texas Ranger and old KGC, Ford commanded the Confederate forces in the valley. Col. Daniel Showalter, the California filibusterer, had commanded Ford's advance position at Palmito Ranch protecting Brownsville, but his troops from "Arizona" had more trouble with Cortina than the Federals. Moreover, Ford had to find a gentlemanly way to remove him because he had been hitting the bottle very hard.[13]

After the surrenders elsewhere, everyone realized that it would be simply a matter of time before the Confederates west of the Mississippi followed suit, and the Federal forces had become increasingly nervous about the presence of the French south of the Rio Grande. In May 1865, the Federal command decided to march several hundred soldiers up the Rio Grande toward Brownsville, likely presuming that any Confederates were about as eager as the Unionists to be among the last men killed or injured in the war. Southerners led the way, as the former First Missouri Colored, and a detachment of the Second Texas Cavalry drove the rebels from White's Ranch west toward Palmito Ranch, with a battalion of the Thirty-fourth Indiana behind them. At Palmito Ranch, though, what was left of Ford's "Cavalry of the West" descended upon the ill-prepared and badly led Union column. Had it not been for the rear guard of the black soldiers, the outcome would have been even worse.[14]

Despite their periodic rhetorical flourishes about republicanism, they, like Bickley, naturally took a greater interest in the success of the imperial forces of Napoleon III. In fact, as the Federals moved on Palmito Ranch, Cmdr. A. Veron brought French Imperial troops from Matamoros across the Rio Grande to help man Ford's artillery.[15] After all, their imperial project of imposing a monarchy on Mexico jibed with the clearest statement of Bickley's intent.

The war of unprecedented destruction and death ended with the Confederate decision to have one final utterly gratuitous bloodbath that they knew would have no impact on the war's outcome. Despite mixed and murky motives, the last Confederate military effort aimed at keeping open the Rio Grande for a mass Confederate exodus into Mexico. It would be another two weeks before Gen. Jo Shelby's Missouri brigade weighted its colors in the waters of the Rio Grande and crossed over into another civil war.[16] At the war's end, thousands of these latter-day *filibusteros,* who had appealed to the legacy of Orsini in clamoring for tyrannicide, scurried into Mexico to assist the very monarch Orsini had tried to kill.

The triumph of the Union and the salvation of the American Republic had required the rejection of filibustering and slavery. That said, the closing clash of the Civil War both recalled the legacy of 1846 and the war with Mexico and clearly anticipated the course the United States took in Latin America in 1898 and after. The long contest over the valley of the Rio Grande not only defined the boundaries of the nation but also contributed to defining its character.

THE OUVRIER FROM BROTHERHOOD TO SOLIDARITY

After the war, fraternalism reemerged with a vengeance, helping to define new standards of manhood and middle-class respectability. Veterans established new organizations, such as the Grand Army of the Republic, which donned many of the trappings of politically motivated secret societies. The survival of the Union required the rejection of secession but not necessarily expansionism or racism. Saving the American Republic had not required its radical redefinition.[17] Nevertheless, that outcome was not entirely uncontested.

The legacy of Hugh Forbes proved paradoxically much more real, but with a more elusive importance. From the eighteenth century, the secret society tradition offer a template for new political party organizations, and it continued among nineteenth-century Europeans, where it helped define a national identity and a social vision. Among the Germans, Italians, and others, they pressed for independence and national unity and pursued those goals in the United States as overseas. The wartime Union Leagues and related societies provided the mass base of the Republican Party. As overseas, *republicanism* in America became a watchword for change that would institutionalize the kind of representative government that individual liberty seemed to require.

On both sides of the Atlantic, secret societies also provided the means for agitation of radical social reform. The 1848–49 revolutions divided these more radical concerns from the pure and simple nationalism of Giuseppe Mazzini, whose views, hoped the *New York Times,* left socialism "finally read out from the current scheme of politics." In reality, the "real forces" among the English and the French inspired by the hope of international cooperation drew radicals such as Karl Marx and Friedrich Engels. In September 1864, they launched the International Workingmen's Association (IWA), which incorporated surviving secret societies and embodied a vision going back to Filippo Buonarroti and the French Revolution.[18]

The American Civil War marked those ideological distinctions sharply, largely over the role of race in a reconstructed republic, but the Franco-Prussian War of 1870–71 severed the goals of nationalism and social radicalism very sharply. The conflict toppled Napoleon III and the Second French Empire, establishing German national unity. Garibaldi—and many others—who had supported German nationalism against French imperialism, responded eagerly when French officials declared the country a republic. Old and ailing, Garibaldi still responded, calling out international volunteers and taking up arms for the French.[19]

With the spring of 1871, the Garde Nationale of Paris rose in revolt against the narrow base of the so-called republic, its denial of self-government to the people of the capital, and all the social problems exacerbated by the war. The Paris Commune represented, in many ways, the social revolution to which many of the old radicals of 1848 had aspired. In the course of its brief and tumultuous history, it threw forth as its minister of war Gen. Gustave Paul Cluseret, Forbes's successor of sorts in the leadership of émigré circles in the United States. After the Civil War, he joined the Irish movement and urged English radicals in London to attempt a coincident insurrection. Returning to France, he joined the International Workingmen's Association. After attempting in 1871 to encourage the risings in Lyon and Marseille, he hurried to Paris, where the commune placed him in charge of the military defense of the city.[20]

New York newspaperman George Wilkes had long functioned within the vague politics of the Brotherhood of the Union and was periodically identified with its members. With the outbreak at Paris, he hurried to the city from Brussels to see the unfolding of a new social order. While he consistently praised the commune, he believed, just as surely as its defamer, that the IWA had secretly pulled its strings.[21]

Forbes's aspirations for revolutionary nationalism and his undaunting faith in internationalist means seem to have persisted. Four years later, newspaper accounts of nationalist turmoil in the Balkans reported the wounding of a "Colonel Forbes" at the head of some British volunteers. At Garibaldi's 1881 funeral, "his old-Etonian white-suited sidekick" turned up, though "in reduced circumstances." Certainly, Forbes remained identified with the Italian republicans at the time of his death at Pisa, on July 22, 1892. "A patriotic society at Pisa decided to go into mourning for three months on the death of Hugh Forbes," wrote one historian. "They did well; he had been no fair-weather friend of Italy. England, too, might have mourned the extinction of that particular type of early Victorian Englishman."[22] So might have the friends of liberty in America, who were already busily constructing new organizations.

In New York City, similar concerns transformed the various associations that had been in the antebellum émigré coalition headed by Hugh Forbes.

The Ouvrier Circle of the Brotherhood of the Union had already operated under many different names, including the New York City Industrial Congress, the Cosmopolitan Conference or Commonwealth Association, the National Land Reform Association, the Workingmen's Republican Union, and the Patriotic Union League. To that, it now added Section 9 of the IWA. Throughout, the Ouvrier saw itself as the means to an end, that is, an exclusive body pursing the goal of a more inclusive and democratic society.

Lippard's local lieutenants in the Brotherhood of the Union at Philadelphia also went through a succession of different forms. There, too, its leading figures became active in the politics of Republicanism and Unionism. At the end of the decade, it became Section 26 of the IWA, as well as the local core of the cooperative Sovereigns of Industry and a pioneer in the expansion of the Knights of Labor and the Greenback-Labor movement.[23] In the nation's largest cities, these particular circles lasted through thirty years in different incarnations.

The Knights of Labor had roots running back through the IWA into the Brotherhood of the Union. Although it began in the needle trades among garment cutters, the project always had the eager support of such former brothers and IWA members as Thomas Phillips, the radical shoemaker. After the war, they launched the Knights of Labor upon principles said to have been pioneered by the old Brotherhood. Over the years, the local Brotherhood remained "much favored by the Knights of Labor, especially in Camden," which supported seven hundred members in three circles of the Brotherhood, with an additional three hundred women in the auxiliary Home Communion.[24] The Knights, however, reached nearly eight hundred thousand members of "the producing classes" and, as a by-product, created the American Federation of Labor and the modern American labor movement.

The Brotherhood of the Union itself survived in several other aspects. Members who had led the independent book printers' union in antebellum New York became assimilated into the National Typographical Union. Well into the twentieth century, a secret "Brotherhood of the Union" continued to play a role in that union.[25]

Before the war, John Otis Wattles of the old True Brotherhood had urged radical spiritualists to foster what he called "Eternal Progression." As early as 1863, they discussed launching a society modeled on the freemasons, but open to all, "irrespective of sex or race." After the war, the spiritualists launched the Order of Eternal Progress, which aspired to be not a "secret order of Spiritualists, but . . . an order for Progressive Minds." It admitted "man and woman upon a perfect equality."[26] The strange order seems to have contributed heavily to the American section of the IWA and provided the foundation for Ezra Hervey Heywood's various Labor Reform Leagues.

Separate and apart from these specific organizations, though, the secret society tradition among social reformers continued to inspire, giving rise to new formations. The largest, the Patrons of Husbandry, organized local farmers into their own "Grange" beneath a national umbrella organization in which women were welcome members.[27]

By then, a number of far more prominent societies emerged. Veteran Fourierists revived their old protective unions as the Sovereigns of Industry, which followed the same regional pattern, centered on New England and Pennsylvania. Pennsylvania also provided the Junior Sons of '76 and the Mechanical Order of the Sun, the latter providing the foundations for what became the Ancient Order of United Workmen.[28]

Labor organizations emerged from their wartime persecutions eager to establish a viable national body, while retaining the protective form of a secret society locally or at the national craft level. Alongside their National Labor Union appeared an independent Colored National Labor Union, and the two bodies circled the hope of concerted action. However, in 1871, the NLU launched an ill-prepared attempt to launch an independent labor party, while blacks remained understandably hopeful as to the future of the Republican Party. Indeed, 1872 found the new National Labor Reform Party manipulated by a faction of the Democratic Party. In its wake, the remnants decided to move toward forming or joining a secret society.

As suited a fraternal, ritually defined division between insiders and outsiders, all these associations had to define how inclusive their fraternity would be. The Grange admitted women and had designated local offices to be filled by them. The Order of Eternal Progress, the IWA, the Sovereigns, trade unions, and other groups admitted women, sometimes without officially mandating so restrictive a role for them.

In the American context, however, exclusions tended much more likely to be about race. Many radicals who embraced internationalism, labor solidarity, and the mystique of a lost past expected this to include Africa and Africans. Dr. James McCune Smith and other black leaders certainly had every reason to expect it would be so.[29]

The radical venerations of Africa implicit in Egyptian masonry provided an essential bridge to the concerns of African American organizations. These interests in Egypt as a seminal civilization turned up with remarkable persistence, forming essential features in the thought of postwar transatlantic radical thinkers such as Albert L. Rawson, Charles Sotheran, Caleb Pink, and Gerald Massey.[30]

Yet race proved a remarkably persistent component in defining fraternalism and solidarity. Local unions reflected the ethnic composition of their crafts, but often—though not always—excluded blacks in deference to Southern whites. The Patrons of Husbandry did not leave this to local or state organizations but explicitly and officially excluded blacks from membership.[31]

This paradox created the Industrial Brotherhood. Missouri Grangers faced the problems of industrialization alongside the turmoil of Reconstruction and wanted to organize wageworkers and black farmers, albeit into separate lodges. Although defeated in February 1874 when they took their case to the National Grange at St. Louis, they found many allies beyond the state and launched their own order. Shortly after, what was left of the National Labor Union decided to join the new secret society. For the next four years, the Industrial Brotherhood carried the continuity of a national American labor movement.[32]

During that time, the interracial Industrial Brotherhood made some impressive strides, particularly in the South. It naturally spread into adjacent Arkansas, especially the northwestern corner. The *Independent Workingman* of Nashville, Tennessee, also supported the order's rejection of a "too selfish" policy with regard to working women "where we have made the mistake all the time." "I am more than satisfied of the correctness of your opinion in regard to the necessity of an association to unite the laboring classes," added the *Valley Farmer* from Tuscumbia, Alabama. "There is no country under Heaven that needs reformation more than this part of the South." At Richmond, Virginia, black labor leader Charles Thompson helped establish and lead a large and powerful organization of tobacco workers under the auspices of the Industrial Brotherhood.[33]

Still, the great trend in the postwar workers' movement involved the progressive shedding of the vestiges of secret societies. In 1878, the Industrial Brotherhood merged into a no-longer-secret Knights of Labor, which had also rejected the sanctions of race and sex. They had once seemed a reasonable means to achieve a more inclusive social republic, but reformers and revolutionaries alike began to think that means and ends could not be so easily separated, that one's means tended to reshape the ends.

Just as the Industrial Brotherhood seemed to wink out of existence, an order calling itself the Brotherhood of Freedom flourished in northwestern Arkansas. Although also a secret society, its composition and stated purposes argued for its continuity with the older association. The Brotherhood of Freedom, in turn, merged into that state's Agricultural Wheel, which made a serious bid for power through the Union Labor Party in the later 1880s.

The national Union Labor Party represented the work of a secret circle of leading proponents of third-party politics, mostly veteran Greenbackers. This inner circle, the Charitable Thirteen, established the Order of the Videttes to provide the new party with what the Greenback movement had lacked, a hardened cadre. Populism often formulated its social critique in terms of conspiracies and secret cabals at the top of society. These reflected what Richard Hofstadter once called a "paranoid style."[34] However, terrified late-nineteenth-century farmers resorted to a fear of conspiracy not because they were radicals but because they were embattled middle-class people operating within an American context.

The political concerns that shape our historical memory are predisposed to permit elites the widest freedom of action in the present. These accord low priorities to people and experiences marginal to what become the dominant concerns. The process freely cedes to specialists any substantive memories of maroons, interracial fraternization, autonomous protonationalist organizations among African Americans, or anarchist or socialist groups. In terms of a general historical memory, such things serve mostly as an ornamental flash against the otherwise predominant drabbery of balance books and election returns. In contrast, the most prominent secret society of the period existed sparsely and episodically, where it actually did exist, and the KGC's founder was less an ideologue than a confidence man molding a message to ingratiate himself to the elite.

In the end, a George N. Sanders may have actually thought that "red republicans" were inspired by secret societies, but their charms played out on the political Left pretty quickly. Of course, if the social problem was a mere conspiracy, its resolution required no extensive social reconstruction. Actual radicals, though, agitated for the people to take power, and this rendered secret societies ultimately useless to the political Left. Mass actions independent of the usual ruling structures and practices could not be conjured from the shadows. Marxism and other radical social critiques bypassed older fraternal models for themselves and increasingly understood what they were challenging in terms of a social analysis rather than conspiracies. Matters were very different among the children of Bickley.

THE STRUGGLE FOR ORDER

The project of actually understanding history in terms of broader social, economic, cultural, and political trends implies an often disorderly world in which good and evil are rarely clear without serious thought and discussion. In contrast, the confident, and ultimately arrogant, faith in an innate human nature offers a much simpler world in which secret societies and conspiracies may rather easily derail or advance the natural unfolding of what amounts to a divine plan. This sense, in turn, justifies secret societies or alleged secret societies to meet this danger. The importance of these bodies ultimately turns on their reflection of, and association with, those broader currents.[35]

Paradoxically, the most tangible legacy of the secret society tradition in American history has less to do with secret societies than with an often orchestrated fear of vague conspiracies among outsiders to the constitutional structures of power. Those concerns systematically justify constitutionally sanctioned authorities to employ constitutionally unsanctioned secrecy. In part, fear of conspiracy among those without any legitimate authority—Illuminati phantoms through international communism to the possible terrorist next door—justifies the making of fortunes and the acquisition of unaccountable power by those exercising such authority.

Before the rise of the modern American state, popular associations—or what professed to be such associations—presumed to exercise such power. Bickley's strand of that secret society tradition was translated by the American filibusterers, though the Order of the Lone Star and similar organizations vying for Cuban independence equated this with a takeover by the *Norteamericanos,* demonstrating a remarkable capacity for counterfeiting nationalism. Bickley's KGC carried this full circle into a secession disconnected from any popular mandate. By then fraternal hucksterism had become a sort of in-joke in which everyone seemed to be in the know—such as the Sons of Malta—but it also opened the door for a top-down redefinition of nation in the name of a now disembodied "people."

Certainly, the role in creating such a thing in an American context naturally owed its key arguments to a confidence man, who may have believed little of what he said about blacks, Jews, Catholics, Latinos, secularists, or monarchism. Ultimately an entrepreneur, Bickley could counterfeit whatever might seem marketable, although we have no reliable information on his order independent from his own boasting and boosterism, the bluffs of the Confederate government, and the paranoid self-justifications of Federal officials. Still, in the end, the KGC needed little more to realize its dream of a Southern incursion into Mexico, though that incursion bore fruit, but only in its own season and on its own terms.

Counterfeit though it, too, may have been, the Confederate nationalism of the KGC played a vital role in Civil War history. As with the filibusters solicitous over the future of Cuba, the KGC became a vehicle to coerce that part of the population unwilling to accept its secessionist agenda. Even more important, the KGC in the North paid the price of prominence for becoming the shadow of its own outrageously inflated claims. In fear of it, Unionists clustered in a common coalition, determined to keep Lincoln and his supporters in power by any means necessary.

The origins and waging of the Civil War assumed the power of secret societies that did not exist, eclipsed that of those that did, and cast into obscurity the leaders of such efforts. Nine years after the death of the largely forgotten George Lippard, who had been one of its most famous men of letters in the country, his embarrassing admirer, "Doctor" Bickley, followed the Civil War's end from his prison cell. From there, he ordered the KGC "to suspend all operations until the year 1870," and proposed that the Union cement its hard-won peace by finding a common enemy and waging a war of expansion against it. Bickley's own ambitions for a postwar KGC centered on building a university, for which, one assumes, he would raise funds. In October 1865, Bickley secured his release, and he turned up from time to time, talking about his imperial ambitions and entrepreneurial prospects. Mexico still seemed to loom as unfinished business for him. Still, Bickley died in August 1867, a forgotten and broken man.[36]

The specter of Bickley's fantasy rode from the shadow of its republicanism and galloped into an invisible empire. Shortly after disguised KGC night riders terrorized political enemies of the elite in central Kentucky and Tennessee, a new manifestation of the "Knights of the Circle" emerged using the Greek for *circle—Kuklos*—with the alliterative addition of *Klan.* It pursued similar nocturnal activities there and in that other KGC stronghold, Texas.[37] Ghosts of a past that never really was, they rode roughshod through historical memory, pounding beneath their hooves recollections of groups and events far more real than the KGC, but far more discomforting to the status quo.

As with Bickley's original KGC, the Knights of the Ku Klux Klan worked because they were part of a long tradition of extralegal establishment violence. Regulators, Anti–Horse Thief, White Caps, Citizens' Committees, Bald Knobbers: almost always involved combinations of self-described taxpayers and property owners circumventing the rule of law to get at their social inferiors. An early writer on such activities in Texas suspected that many involved secret societies with rituals and offered specific evidence that such activities took place in San Saba County.[38]

So, too, the legacy of George Sanders and others who conflated social discontent and radicalism resurfaced after the war. Georgian William Dugas Trammell, for example, later claimed to have been the only American to have fought for the Paris Commune. We have no other source for this that does not rest ultimately on his own statement, and he also claimed—with documentable falseness—to have been a "vice president" of the International. His *Ça Ira,* a notably garbled novel on the commune, recast the conflict in the context of the Confederacy's fight against the centralization of government and the International as part of a secret society tradition with the Ku Klux Klan as its cornerstone.[39]

Karen Halttunen's study of antebellum guidebooks demonstrates the persistent and predictable warnings to those seeking success in life about the dangerous of trusting "confidence men." However, as she points out, these warnings wink out of such titles quickly because of "the growing acceptance of the idea that the young American on the make had to become a kind of confidence man himself in order to succeed."[40]

From that day forward, apologists cited "the lack of effective law enforcement" against "horse thieves and counterfeiters, murderers and rapists, loose women and 'uppity' free Negroes." There existed the need to repress "trade unionists, civil rights supporters, feudists, outlaws, cattle rustlers, gold thieves, Comanches, Kiowas, and Apaches." In response, those who "espoused high ideals: self-preservation, self-protection, popular sovereignty, and democracy" formed the Klan, along with various kindred associations. Historical works as late as 1994 repeated such assertions without, as it were, blinking.[41] So would end yet another American century.

In the backcountry, though, the circumstances that produced Bickley's aspirations persisted. There, ambitious and unscrupulous men on the make still plied the alchemy of professional respectability and traditionalism. A generation later, Bickley's old stomping grounds in North Carolina produced John Romulus Brinkley, the similarity in name being surely coincidental. Like his predecessor, "Doctor" Brinkley gave himself the title and a father who had been in the medical service during the most recent war. As with Bickley, both claims seem entirely spurious. Brinkley's kindly old ex-Confederate daddy died while pursuing his medical duties and allegedly had a family library consisting only of the Bible, building his middle-class professionalism on the virtues of ignorance.[42] Although secret societies had become largely passé, Brinkley became one of the most famous surgeons in the country with his exclusive restorative treatments for male erectile dysfunction.

Regrettably, the implications of all this for erectile dysfunction remain remarkably underdiscussed. Certainly, "Doctor" Brinkley actually entered politics himself and, in 1930, rode the tide of mass resentment against the American Medical Association almost into the governorship of Kansas.[43] Through newspaper and radio, respectively, Bickley and Brinkley offered a powerful new alchemy of folksy ignorance suffused with an expertise exclusive to the initiates.

Historians should probably find it more disconcerting than they do that we remember the KGC. A vehicle for a confidence trickster that hardly even existed is remembered, whereas the far more real organizations of Forbes, Cluseret, and their comrades are forgotten? In part, the former offered something far more real: an approach that provided targeted audiences with what made them comfortable and contented with the general structure of the status quo.

Paradoxically, Bickley and his peers offered the basic features of what began emerging in the postwar American middle class. Ongoing social changes disintegrated or seriously changed familiar institutions, and identities combined with their horror at the inhumanity of industrial capitalism to create their search for an authenticity untainted by modernism. They sought regeneration in philanthropy, social work, arts and crafts, or rediscovery of secret truths. As the title of Jackson Lears's *Rebirth of a Nation* suggests, the half century following the Civil War proved essential to this process, as technologies unimaginable to Bickley emerged. The emergence of a corporate-dominated mass culture simultaneously tended to bury people, movements, and ideas that may have challenged the social order, while fostering what strengthened the assumptions essential to the system.[44] A "social Darwinism" emerged that placed economic and social questions as far beyond question as natural laws and eventually would even subjugate natural laws to the subjective measure of consumer comfort.

* * *

History represents the consensus among those with a vested interest in a particular understanding of the past and the power to make that interest matter. For this reason, annals of power tend to structure a popular sense of history, and only events as disruptive as civil wars and revolutions provide discomforting glimpses of people and events ordinarily accorded little importance.

While the American Civil War had been such an event, its recent wave of popular interest has coincided with declarations of an end to history, ideology, or whatever else requires serious social analysis and political debate. This perspective of an ultimately meaningless past particularly eases its distillation into an ultimately arbitrary celebration of heritage, yet another signifier of consumer identity. What emerges is a view of the conflict in which the immensely more marketable con-artist fictions of Bickley entirely eclipse the radicalism of a Forbes or a Cluseret. So it is that the real secret societies of the past may be made such by the conventions of the present.

NOTES

INTRODUCTION

1. Allen E. Roberts, *House Undivided: The Story of Freemasonry and the Civil War* (Richmond, VA: Macoy Publishing and Masonic Supply, 1961); Michael A. Halleran, *The Better Angels of Our Nature: Freemasonry in the American Civil War* (Tuscaloosa: University of Alabama Press, 2010), 52–53. Note, though, that the percentage of the male population eighteen to forty-five cited by Halleran seems to be white men only.

2. Mark C. Carnes, *Secret Ritual and Manhood in Victorian America* (New Haven: Yale University Press, 1989).

3. Horace Greeley, *The American Conflict: A History of the Great Rebellion in the United States of America, 1860–'65,* 2 vols. (Hartford: O. D. Case; London: Stevens Brothers, 1867), 1:350; see also 1:493, 2:18–19.

4. Warren Getler and Bob Brewer, *Shadow of the Sentinel: One Man's Quest to Find the Hidden Treasure of the Confederacy* (New York: Simon and Schuster, 2003) and *Rebel Gold: One Man's Quest to Crack the Code behind the Secret Treasure of the Confederacy* (New York: Simon and Schuster, 2004); Frank Klement, *Dark Lanterns: Secret Political Societies, Conspiracies, and Treason Trials* (Baton Rouge: Louisiana State University Press, 1984).

PROLOGUE

1. "The Eastern War and the United States," *New York Times,* March 29, 1854, 4; Robert C. Binkley, *Realism and Nationalism, 1852–1871* (Boston: Beacon Press, 1961), 137–38; Adam Zamoyski, *Holy Madness: Romantics, Patriots, and Revolutionaries, 1776–1871* (New York: Penguin Books, 1994), 386; "The Sanders Dinner to the Revolutionary Exiles in London" (from Brussels's *Nation*), *New York Times,* March 29, 1854, 1; Edward Hallett Carr, *The Romantic Exiles: A Nineteenth Century Portrait Gallery* (Boston: Beacon Press, 1961), 140–43; Michael J. Kline, *The Baltimore Plot: The First Conspiracy to Assassinate Abraham Lincoln* (Yardley, Pa.: Westholme Publishing, 2008), 380–81.

2. J. M. Roberts, *The Mythology of the Secret Societies* (1972; reprint, St. Albans: Paladin, 1974), 32–47, 58–59; "The Order of Freemasons," *New York Times,* June 12, 1870, 7.

3. For this and the following paragraph, see Roberts, *Mythology of Secret Societies,* 48–59, 62–82, 115–27.

4. Steven C. Bullock, *Revolutionary Brotherhood: Freemasonry and Transformation of the American Social Order, 1730–1840* (Chapel Hill: University of North Carolina Press, 1996); Bernard Fay, *Revolution and Freemasonry, 1680–1800* (Boston: Little, Brown, 1935).

5. Roberts, *Mythology of Secret Societies,* 133–73, 176–80.

6. Ibid., 173–76; Robert Darnton, *Mesmerism and the End of the Enlightenment in France* (Cambridge: Harvard University Press, 1968); James H. Billington, *Fire in the Minds of Men: Origins of the Revolutionary Faith* (New York: Basic Books, 1980), 98–100.

7. Billington, *Fire in the Minds of Men,* 96–97; Susanne Kleinert, "Nicolas de Bonneville: Studien zur ideengeschichtlichen und literaturtheoretischen Position eines Schriftstellers der Französischen Revolution," in *Studia Romanica* (Heidelberg) 42 (Winter 1981); R. B. Rose, *The Enragés: Socialists of the French Revolution?* 2nd ed. (1965; reprint, Sydney: Sydney University Press, 1968); Gary Kates, *The Cercle Social, the Girondins, and the French Revolution* (Princeton: Princeton University Press, 1985); Philippe Le Harivel, *Nicolas de Bonneville: Pre-romantique et revolutionnaire, 1760–1823* (Paris: Libraire Istra, 1923).

8. Armando Saitta, *Filipp Buonarroti, contributo alla storia della sua vita e eel suo pensiero,* 2 vols. (Rome: Instituto Storico Italiano per L'Eta Moderna e Contemporanea, 1972); Elizabeth L. Eisenstein, *The First Professional Revolutionist, Filippo Michele Buonarroti, 1761–1830* (Cambridge: Harvard University Press, 1959); Arthur Lehning, *From Buonarroti to Bakunin: Studies in International Socialism* (Leiden: E. J. Brill, 1970), 30–121; J. Höppner and W. Seidel-Höppner, *Von Babeuf bis Blanqui: Französischer Sozialismus und Kommunismus vor Marx,* 2 vols. (Leipzig: Verlag Philip Reclam jun, 1975); Roberts, *Mythology of Secret Societies,* 238–61.

9. Buonarroti later told of how the two friendly revolutionists had an exchange in which he had promised to play Brutus to Bonaparte's Caesar.

10. For Buonarroti's activities during this period, see Roberts, *Mythology of Secret Societies,* 276–81. See also Eisenstein, *First Professional Revolutionist,* 25–54.

11. In addition to several French titles, see Guido Artom, *Napoleon Is Dead in Russia,* trans. Muriel Grindrod (New York: Atheneum, 1970; London: George Allen and Unwin, 1970); Roberts, *Mythology of Secret Societies,* 281–85; and Charles Nodier, *History of the Secret Societies of the Army* (London: printed for Longman, Hurst, Rees, Orme, and Brown, 1815).

12. Roberts, *Mythology of Secret Societies,* 296–307.

13. Unraveling the activities of the underground during the Bourbon Restoration and the reactionary alliance by the leading states. Roberts, *Mythology of Secret Societies,* 314–54.

14. *Conspiration pour l'égalité dite de Babeuf: Suivie du procès auquel elle donna lieu, et des pièces justificatives, etc.* (Brussels: La Librairie Romantique, 1828), with the English version as *Buonarroti's History of Babeuf's Conspiracy for equality; with the author's reflections on the cause & character of the French Revolution, and his estimate of the leading men and events of that epoch. Also, his views of democratic government, community of property,*

and political and social equality, translated and illustrated by original notes by Bronterre [pseud.] (London: H. Hetherington, 1836).

15. While membership in the order did not necessarily entail a rejection of religious, nationalistic, or hierarchical values, its recruitment of men of different classes, religions, and nations clearly indicated a high degree of tolerance and implied that other values transcended those more widely accepted in the society. Then, too, freed from the perceived social necessity of maintaining the pretense of unquestioning loyalty to institutions of the prevailing order, many masons openly and frankly discussed subjects barred from general discourse.

16. Kenneth R. H. Mackenzie, *Royal Masonic Cyclopaedia of History, Rites, Symbolism, and Biography,* 6 vols. in 1 (London: John Hogg, 1877), 43, 188–90, 469, 491, 504; publishers' introduction to Jacques Étienne Marconis, *The Sanctuary of Memphis* (n.p., n.d.), translated from *Le Sanctuaire de Memphis, ou Hermes. Développements completes des Mysteres Maçonniques* (Paris: Bruyer, 1849), 3; Karim Wiasa, "Freemasonry in Egypt, 1798–1921: A Study in Cultural and Political Encounters," *Bulletin of the British Society for Middle Eastern Studies* 16 (1989): 160n; Arthur E. Waite, *A New Encyclopaedia of Freemasonry,* 2 vols. in 1 (New Hyde Park, N.Y.: University Books, 1970), 2:133, 241–48.

17. See particularly Eisenstein's insightful overview in *First Professional Revolutionist,* 144–60.

18. Joseph Mazzini, "Duties to Country," in *The Duties of Man, and Other Essays* (London and Toronto: J. M. Dent & Sons; New York: E. P. Dutton, 1907), 52, 53.

19. Ibid., 53, 57.

20. Alan B. Spitzer, *The Revolutionary Theories of Louis Auguste Blanqui* (New York: Columbia University Press, 1957), 4–5, 129–33; Patrick H. Hutton, *The Cult of the Revolutionary Tradition: The Blanquists in French Politics, 1864–1893* (Berkeley and Los Angeles: University of California Press, 1981), 18.

21. Alessandro Galante Garrone, *Philippe Buonarroti et les révolutionnaires du XIXe (1828–1837),* trans. Anne and Claude Manceron (Paris: Champ Libre, 1975).

22. Julius West, *A History of the Chartist Movement* (London: Constable, 1920), 230–31, 234–35. J. F. C. Harrison, *Bibliography of the Chartist Movement, 1837–1976* (Hassocks, England: Harvester Press; Atlantic Highlands, N.J.: Humanities Press, 1978), provides an already rather dated guide to the extensive literature on Chartism.

23. Arthur Lehning, "The International Association (1855–1859): A Contribution to the Preliminary History of the First International," 169–70, reprinted in Lehning's *From Buonarroti to Bakunin,* 151–260.

24. Boris I. Nicolaevsky, "Secret Societies and the First International," in *The Revolutionary Internationals, 1864–1943,* ed. Milorad M. Drachkovitch (Stanford: Stanford University Press for the Hoover Institution on War, Revolution, and Peace, 1966), 38, 39–40, 41–42; Lehning, "International Association," 170–73, 174–75, 178–79. See also Andrew Prescott, "'The Cause of Humanity': Charles Bradlaugh and Freemasonry," *Ars Quatuor Coronatorum* 116 (2003): 15–64, available at http://www.freemasons-freemasonry.com/andrew_prescott.html; and Robert F. Gould, *Gould's History of Freemasonry throughout the World,* revised by Dudley Wright, 6 vols. (New York: Charles Scribner's Sons, 1936) 3:61, 67.

25. Christine Lattek, *Revolutionary Refugees: German Socialism in Britain, 1840–1860*

(London: Routledge, 2006), 33–35; Richard Brown, *Chartism* (Cambridge: Cambridge University Press, 1998), 99, 102; West, *History of the Chartist Movement*, 230–31, 234–35. See also Sabine Freitag, *Exiles from European Revolutions: Refugees in Mid-Victorian England* (London: German Historical Institute, Berghahn Books, 2003). In 1850, the Fraternal Democrats merged into the National Reform League of James Bronterre O'Brien, aimed at nationalization and democratization of land.

26. For the specific rhetoric behind this, see Vernon Stauffer, *New England and the Bavarian Illuminati* (New York: Columbia University Press, 1918).

27. Mark A. Lause, "'The Unwashed Infidelity': Thomas Paine and Early New York City Labor History," *Labor History* 27 (Summer 1986): 385–409. Extracts from Babeuf appeared in *Peace-Republicans' Manual; or, the French Constitution of 1793 . . . Translated Extracts from Pieces Seized in Baboeuf's Rooms . . .* (New York: sold by J. Tiebout & Sons, 1817), 85–94.

28. Lause, "'The Unwashed Infidelity,'" 385–409.

29. The organization is frequently mentioned at the edges of labor and land reform activities through the 1840s, though it seems to have declined somewhat after 1848. "Strikes for Wages—Mechanics Association," *Scientific American* 5 (June 8, 1850): 301.

30. Lehning, "International Association," 327n4.

31. William B. Greene, *The Blazing Star, with an Appendix Treating of the Jewish Kabbala, Also a Tract on the Philosophy of Mr. Herbert Spencer, and One on New-England Transcendentalism* (Boston: A. Williams, 1872), 20–21.

32. Charles L. Hunt to Mary C. Hunt, May 28, 1845, August 8, September 13, October 6, 19, 1847, January 17, February 26, March 12, 16, 1848, Box 2, Hunt Family Papers, Missouri History Museum Library, St. Louis; Rev. John Rothensteiner, *History of the Archdiocese of St. Louis*, 2 vols. (St. Louis: by the author, 1928), 1:807, 2:272, 273. See also John Bartier, "Belgium in 1848," in *The Opening of an Era: 1848, an Historical Symposium*, ed. François Fejtö (1948; reprint, New York: H. Fertig, 1966), 160–66.

33. Bartier, "Belgium in 1848," 165; Charles L. Hunt to Mary C. Hunt, February 26, March 12, 16, 1848, Hunt Family Papers. See also Charles L. Hunt to Mary C. Hunt, January 17, 1848, for his general itinerary, in ibid. Karl Marx, *Free Trade: A Speech Delivered before the Democratic Club, Brussels, Belgium, Jan. 9, 1848*, trans. Florence Kelley Wischnewetzky (Boston: Less and Shepard, 1888).

34. Carr, *Romantic Exiles*, 140–43; "New-York City: The First French Republic—Anniversary by the Society of the Mountain," *New York Times*, September 24, 1855, 1. For a more representative Southern view, see Timothy M. Roberts, "'Revolutions Have Become the Bloody Toy of the Multitude': European Revolutions, the South, and the Crisis of 1850," *Journal of the Early Republic* 25 (Summer 2005): 259–83.

CHAPTER 1. THE BROTHERHOOD OF THE UNION

1. *B.G.C.* (Philadelphia: [Brotherhood of the Union], [1850?]), 36–42. Copy in the archives of the Brotherhood of America, Historical Society of Pennsylvania, Philadelphia.

2. [John Bell Bouton], *The Life and Choice Writings of George Lippard* (New York: H. H. Randall, 1855), 7–10, 12, 13; David S. Reynolds, *George Lippard* (Boston: Twayne, 1982) and his anthology *George Lippard, Prophet of Protest: Writings of an American Radical, 1822–1854*, ed. David S. Reynolds (New York: P. Lang, 1986). Frederick S. Frank also in-

cludes a good recent bibliography in his "George Lippard," in *Gothic Writers: A Critical and Bibliographical Guide*, ed. Douglass H. Thomson, Jack G. Voller, and Frederick S. Frank (Westport, Conn.: Greenwood Press, 2002), 261–69.

3. Bouton, *George Lippard*, 10, 14–17, 18–19; George Lippard, "Twenty-three Thoughts," *Quaker City*, April 28, 1849, 3.

4. Bouton, *George Lippard*, 19, 20, 27, 44–45, 46; *Popular American Literature of the 19th Century*, ed. Paul C. Gutjahr (New York: Oxford University Press, 2001), 287, which reprints much of it on 288–402. In May 1849, only a few years after this Philadelphia incident, a play sparked the Astor Place Riot in New York City.

5. R. H. Stoddard poems "The Village School House" and "Death" and his notice on Poe's loss in *Quaker City*, February 24, March 24, October 20, 1849, 2.

6. "To Those Who Work," *Quaker City*, June 2, 1849, 2, but see also Blanc, "The Illuminati; or, The Free-Masonry of the French Revolution," *Quaker City*, May 26, 1849, 3; "Cagliostro, of the Sorcerer of the French Revolution (an Historical Picture)," *Quaker City*, June 2, 1849, 4; "Mesmer," *Quaker City*, September 1, 1849, 4; and, on Charles Brockden Brown, "The Heart Broken," *Quaker City*, June 2, 1849.

7. Lippard personally verified for the integrity of Capron and Barron. *Quaker City*, January 19, 1850, 2; Capron's serialized "An Address Delivered before Cayuga Circle No. 1 B. U. (H. F.) C.A. of Auburn, New York, and 76 of the Continent, January 1, 1850," *Quaker City*, February 22, 1850, 1–2, March 2, 1850, 4; capped by his comments in "The Mysterious Noises," *Quaker City*, April 13, 1850, 2. The historiography of spiritualism is growing and increasingly involved, but the following titles provide a good introduction to the subject: Logie Barrow, *Independent Spirits: Spiritualism and English Plebeians, 1850–1910* (London and New York: Routledge & Kegan Paul, 1986); Bret E. Carroll, *Spiritualism in Antebellum America* (Bloomington: Indiana University Press, 1997); Barbara Weisberg, *Talking to the Dead: Kate and Maggie Fox and the Rise of Spiritualism* ([San Francisco]: Harper San Francisco, 2004); Barbara Goldsmith, *Other Powers: The Age of Suffrage, Spiritualism, and the Scandalous Victoria Woodhull* (New York: Alfred A. Knopf, 1998); John B. Buescher, *The Remarkable Life of John Murray Spear: Agitator for the Spirit Land* (Notre Dame: University of Notre Dame Press, 2006), 178–79, 226–31, 236–49, 253–54 and *The Other Side of Salvation: Spiritualism and the Nineteenth-Century Religious Experience* (Boston: Skinner House Books, 2004),

8. See Yonatan Eyal, *The Young America Movement and the Transformation of the Democratic Party, 1828–1861* (New York: Cambridge University Press, 2007).

9. "To Those Who Work," *Quaker City*, June 2, 1849, 2; "'The Great Secret Society,'" *Quaker City*, June 30, 1849, 3. In general, see Roger Butterfield's "George Lippard and His Secret Brotherhood," *Pennsylvania Magazine of History and Biography* 79 (July 1955): 285–309.

10. "'The Great Secret Society'"; "Recommendation: The Supreme Circle of the Brotherhood of the Union (H. F.) to All the Circles of the Order, and to All the Brothers, in Truth, Hope, and Love," *Quaker City*, December 22, 1849, 2. See also the following items from *Quaker City*: "To Those Who Work," June 2, 1849, 2; "To the Men Who Work—Another Word," August 25, 1849, 2, repeated September 29, 1849, 2; "To the Men Who Work, Once More," October 20, 1849, 2, repeated October 27, 1849, 4; W. H. G., "Letter from Wiskonsan: Brotherhood of the Union," December 1, 1849, 2; "To the Men Who Work, in the North

and South,'" March 9, 1850, 2; "Letter from John Grieg," March 30, 1850, 2; and J. M. W. Geist, "Social Aristocracy," March 30, 1850, 4.

11. Editorial Department, "The Brotherhood," in *The White Banner*, 1 vol. extant (Philadelphia: by the author, 1851), 141; "H. F. Constitution of the—Circle of the Brotherhood of the Union, No.—of the C. of and No.—of the State of—," independently paged at the end of *The White Banner* as 5–6, 20–21, 22, 23–24; *Quaker City*, February 16, 1850, 2.

12. "Advent of the New Era," *Quaker City*, January 5, 1850, 2; *Quaker City*, January 12, 1850, 2; George Lippard, "Thomas Paine, the Author-Hero of the Revolution," *Quaker City*, February 9, 1850, 1–2; *Quaker City*, March 9, 1850, 2; "Mass Meeting in the Chinese Museum, in Behalf of the Tailoresses and Other Sewing Women: Plan of 'Industrial Union,'" March 9, 1850, 2–3, in which the order reprinted *Thomas Paine: Author-Soldier of the American Revolution by George Lippard, Philadelphia, January 25th, 1852* (n.p.: n.p., [1894?]); Clifton K. Yearley Jr., "Thomas Phillips, a Yorkshire Shoemaker in Philadelphia," *Pennsylvania Magazine of History and Biography* 79 (April 1955): 167–96.

13. *Quaker City*, January 5, 1850, 3; *Quaker City*, March 23, 1850, 2.

14. John R. Commons et al., eds., *A Documentary History of American Industrial Society*, 10 vols. (1910; reprint, New York: Russell & Russell, 1958), 8:27, 285, 287, 305–7; Mark Lause, *Young America: Land, Labor, and the Republican Community* (Urbana: University of Illinois Press, 2005), 65–66, 123. For similar movements in the Cincinnati area, see "The Work Goes Bravely On" (from *Cincinnati Nonpareil*), *Quaker City*, March 2, 1850, 2. On Henderson, see *American Biographical History of Eminent and Self-Made Men: Michigan Volume* (Cincinnati: Western Biographical Publishing, 1878), 52–55.

15. "What 'Socialism' Really Is," *Quaker City*, March 30, 1850, 2; *Quaker City*, April 27, 1850, 2; "The Working Men's Meeting," *Boston Herald*, April 9, 1850, 2.

16. *Quaker City*, April 20, 1850, 2.

17. Four circles may have formed at Pittsburgh; Morrisville, Vermont; Eaton Rapids, Michigan; and Nacogdoches, Texas, from which Lippard received correspondence but for which we have no assigned number. The order assigned numbers 104, 162, and 186 to two circles. The unassigned numbers, in addition to Nos. 2–55 were 66, 67, 105, 151, 159, 160, 161, and 185. On circle formations, see the appendix.

18. The rolls contained no names for many of the numbered circles, indicating that it never functioned well enough to elect officers or report them. Others include names that were so obscure as to have had no significant impact on the local historical record. Moreover, a few names turn up associated with two or more circles.

19. Bouton, *George Lippard*, 57, 69–70.

20. Lippard, "Twenty-three Thoughts"; "Brotherhood of the Union: Organization of the First Circle in the State of New Jersey," *Quaker City*, December 29, 1849, 2; *B.G.C.*, 36, 44, 48, 50, 51, 58; "H. F. Constitution," in *The White Banner*, independently paged at the end of the volume as 3–24. See also John H. Keyser's letter, "Wages, Slavery, and Chattel Slavery," *Liberator*, April 21, 1848, 63.

21. Ibid., 66; "The First Annual Convocation" tract, 12, 13, Brotherhood of America Papers, Historical Society of Pennsylvania, Philadelphia; *Tenth Annual Report of the Bureau of Statistics of Labor and Industries of New Jersey, for the Year Ending October 31st, 1887* (Somerville, N.J.: Unionist-Gazette Printing House for the State of New Jersey, 1888), 146.

22. Lause, *Young America*, 92, 94, 95. See also "Land Reform," *Erie Observer*, June 15, 1848, 2.

23. *Adonai: The Pilgrim of Eternity*, in *The White Banner*, 74–79.

24. Cora Montgomery letters, *Quaker City*, April 14, July 21, 1849, September 22, 29, December 29, 1849, February 2, 1850, all on 2, as well as her serialized story "Red Hand: A Romance of Indian History," March 9, 1850, 1–2; March 16, 1850, 1, 4; March 23, 1850, 1–2.

25. *Tenth Annual Report of the Bureau of Statistics of Labor and Industries*, 146–47; *Adonai: The Pilgrim of Eternity*, in *The White Banner*, 96; "H. F. Constitution," in *The White Banner*, independently paged at the end of the volume as 3; Charles Goepp and Theodore Poesche, *The New Rome; or, The United States of the World* (New York: G. P. Putnam, 1853).

26. "Legends of Every Day," in *The White Banner*, 107–9.

27. Shelley Streeby, *American Sensations: Class, Empire, and the Production of Popular Culture* (Berkeley and Los Angeles: University of California Press, 2002), 21–22, 166; untitled item by A. J. H. Duganne on Knights, *Quaker City*, September 1, 1849, 3. See also A. J. H. Duganne, *The Knights of the Seal; or, The Mysteries of the Three Cities: A Romance of Men's Hearts and Habits* (Philadelphia: Colon and Adriance, Arcade, 1845), on the dangers of alien conspiracies.

28. Editorial Department, "The Brotherhood," in *The White Banner*, 142; "H. F. Constitution," in *The White Banner*, independently paged at the end of the volume as 3; *Tenth Annual Report of the Bureau of Statistics of Labor and Industries*, 146.

29. Bouton, *George Lippard*, 64; Editorial Department, "The Brotherhood," in *The White Banner*, 145; January 29, February 12, April 11, 1853, in the manuscript journal of the order, Brotherhood of America Papers.

30. *Quaker City*, July 7, 1849, 3; Cora Montgomery, "Letter from the Far West," July 21, 1849, 2. "America was peopled thousands of years ago by a highly civilized race. This race was destroyed by wandering hordes analogous to the Arab and Tartar races. A dim record of their history may be traced in the mounds and buried cities of the west and south." Lippard, "Twenty-three Thoughts," 3.

31. Bouton, *George Lippard*, 93–95.

32. Cosmopolite, "Essay on Ultra-Democracy," *Quaker City*, June 16, 1849, 1; J. E. I., "The Late Mr. Detwiler of Baltimore," *Quaker City*, March 16, 1850, 2.

33. Lippard to Macfarland, October 18, 1852, and, for Lockport, September 13, December 31, 1852, journal of the order, Brotherhood of America Papers. On Durkee, see "National Industrial Congress—VII Session," *New York Daily Tribune*, June 3, 1852, 6.

34. Nelson W. Evans, *A History of Scioto County, Together with a Pioneer Record of Southern Ohio* (Portsmouth, Ohio: for the author, 1903), 221, 226, 239 (Appler), 156, 216, 471, 472 (Camden), 455 (Work), 517 (Friar, Camden). Other members of the Rainbow Circle were F. W. Frazier and S. F. Rawson.

35. Bouton, *George Lippard*, 66, 117; Lippard support for Joel Jones, "the People's Candidate for Mayor," noted in two untitled items, *Quaker City*, October 6 and 20, 1849, both on 2; Rev. C. Chauncey Burr, "An Essay on the Writings of Genius of George Lippard," *Quaker City*, November 24, 1849, 1–2; *Quaker City*, March 23, 1850, 2.

36. See Lause, *Young America*, 72–84.

37. "Politics and Policy," *National Era*, April 17, 1851, 61.

38. Ibid.; "The Proposed League of Freedom," *National Era*, May 8, 1851, 73; "Proposals for the Formation of a New Anti-Slavery Association," *National Era*, June 10, 1852, 96; "Organizing in Iowa," *National Era*, April 5, 1855, 53; "Comment on the League," *Huntress*, May 24, 1851, 2; "The Proposed 'League of Freedom,'" *Huntress*, June 7, 1851; "Affairs in Massachusetts," *Independent*, February 15, 1855, 56.

39. *Proceedings of the Seventh National Industrial Congress, Held in Washington, D.C., Commencing in Wednesday, June 2d, and Ending on Monday, June 7th, 1852* (Washington: [National Industrial Congress], [1852]), 2; letters to Pierce from Price, June 7, 1852; Gordon, June 14, 1852; Devyr, June 18, 23, 1852; A. G. H. Duganne, July 2, 1852; Price (with Croly, A. G. Levy, Commerford, and David Marsh), July 5, 1852; E. W. Capron, July 27, 1852.

40. "News Gatherings," *New York Times*, July 2, 1852, 4; "Meeting of Land Reform," *New York Times*, August 11, 1852, 5; "Meeting of Land Reformers in New York—Important Action" (from *New York Tribune*), *Dollar Weekly Nonpareil*, August 12, 1852, 2; "Land Reform," *New York Daily Tribune*, August 11, 1852, 5; "Land Reform Meeting at Military Hall, Bowery," *New York Daily Tribune*, August 18, 1852, 7; "City News," *New York Herald*, August 19, 1852, 2; memorial to the Senate, SEN32A-J2, Box 150, f 8/9/52–2/22/53. Alvan E. Bovay, the former secretary of the NRA, also supported Scott, but "felt defeat in the air every day." Quoted in Frank A. Flower, *History of the Republican Party* (Springfield, Ill.: Union Publishing, 1884), 151. See also Theodore Clarke Smith, *The Liberty and Free Soil Parties in the Northwest* (New York: Longmans, Green, 1897), 256–57.

41. "Meeting of the Independent Democrats at the Chinese Building," *New York Daily Tribune*, August 7, 1852, 5; "Land Reform Meeting at Military Hall, Bowery," *New York Daily Tribune*, August 18, 1852, 7; Lause, *Young America*, 109–10.

42. Two pieces titled "Free Soil National Convention," *Pittsburgh Evening Chronicle*, August 11, 12, 1852, both starting 2; John R. Irelan, *The Republic; or, A History of the United States of America*, 18 vols. (Chicago: Fairbank and Palmer Publishing, 1888), 13:325–32. "Independent Democratic Nominations" with "Free Democratic National Convention," *National Era*, August 19, 1852, 134–35; "Proceedings of the Free Democratic National Convention," *National Era*, August 26, 1852, 137–38.

43. "The Pittsburgh Convention," *American Whig Review* 16 (October 1852): 366–74; "Gerrit Smith, Again" and "A Second Letter for Gerrit Smith," *New York Tribune*, August 17, 1852, 4, 6; "Butler to Chase," *New York Times*, August 9, 1852, 2; "The Free Democratic Electoral Ticket," *New York Times*, October 6, 1852, 1; "Massachusetts Politics, National and State," *New York Times*, October 6, 1852, 2; "Movements of Senator Hale," *New York Times*, October 27, 1852, 1; "Free Soil National Convention," *Pittsburgh Evening Chronicle*, August 10, 1852, 2; "'We'll Be with You,'" *Pittsburgh Evening Chronicle*, August 14, 1852, 2; "Meetings," *National Era*, August 5, 1852, 176; "The Organization," *National Era*, December 16, 1852, 202; "Great Free Soil Demonstration," *New York Herald*, May 7, 1853, 7; "The Presidential Election," *Boston Herald*, November 1, 1852, 4; *Free Democratic Extra: For President, John P. Hale* (n.p.: Free Democratic Press, [1852]).

44. "Meeting of Independent Democrats at the Chinese Building," *New York Tribune*, August 2, 1852, 5; "Land Reform Meeting in Military Hall," *New York Tribune*, August 18, 1852, 7; "Land Reform Meeting in Military Hall," *New York Herald*, August 19, 1852, 2; "Free Democratic Convention at Syracuse," *New York Herald*, September 30, 1852, 1; *Free Demo-*

cratic Extra. See also "Gerrit Smith's Platform," in *The Jubilee Harbinger for 1854* (Philadelphia: n.p., [1854]), 311, this bound volume being consecutively paged but undated issues of the *Monthly Jubilee*; "The Free Democracy," *New York Times,* September 30, 1852, 1; *New York Times,* October 1, 1852, 4; "The Free Democracy," *New York Times,* October 1, 1852, 8; "Meeting of the Free Democracy," *New York Times,* October 7, 1852, 8; John C. Spurlock, *Free Love, Marriage, and Middle-Class Radicalism in America, 1825–1860* (New York: New York University Press, 1988), 9, 148; and Martin H. Blatt, *Free Love and Anarchism: The Biography of Ezra Heywood* (Urbana: University of Illinois Press, 1989), 115–16.

45. "Free Soil State Convention at Pittsburgh," *New York Tribune,* August 11, 1852, 5; "State Convention," *Pittsburgh Evening Chronicle,* August 11, 1852, 2; "Free Soil: Pennsylvania State Convention," *Pittsburgh Evening Chronicle,* August 12, 1852, 2; "Meeting in Philadelphia," *National Era,* July 15, 1852, 114; "Pennsylvania Free Soil State Convention," *National Era,* August 19, 1852, 133; "An Address to the Citizens of the State of Pennsylvania," *National Era,* August 26, 1852, 138; "Pennsylvania," *National Era,* October 14, 1852, 165.

46. Brotherhood of the Union, Third Annual Convocation of the Supreme Circle, Oct. 4, 1852, A. O. 1856 ([Philadelphia: Brotherhood of the Union, 1852]), unnumbered eight-page tract; Supreme Circle of the Brotherhood of the Union (H. F.), C. A. Philadelphia, January 1st, 1852 (n.p.: the order, [1852?]).

47. "Free Democratic Nominations," *New York Times,* September 8, 1852, 2; "Free Soil and Democratic Nominations," *New York Times,* October 13, 1852, 1; *New York Times,* October 13, 1852, 5; "Mr. Horace Mann," *New York Times,* November 20, 1852, 4; "Grand Mass Meeting of the Free Soilers in Faneuil Hall," *Boston Herald,* October 14, 1852, 2; "From J. E. Snodgrass" and "From L. A. Hine," *Liberator,* October 22, 1852, 171; campaign tract; *Free Democratic Extra;* "Land and People," *New York Tribune,* November 6, 1852, 4. G. Howe toiled for the cause from Worchester and Boston.

48. "Proceedings of National Industrial Congress," in *The Jubilee Harbinger for 1854,* 377, part of Fanny Townsend's "Slices of Wilmington," 371–77; *National Reform Almanac for 1849* (New York: Young America, 1848), 18; "Industrial Congress—Third Session," *New York Daily Tribune,* June 29, 1848, and *New Era of Industry,* June 29, 1848; Henry C. Conrad, *History of the State of Delaware,* 3 vols. (Lancaster, Pa.: Wickersham Company for the author, 1908), 2:444; John T. Scharf, *History of Delaware, 1609–1888,* 2 vols. (Philadelphia: L. J. Richards, 1888), 2:822, 823; William T. Jeandell, the Democratic editor of the *Blue Hen's Chicken,* was also a member of the Wilmington order. *Quaker City,* May 11, 1850, 2.

49. Bouton, *George Lippard,* 45, 57, 67–68, 69, 74, 78.

50. Brotherhood of the Union, *Fourth Annual and First Triennial Convocation of the Supreme Circle,* October 3, 1853, A. O. 1857; journal of the order, October 17, 1853, Brotherhood of America Papers; Bouton, *George Lippard,* 57, 66; Walt Whitman notes dated November 26, 1860, in his *Notebooks and Unpublished Prose Manuscripts,* ed. Edward F. Grier, 6 vols. (New York: New York University Press, 1984), 1:434.

CHAPTER 2. UNIVERSAL DEMOCRATIC REPUBLICANS

1. "Liberal Societies Represented in This Convention," in "Convention of Liberal Societies," *New York Tribune,* October 13, 1854, 3; Richard Josiah Hinton, "John Brown and His Men," *Frank Leslie's Popular Monthly,* June 1889, 695, and, for the later New York City connection, Hinton, *John Brown and His Men* (New York: Funk & Wagnalls, 1894),

162–63; Benjamin Quarles, *Allies for Freedom: Blacks and John Brown* (Oxford: Oxford University Press, 1974), 52–53; Daniel C. Littlefield, "Blacks, John Brown, and a Theory of Manhood," in *His Soul Goes Marching On: Responses to John Brown and the Harpers Ferry Raid,* ed. Paul Finkelman (Charlottesville: University Press of Virginia, 1995), 79; David S. Reynolds, *John Brown, Abolitionist: The Man Who Killed Slavery, Sparked the Civil War, and Seeded Civil Rights* (New York: Alfred A. Knopf, 2005), 240, but see also 113–14, 191, 234, 240–44, and 258.

2. On the Forbes clan, see William Anderson, *The Scottish Nation; or, The Surnames, Families, Literature, Honours, and Biographical History of the People of Scotland,* 3 vols. (Edinburgh: Fullarton, [1859]–63); http://worldroots.com/brigitte/royal/bio/francoiserochefoucauldbiol723.html; Christopher Hippert, *Garibaldi and His Enemies: The Clash of Arms and Personalities in the Making of Italy* (Boston: Little, Brown, 1966), 104; George Macaulay Trevelyan, *Garibaldi's Defence of the Roman Republic,* 3rd ed. (London, Bombay, and Calcutta: Longmans, Green, 1914), vii, 349.

3. "'Roma o morte': Garibaldi, Nationalism, and the Problem of Psycho-Biography," 7, http://ourworld.compuserve.com/homepages/autographe/indexl.htm; War Office, *Printed Annual Army Lists: A List of Officers of the Army and Royal Marines, on Full, Retired, and Half Pay, with an Index, Published Annually, 1827* (London: published by authority, annual), 149; *1829,* 149; *1830,* 145; and *1831,* 148, the last listed as the second ranking man of that rank in the regiment. See also the 1830 presentations to "Lieutenant Forbes" by Vice Adm. Sir Charles Rowley and his presence at an 1843 anniversary banquet at Clarendon Hotel in "The King's Levee," *Times* (London), July 22, 1830, 2; "From the *London Gazette,* Tuesday, May 24," *Times* (London), May 25, 1831, 4; *Times* (London), November 4, 1843, 7.

4. Theodore Dwight, *The Roman Republic of 1849, with Accounts of the Inquisition, and the Siege of Rome, and Biographical Sketches, with Original Portraits* (New York: R. Van Dien, 1851), 198; Hippert, *Garibaldi and His Enemies,* 104. For a misidentification as an Englishman "then traveling en touriste through Italy," see Jessie White Marie, *The Birth of Modern Italy* (New York: Charles Scribner's Sons; London: T. Fisher Unwin, 1909), 161; H. Forbes, "Italian Affairs in the Roman Republic and Its Calumniators," *National Era,* July 4, 1850, 105; this was surely owing to confusion with John Peard.

5. Dwight, *Roman Republic of 1849,* 198–99. See also "Garibaldi's Retreat from Rome," *Manchester Times,* July 13, 1867; "Garibaldi's Heroic Defence of Rome," *Penny Illustrated Paper and Illustrated Times,* June 10, 1882, 366.

6. Hippert, *Garibaldi and His Enemies,* 104; Dwight, *Roman Republic of 1849,* 199; Bernard Cook, "Two Sicilies, Kingdom of, 1848–49"; Lawrence Sondhaus, "War in Northern Italy"; Emiliana P. Noether, "Constitutions and Parliaments, Italy, 1848–1849" and "Roman Republic," in James Chastain, *Encyclopedia of 1848 Revolutions,* posted by Ohio State University at http://www.ohio.edu/chastain/. For the most recent biography, see Alfonso Scirocco, *Garibaldi, Citizen of the World: A Biography* (Princeton: Princeton University Press, 2007).

7. Dwight, *Roman Republic of 1849,* 199–200.

8. Trevelyan, *Garibaldi's Defence of the Roman Republic,* 270, 350; Hippert, *Garibaldi and His Enemies,* 104; Dwight, *Roman Republic of 1849,* 200–202; André Viotti, *Garibaldi: The Revolutionary and His Men* (Dorset, UK: Blandford Press, 1979), 89; "Italian Affairs in the Roman Republic and Its Calumniators," *National Era,* July 4, 1850, 105; "A Roman,"

letter to the editor dated June 25, "Garibaldi and Colonel Forbes," *New York Times,* June 28, 1859, 1; Hugh Forbes, "Catechism of the Patriotic Volunteer," in his *Manual for the Patriotic Volunteer on Active Service in Regular and Irregular War, Being the Arts and Science of Obtaining and Maintaining Liberty and Independence,* 2 vols., 2nd ed. (New York: W. H. Tinson, Printer, 1855), 1:viii, 9, 10, vii.

9. Noether, "Roman Republic"; Hippert, *Garibaldi and His Enemies,* 104, 106, 108; Dwight, *Roman Republic of 1849,* 201–4; "The State of Europe," *Times* (London), July 24, 1849, 6; and the conflicting views in "Garibaldi and His Former English Lieutenant," *New York Times,* June 24, 1859, 2; and "Garibaldi and Colonel Forbes," *New York Times,* June 28, 1859, 1.

10. "A Roman," letter to the editor dated June 25, "Garibaldi and Colonel Forbes," *New York Times,* June 28, 1859, 1; Dwight, *Roman Republic of 1849,* 204–8; Hippert, *Garibaldi and His Enemies,* 110.

11. "Tuscany" under "Austria and Hungary," *Times* (London), October 20, 1849, 6; Dwight, *Roman Republic of 1849,* 208–9; "Garibaldi," *Red Republican* (London), July 6, 1850, 24; "Italian Affairs in the Roman Republic and Its Calumniators," *National Era,* July 4, 1850, 105; quoting Radetzky in Marie, *Birth of Modern Italy,* 161; Forbes to F. B. Sanborn, January 9, 1858, in "Most Important Disclosures," *New York Herald,* October 27, 1859, 3; William J. Linton, *Threescore and Ten Years, 1820 to 1890* (New York: Charles Scribner's Sons, 1894), 121–22, and his *European Republicans: Reflection of Mazzini and His Friends* (London: Lawrence and Bullen, 1892), 124.

12. Trevelyan, *Garibaldi's Defence of the Roman Republic,* 351.

13. Item from the *Tribune* under "Notice to Correspondents," *Red Republican* (London), October 26, 1850, 148; "The United States," *Morning Chronicle,* September 24, 1850; Howard Marraro, *American Opinion on the Unification of Italy, 1846–1861* (New York: Columbia University Press, 1932), 62–63; Forbes to Sanborn, January 9, 1858, in "Most Important Disclosures," *New York Herald,* October 27, 1859, 3; "A Roman," letter to the editor dated June 25, "Garibaldi and Colonel Forbes," *New York Times,* June 28, 1859, 1; Hippert, *Garibaldi and His Enemies,* 110; Forbes, "Catechism of the Patriotic Volunteer," 1:viii; "H. Forbes" of Bradford attended the "Reform Conference at Manchester," *Times* (London), December 4, 1851, 6; Theodore Dwight letter, March 1, 1851, Stuart Lutz Historic Documents, Short Hills, N.J., offered this item, No. 2062, through the International League of Antiquarian Booksellers, available at http://www.ilab.org/db/book2329_2062.html.

14. Notices in *Red Republican* (London), November 16, 23, 1850, January 18, 1851, 173, 180–81, 481. For the French, in addition to items cited elsewhere, see Cosmopolite, "On the French Revolution," *Quaker City,* April 21, 1849, 3; Cosmopolite, "On the French Revolution, Part II," *Quaker City,* April 28, 1849, 3; Cosmopolite, "On the French Revolution, Part III," *Quaker City,* May 12, 1849, 2; Cosmopolite, "On the French Revolution, Part IV," *Quaker City,* May 26, 1849, 2; Cosmopolite, "On the French Revolution, Part V," *Quaker City,* June 2, 1849, 4; Alphonse de Lamartine, "Robespierre," *Quaker City,* June 9, 1849, 4; Alphonse de Lamartine, "The Last Days of Robespierre," *Quaker City,* June 23, 1849, 3; Alphonse de Lamartine, "The Moral of the French Revolution," *Quaker City,* July 14, 1849, 1–2; 1849. On the toasts, see "Advent of the New Era," *Quaker City,* January 5, 1850, 2 (emphasis in the original), which reports on the Italians; untitled item, *Quaker*

City, June 9, 1849, 2; "The Cause of Rome," *Quaker City,* July 14, 1849, 3; and "The Fall of Rome," *Quaker City,* September 1, 1849, 2.

15. *Friend of the People,* February 15, April 5, 1851, 80, 136; *New York Daily Tribune,* December 12, 20, 1850, February 11, 14, 1851. On Day, see Lippard's untitled notice in *Quaker City,* January 5, 1850, 3; Commons et al., *Documentary History of American Industrial Society,* 8:287, 288, 303, and his obituary in the *New York Times,* June 9, 1906, 9. On the British associations, see Jamie L. Bronstein, *Land Reform and Working-Class Experience in Britain and the United States, 1800–1862* (Stanford: Stanford University Press, 1999).

16. Two pieces entitled "The Ingraham Testimonial," *New York Herald,* September 9, October 28, 1853, 4; "New York City," *New York Times,* December 1, 1852, 6; "The Koszta Affair," *New York Times,* September 23, 1853, 1; "New-York City: Republican Festival; Grand Celebration of the Universal Democratic Republicans; Processions, Banquets at the Shakespeare Hotel, Speeches, &c., &c.," *New York Times,* February 25, 1854, 8; and "Anniversary of the French Republic," *New York Times,* February 26, 1855, 2.

17. Lehning, "International Association," 173 (see prologue, n. 8).

18. Marraro, *American Opinion on the Unification of Italy,* 33–67; Marraro, "Garibaldi in New York," *New York History* 27 (April 1947): 179–203, also in *Pages from the Garibaldian Epic,* ed. Anthony P. Campanella (Sarasota: International Institute for Garibaldian Studies, 1984); Dwight, *Roman Republic of 1849,* 208; H. Nelson Gay, "Garibaldi's American Contacts and His Claims to American Citizenship," *American Historical Review* 38 (October 1932): 5–6, 7; John MacMullen, "Recollections of Garibaldi," *Frank Leslie's Popular Monthly,* March 1893, 18, and, for George Perkins Marsh's letter summarizing the issue, 16–17, also in Marraro, "Unpublished American Documents on Garibaldi's March on Rome in 1867," *Journal of Modern History* 16 (June 1944): 118–19, 121–23.

19. "The Hale Dinner," *Boston Herald,* May 6, 1853, 2; "The Ingraham Committee," *New York Times,* October 28, 1853, 1; "Society of Universal Democratic Republicans," *New York Times,* October 28, 1853, 5; McMullen in Chair, "The Ingraham Committee and the Universal Democratic Republicanism," *New York Times,* November 11, 1853, 1; "The Neutrality Laws," *New York Times,* January 11, 1854, 5.

20. Two articles under the heading "Free Democratic State Convention," *New York Herald,* February 23, 24, 1853, 1; "The Free Soil State Convention—Their State Ticket," *New York Herald,* September 2, 1853, 4.

21. "The Organization," *National Era,* December 16, 1852, 202; "Constitution of the Free Democratic League of the City and County of New York," *National Era,* October 27, 1853, 171; "The Free Democratic League," *New York Times,* October 26, 1853, 5; "Meeting of the Free Democratic League," *New York Times,* October 29, 1853, 4; "Review," *Historical Magazine,* 2nd ser., 1 (May 1867): 307–8, 330, 331, 333; "The Origins of the Republican Party," *Historical Magazine,* 3rd ser., 2 (December 1873): 329.

22. Bovay quoted in Flower, *History of the Republican Party,* 147–48, 149–53 (see chap. 1, n. 40).

23. "The Convention of Infidels," *New York Times,* January 7, 1853, 4; "The Society of Universal Democratic Republicanism," *New York Times,* April 12, 1854, 8; "Universal Democratic Republican Societies of United States of North America," *New York Times,* April 27, 1854, 3; "Meeting of Liberal Societies," *New York Times,* May 25, 1854, 4; "Union of the Liberal Societies," *New York Times,* July 6, 1854, 4.

24. "The Society of Universal Democratic Republicans," *New York Herald*, December 21, 1853, 4; "Society of Universal Republicanism," *New York Herald*, January 25, 1854, 8; "The Universal Democratic Republican Society," *New York Herald*, February 28, 1854, 2; "The Universal Republican Democratic Society," *New York Herald*, April 12, 1854, 8.

25. Forbes, "Catechism of the Patriotic Volunteer," 2:59–95, with the party descriptions on 84–85. The one-volume edition of 1854 represented a manuscript put together in the wake of his Italian experience.

26. "New-York City: Union of the Liberal Societies," *New York Times*, July 6, 1854, 4.

27. *Journal of the Senate of the United States of America, 1789–1873*, March 29, 1854, xxx; "The Society of Universal Democratic Republicanism," *New York Times*, April 12, 1854, 8; "Meeting of Liberal Societies," *New York Times*, August 31, 1854, 8; "Convention of Liberal Societies," *New York Times*, September 21, 1854, 1; "Red Republican Demonstration: Celebration of the 22d September; Speech of Coussidiere—a Look at the French Men of War," *New York Times*, September 23, 1854, 1; "Liberal Societies," *New York Times*, September 28, 1854, 4; "Convention of Liberal Societies," *New York Times*, October 13, 1854, 8; "Circular of the Convention of Liberals in America: To the Citizen Victor Hugo, Barbier, Tekeli, Piancianc, Switoslawski, Members of the Committee in and of the Political Refugees in England," *Liberator*, October 27, 1854, 172; Forbes, *Manual for the Patriotic Volunteer*, 2:66–67.

28. "New-York City: Republican Festival; Grand Celebration of the Universal Democratic Republicans; Processions, Banquets at the Shakespeare Hotel, Speeches, &c., &c.," *New York Times*, February 25, 1854, 8; "Meeting of Liberal Societies," *New York Times*, May 25, 1854, 4; "Cuban Liberty: Third Anniversary of the Defeat of the Cuban Patriots," *New York Times*, September 4, 1854, 6; "Cuban Athenaeum Anniversary," *New York Times*, October 9, 1854, 6; "Anniversary of the French Republic," *New York Times*, February 26, 1855, 2; "Scintillations from the Lone Star," *New York Times*, March 13, 1855, 4.

29. "New-York City: Republican Festival; Grand Celebration of the Universal Democratic Republicans; Processions, Banquets at the Shakespeare Hotel, Speeches, &c., &c.," *New York Times*, February 25, 1854, 8; "Meeting of Liberal Societies," *New York Times*, May 25, 1854, 4; "Cuban Liberty: Third Anniversary of the Defeat of the Cuban Patriots," *New York Times*, September 4, 1854, 6; "Cuban Athenaeum Anniversary," *New York Times*, October 9, 1854, 6; "Sickles Abroad," *New York Times*, November 7, 1854, 4; "Capt. Rynders and the Lone Star," *New York Times*, February 26, 1855, 2; "Anniversary of the French Republic," *New York Times*, March 13, 1855, 4; "Scintillations from the Lone Star," *New York Times*, March 16, 1855, 1; "The Empire Club Chief," *New York Times*, January 14, 1885, 1; "Praise of Capt. Rynders," *New York Times*, January 15, 1885, 5. On Sickles's shooting of his wife's lover, see "Les souteneurs de la famille aux États-Unis," *Le Libertaire*, March 12, 1859, 1–2.

30. "Democratic Glorification," *New York Daily Tribune*, November 11, 1854. See also "Tammany Union and Harmony Demonstration," *New York Daily Tribune*, March 8, 1855.

31. Amy Bridges, *A City in the Republic: Antebellum New York and the Origins of Machine Politics*, 2nd ed. (Ithaca: Cornell University Press, 1987), 116–17n60; "Liberal Societies" and "The 'Practical Democrats,' Meeting in the Park: The Platform of the Party," *New York Times*, September 28, 1854, 4.

32. "The Liberal Societies on Politics," *New York Times*, October 20, 1854, 3; "A Letter to

the American Slaves from Those Who Have Fled from American Slavery," in *Proceedings of the Black State Conventions, 1840–1865,* ed. Philip S. Foner and George E. Walker, 1:50.

33. "The City Poor: Meeting of the Unemployed," *New York Times,* December 22, 1854, 2; "The Labor Movement: Second Meeting of the Unemployed," *New York Times,* December 23, 1854, 3; "Meeting of the Unemployed Workingmen in the Park," *New York Times,* December 23, 1854, 5.

34. "New-York City: Meeting of the Liberal Societies—the Soule Affair—Maine Law," *New York Times,* November 16, 1854, 8; "The Liberal Societies in Conclave," *New York Times,* December 15, 1854, 4; "Meeting of the Liberal Societies," *New York Times,* January 17, 1855, 4; "Labor: Condition of the Unemployed Poor," *New York Times,* March 1, 1855, 2; "City Politics: Clear the Track, Hi! Hi! Meeting of the American Democracy," *New York Times,* September 18, 1855, 8.

35. "The Saratoga Convention," *New York Daily Tribune,* August 17, 1854, 4; "Anti-Nebraska Meeting at Saratoga," *New York Daily Tribune,* August 18, 1854; "Temperance Meeting in Saratoga," *New York Daily Tribune,* August 18, 1854; "Anti-Nebraska Convention at Auburn," *New York Daily Tribune,* September 27, 1854, 4–5; and, on the seceding group, *New York Daily Tribune,* September 27, 28, 1854. See also September 27, 28, 1855, on the Syracuse convention.

36. On Eleventh Ward Republicans, see "Free-Soil Republican Club," and for Seaman's presence, see "Republican Demonstration," both in *New York Daily Tribune,* September 14, 1855, 5; for Tobbitt and Freeman Hunt, "Republican Organization in Brooklyn," *New York Daily Tribune,* October 5, 1855, 5; and Watson G. Haynes at "Republican Mass Meeting" in Brooklyn, *New York Daily Tribune,* November 3, 1855.

37. "Free Democratic Convention," *Ohio State Journal,* January 18, 1853, 3, "Free Democratic Convention in Pennsylvania," *New York Herald,* May 25, 1854, 8; untitled piece on Pennsylvania, *Boston Herald,* June 4, 1853, 4; "Free Democratic Convention" on Massachusetts, *Boston Herald,* September 15, 1853, 4; "Free Democratic Convention" on Vermont, *Boston Herald,* July 14, 1854, 2; "Extract from Our Correspondence," *National Era,* February 16, 1854, 27; "To the Free Democracy of the State of New York," *National Era,* August 16, 1855, 13; review of Robert S. Dabney, *A Defence of Virginia* (New York: E. J. Hale & Son, 1867), *Historical Magazine,* 2nd ser., 3 (January 1868): 61; "More Fusion," *New York Times,* August 7, 1855, 4; *Brooklyn Daily Eagle,* August 8, 1855, 2.

38. M. Leon Perkal, "American Abolition Society: A Viable Alternative to the Republican Party?" *Journal of Negro History* 65 (Winter 1980): 58; "Radical Abolition Convention" (from *Syracuse Chronicle*), *Frederick Douglass' Paper,* June 29, 1855, 5; "Great Anti-Slavery Convention" (from *New York Tribune*), *Frederick Douglass' Paper,* July 6, 1855, 3; "The Abolition Convention," *New York Times,* June 24, 1855, 1; "Anti-Slavery Convention," *New York Times,* June 28, 1855, 4; "Radical Anti-Slavery Convention," *Liberator,* July 6, 1855, 107; "Convention at Syracuse," *Radical Abolitionist* 1 (August 1855): 5–?; *Proceedings of the Convention of Radical Political Abolitionists, Held at Syracuse, N.Y., June 26th, 27th, and 28th, 1855* (New York: Central Abolition Board, 1855), including addresses on 23–51, nonextension on 37–38, opposition to dissolution of the Union on 42–44, and various letters of support, including one from John McIntrosh and twenty others, on 63.

39. "Les collectivistes Français Chapter V: Le précurseurs théoriques du parti ouvrier," *La Revue Socialiste* 5 (January–June 1887): 221n.

40. "National Industrial Congress," *New York Daily Tribune,* June 8, 1855, 5; Crisfield Johnson, comp., *History of Cuyahoga County* (Cleveland: by the author, 1879), 190, 428 (Brainerd), 190, 204 (Calkins), 324, 325, 326 (Buhrer). On Brainerd, see Ruth Miller Elson, *Guardian of Tradition: American Schoolbooks of the Nineteenth Century* (Lincoln: University of Nebraska Press, 1964), 38. On Bouton, see *American Authors, 1600–1900,* 98; *National Reform Almanac for 1849,* 20 (see chap. 1, 48); and NIC proceedings.

41. Bruce Levine, *The Spirit of 1848: German Immigrants, Labor Conflict, and the Coming of the Civil War* (Urbana: University of Illinois Press, 1992); Mosha Honeck, "We Are the Revolutionists: Forty-eighters, Abolitionists, and the Struggle to Overthrow Slavery" (Ph.D. diss., University of Heidelberg, 2008). For the activities of Wilhelm Weitling's *Arbeiterbund,* see the untitled items, the second from the *Mechanic's Advocate* (Albany), in *Quaker City,* May 26, 1849, 3, and May 11, 1850, 4.

42. See Bridges, *City in the Republic,* 117, 116n61, 117nn63–64; Commons et al., *Documentary History of American Industrial Society,* 8:27, 287, 288, 301; Thomas Ainge Devyr, "American Section," in *The Odd Book of the Nineteenth Century; or, "Chivalry" in Modern Days, a Personal Record of Reform—Chiefly Land Reform, for the Last Fifty Years* (New York: the author, 1882), 161ff; the British and American sections of Devyr's book are independently paged.

43. Carlos Larralde and Jose Rodolfo Jacobo, *Juan N. Cortina and the Struggle for Justice in Texas* (Dubuque: Kendall/Hunt, 2000), 36–37, 37–38, 40, 39 (quoting the *Corpus Christi Ranchero,* November 19, 1859), 42 (on the *curanderos*).

44. Tom Chaffin, *Fatal Glory: Narciso Lopez and the First Clandestine U.S. War against Cuba* (Charlottesville: University Press of Virginia, 1996), 121–22; Richardson Hardy, *The History and Adventures of the Cuban Expedition, from the First Movements Down to the Dispersion of the Army at Key West, and the Arrest of General Lopez; Also, an Account of the Ten Deserters at Isla de Mugeres* (Cincinnati: L. Stratton, 1850).

CHAPTER 3. LONE STARS AND GOLDEN CIRCLES

1. Agate [Whitelaw J. Reid], Washington, D.C., August 1, "Letter from Washington. 'Gen. Bickley': From Passages in the History of a Notorious Humbug," *Cincinnati Daily Gazette,* August 6, 1863, 1; Horace Greeley, "'Columbia, the Land of the Free,'" *Independent . . . Devoted to the Consideration of Politics, Social and Econ . . .* 12 (August 30, 1860): 1.

2. On Beckley (1757–1807), see *Justifying Jefferson: The Political Writings of John James Beckley,* ed. Gerard W. Gawalt. Clayton E. Jewett gives his name as "William Lamb Bickley" in *Texas in the Confederacy: An Experiment in Nation-Building* (Columbia: University of Missouri Press, 2002), 50.

3. Harvey Wickes Felter, *History of the Eclectic Medical Institute, Cincinnati, Ohio, 1845–1902* (Cincinnati: Alumnai Association of the Eclectic Medical Institute, 1902), 110; Emory L. Hamilton, "Frontier Forts of Southwest Virginia," *Historical Sketches of Southwest Virginia,* no. 4 (1968): 1–26.

4. The year of his birth is given as 1819 in "Department of the East," *New York Times,* March 21, 1865, 4; "The Knights of the Golden Circle" (from *Houston Telegraph* of November 1), *Liberator,* November 23, 1860, 1; Felter, *History of the Eclectic Medical Institute,* 110; *An Authentic Exposition of the "K.G.C." Knights of the Golden Circle; or, A History of Secession from 1834 to 1861, by a Member of the Order* (Indianapolis: Asher, 1861), 77. Of

his siblings, Virginia, William, and John died in 1821, 1822, and 1831, respectively, leaving Joseph, born in 1828, possibly to reach adulthood. Ancestry.com.

5. James Hagy, "George Washington Lafayette Bickley: The Early Years," *Historical Sketches of Southwest Virginia* (Historical Society of Southwest Virginia), no. 6 (March 1972): 64–74, available at http://www.rootsweb.com/~vawise2/sketches/HSpubl44.html; http://www.newrivernotes.com//swva/hssv-6.htm#bickley; "The Extraordinary Life of an American Adventurer," *Abingdon Virginian,* October 4, 1867, reprinted in Felter, *History of the Eclectic Medical Institute,* 112.

6. Felter, *History of the Eclectic Medical Institute,* 110–11, and "Extraordinary Life of an American Adventurer," 112; letters of Elizabeth Galt and Martha Bickley to John Bickley, December 25, 1830, June 1834, and G. W. L. Bickley, December 14, 1862, Bernard Gibson Collection, cited in Hagy, "George Washington Lafayette Bickley"; "Department of the East," *New York Times,* March 21, 1865, 4.

7. Felter, *History of the Eclectic Medical Institute,* 111; Bickley letter, December 14, 1862, Bristol, Tenn., cited with other material in Hagy, "George Washington Lafayette Bickley"; "Department of the East," *New York Times,* March 21, 1865, 4.

8. Felter, *History of the Eclectic Medical Institute,* 111; Bickley letter, December 14, 1862, Bristol, Tenn., cited with other material in Hagy, "George Washington Lafayette Bickley." Note "Typographical" not "Topographical" "Department of the East," *New York Times,* March 21, 1865, 4. General Scott said "he did not know such a person" and had never heard of the KGC. "A Soldier of Fortune," *New York Times,* April 7, 1860, 4.

9. Felter, *History of the Eclectic Medical Institute,* 33, 34, 79, 110–11; "Extraordinary Life of an American Adventurer," 112; "Department of the East," *New York Times,* March 21, 1865, 4; George W. L. Bickley, *History of the Settlement and Indian Wars of Tazewell County, Virginia* (1973; reprint, Parsons, W.Va.: McClain, 1974), 132.

10. Bickley, *History of the Settlement and Indian Wars,* vii–viii, ix, x, 129, 133–34, 263, on the historical society; Felter, *History of the Eclectic Medical Institute,* 111; "Department of the East," *New York Times,* March 21, 1865, 4.

11. Felter, *History of the Eclectic Medical Institute,* 33, 34, 79, 110–11; "Extraordinary Life of an American Adventurer," 112; "Department of the East," *New York Times,* March 21, 1865, 4.

12. Evans, *History of Scioto County,* contains biographies of her father and mother (Aaron Kinney and Mary Clingman), 751–53, and her brothers: Washington, 753–54; Peter, 754–56; Eli, 756–57; Henry Richie, 757–58; and Philander Chase Kinney, 758–59; the quote being from 758, with the references to the marriages of her sisters—Elizabeth to Wilson Gates and Ann Elizabeth to David Cady—and the toll of the cholera epidemic of August 1849 on 752, 753 (see chap. 1, n. 34).

13. Ibid., 751; "Extraordinary Life of an American Adventurer," 112. See the later reference to the testimony of her brother Eli Kinney.

14. John H. Keyser's letter, "Wages, Slavery, and Chattel Slavery," *Liberator,* April 21, 1848, 63; Bickley, *History of the Settlement and Indian Wars,* 132; ms. rolls of the Brotherhood of the Union, Brotherhood of America Papers, Historical Society of Pennsylvania, Philadelphia.

15. *Cincinnati Daily Nonpareil,* April 17, 1852; ms. rolls of the Brotherhood of the Union in Brotherhood of America Papers; George L. W. Bickley, *Address Delivered before the*

Grand Circle of Ohio, Brotherhood of the Union, at the Dedication of Brotherhood Hall, Cincinnati, March 8, 1853 (Cincinnati: Abbott and Benrley, Printers, 1853). Thanks to Ken Burchell.

16. Felter, *History of the Eclectic Medical Institute*, 111; "The K.G.C.'s," *Marshall Texas Republican*, November 17, 1860, 2; "Department of the East," *New York Times*, March 21, 1865, 4. Although variously described as published in 1851–52 or even starting as late as 1854, extant numbers indicate that *Bickley's West American Review*, printed by Morgan & Overend in Cincinnati, was launched in 1853.

17. George W. L. Bickley, *Adalaska; or, The Strange and Mysterious Family of the Cave of Genreva* (Cincinnati: H. M. Rulison, 1853), 19, 102.

18. Felter, *History of the Eclectic Medical Institute*, 111; "Department of the East," *New York Times*, March 21, 1865, 4n5.

19. Bickley, *History of the Settlement and Indian Wars*, 46, and this bizarre speculation continues on 46–48.

20. The interests of American agriculture, particularly in those areas that had been farmed for decades, in scientific soil regeneration came to focus on the isolated islands of the Caribbean and Pacific frequented by seabirds and buried in their droppings. Jimmy M. Skaggs, *The Great Guano Rush: Entrepreneurs and American Overseas Expansion* (New York: St. Martin's Griffin, 1994), 71. See also Brian R. Hamnett, "Mexico's Royalist Coalition: The Response to Revolution, 1808–1821," *Journal of Latin American Studies* 12 (May 1980): 55–86.

21. *New York Morning News*, December 27, 1845; Frank L. Owsley and Gene A. Smith, *Filibusters and Expansionst: Jeffersonian Manifest Destiny* (Tuscaloosa: University of Alabama Press, 1997). See also Nelson Reed, *The Caste War in the Yucatan* (Stanford: Stanford University Press, 1964); J. Preston Moore, "Pierre Soule: Southern Expansionist and Promoter," *Journal of Southern History* 21 (May 1955): 208, 214; Donald S. Frazier, *Blood and Treasure: Confederate Empire in the Southwest* (College Station: Texas A&M University Press, 1995), 11; W. J. Hughes, *Rebellious Ranger: Rip Ford and the Old Southwest* (Norman: University of Oklahoma Press, 1964).

22. Reed, *Caste War in the Yucatan*, 111, 113–14

23. For the three Cuban expeditions, see Robert L. Scheina, *Latin American Wars: The Age of the Caudillo, 1791–1899* (Washington, D.C.: Brassey's, 2003), 1:214–19; Robert E. May, *The Southern Dream of a Caribbean Empire, 1854–1861* (Baton Rouge: Louisiana State University Press, 1973), 25, 26, 27, 28–29; Chaffin, *Fatal Glory* (see chap. 2, n. 44).

24. One Captain Weymouth of New York, a freemason and known member of the OLS, died after being wounded in a New Orleans coffeehouse. *New York Times*, August 5, 1852, 1; "Cuba and Emancipation," *New York Times*, August 10, 1852, 2; "Topics of the Press," *New York Times*, August 28, 1852, 8; "The Aggressive Policy of the United States" (from *London Morning Chronicle*), *New York Times*, November 16, 1852, 2; "Scintillations from the Lone Star," *New York Times*, March 13, 1855, 4; "The Knights of the Golden Circle" (from *London Spectator*, August 17), *New York Times*, August 30, 1861, 2.

25. "Cuba and the Ostend Manifesto," *Harpers New Monthly Magazine* 40 (December 1869–August 1870), 900; J. Quero Molareas, "Spain in 1848," in *The Opening of an Era: 1848*, ed. François Fejtö (New York: Grosset and Dunlap, 1975), 143–60. Alleged authorship of Edward Fitch Underhill, Hermann von Holst, *The Constitutional and Political History of the United States*, trans. John J. Lalor, vol. 5, *1854–1856: Kansas-Nebraska Bill—Buchanan's*

Election (Chicago: Callaghan, 1885), 44n–45n; the mockingly satirical A. Gnonuthin, "Our Champion, the Immortal Ganders!" *United States Democratic Review* 34 (December 1854): 539–47, describing 1848–49 as the one-man project of George N. Sanders.

26. George N. Sanders, "European Democracy and American Slavery," *Leader* 5 (July 1, 1854): 611; Joseph Barker, "'Pro-Slavery' Influences of the Leader," *Leader* 5 (July 29, 1854): 710; "Mr. G. N. Sanders's Letter," *Leader* 5 (August 26, 1854): 807. Kline describes Sanders, a white supremacist advocate of imperial expansion and military dictatorship, as a "left wing political radical." Kline, *Baltimore Plot*, 88 (see prologue, n. 1). See also H. Donald Winkler, *Lincoln and Booth: More Light on the Conspiracy* (Nashville: Cumberland House, 2003), 28–29, 35–36, 38–39, 166, 250–58, 260–61; Elizabeth D. Leonard, *Lincoln's Avengers: Justice, Revenge, and Reunion after the Civil War* (New York: W. W. Norton, 2005), 64–65; and William A. Tidwell, with James O. Hall and David W. Gaddy, *Come Retribution: The Confederate Secret Service and the Assassination of Lincoln* (Jackson: University Press of Mississippi, 1988), 348n10. Examples include the Chartist and racist John Campbell, "Lecture on the French Revolution," *Quaker City,* February 9, 1850, 3, February 23, 1850, 3; and also Campbell, *Negro-mania* (Philadelphia: Campbell and Powers, 1851), the second publisher being his Chartist colleague E. Powers.

27. John Salmon Ford, *Rip Ford's Texas,* ed. Stephen B. Oates (Austin: University of Texas Press, 1963), 217; Henninger correspondence in "Society of Universal Democratic Republicans," *New York Times,* October 28, 1853, 4; and "Col. Schlessinger," *New York Times,* April 25, 1856, 3.

28. May, *Southern Dream of a Caribbean Empire,* 23, 24–25. Pierre Soulé won his revolutionary credentials in opposition to Bourbons in France during the 1820s. George W. Bugay, *Off-Hand Takings; or, Crayon Sketch of the Noticeable Men of Our Age* (New York: DeWitt & Davenport, 1854), 223.

29. "The Knights of the Golden Circle" (from *London Spectator,* August 17), *New York Times,* August 30, 1861, 2; Frazier, *Blood and Treasure,* 11; May, *Southern Dream of a Caribbean Empire,* 147; Hughes, *Rebellious Ranger,* 121; Ford, *Rip Ford's Texas,* 196–99, 201–2, 203–4, 215–16.

30. William Walker, *The War in Nicaragua* (New York: S. H. Goetzel, 1860); Robert E. May, *Manifest Destiny's Underworld: Filibustering in Antebellum America* (Chapel Hill: University of North Carolina Press, 2002). See also the appendix.

31. May, *Southern Dream of a Caribbean Empire,* 138, 147, 148.

32. On the filibustering ventures into Central America, see Scheina, *Latin American Wars,* 221–33.

33. W. R. Gore, "The Life of Henry Lawrence Kinney" (master's thesis, University of Texas, 1948); Henry Lawrence Kinney Papers, Panhandle-Plains Historical Museum, Canyon, Texas; "The Nicaraguan Expedition: The Arrest of Colonel Kinney," *New York Herald,* April 29, 1855, 1.

34. May, *Southern Dream of a Caribbean Empire,* 90, 94, 100, 102, 103, 106, 113–14; "The First French Republic—Anniversary by the Society of the Mountain," *New York Times,* September 24, 1855, 1; "Sympathy for Walker," *New York Times,* December 22, 1856, 2; "Filibustering," *Putnam's Monthly Magazine,* April 1857, 425–35. See also Gnonuthin, "Our Champion, the Immortal Ganders!"; "Gen. Walker Surrendered," *New York Observer and Chronicle,* December 31, 1857, 422; "Filibustering," 432; and the cartoon of Rynders in "The Naturalization Question . . .," *Harper's Weekly,* September 17, 1859, xx.

35. "Miscellaneous," *New York Times,* April 20, 1860, 4; "The K.G.C." (from *New Orleans Courier*), *Alexandria Louisiana Democrat,* March 21, 1860, 4; "The K.G.C.: A Few Remarks Thereon" (from *Vicksburg Sun*), *Natchez (Miss.) Daily Free Trader,* March 30, 1860, 2; Felter, *History of the Eclectic Medical Institute,* 111–12; "Knights of the Golden Circle" (from *Norfolk Day Book*), *Little Rock Old-Line Democrat,* September 20, 1860, 2; Klement, *Dark Lanterns,* 9n9 (see introduction, n. 4).

36. "Department of the East," *New York Times,* March 21, 1865, 4.

37. Untitled notice (from *Cincinnati Daily Republican*), *New York Times,* October 27, 1852, 5; "Designs upon Cuba," *New York Times,* March 8, 1853, 4; Istvan Deak, *The Lawful Revolution; Louis Kossuth and the Hungarians, 1848–1849* (New York: Columbia University Press, 1979), 342–45.

38. *The Sons of Malta Exposed: Being a Complete Expose of the Secret Doings of the I.O.S.M.; or, The Mysterious Order, Meaning of the Letters G.R.J.A., the Mystic Veil, &c. &c. &c.* (New York: for the author, 1860), 12, 24–25, 27, 15, 16. On the pin, see Agate [Whitelaw J. Reid], Washington, D.C., August 1, "Letter from Washington. 'Gen. Bickley': From Passages in the History of a Notorious Humbug," *Cincinnati Daily Gazette,* August 6, 1863, 1. A description of the Grand Conductor's costume sounds remarkably similar to Bickley's design for the KGC.

39. "Doomed Cities of Antiquity," *New York Times,* January 16, 1855, 8. He began with the "Seven Churches of Asia," the communities of believers mentioned in the book of Revelation: "What thou seest, write in a book, and send it unto the seven churches which are in Asia; unto Ephesus, and unto Smyrna, and unto Pergamos, and unto Thyatira, and unto Sardis, and unto Philadelphia, and unto Laodicea" (1:11). A Mr. Bickley discussed scientific instruments used at Kew Observatory, cited in "Philosophical Instruments," *Scientific American* 2 (March 31, 1861): 211.

40. Felter, *History of the Eclectic Medical Institute,* 41. For this division, see John S. Haller, *A Profile in Alternative Medicine: The Eclectic Medical College of Cincinnati* (Kent: Kent State University Press, 1999), 30–31, 95.

41. G. W. L. Bickley, "*History of the Eclectic Medical Institute,*" *Eclectic Medical Journal* (1857), 155–56, quoted in Felter, *History of the Eclectic Medical Institute,* 41–42.

42. Felter, *History of the Eclectic Medical Institute,* 44, 45, 79, 111; Klement, *Dark Lanterns,* 8n5; Felter, *History of the Eclectic Medical Institute,* 44, 45–46, 79, 111. G. W. L. Bickley, eclectic physician, boarding at 297 West Fifth Street. *Williams' Cincinnati Directory, City Guide, and Business Mirror; or, Cincinnati in 1858* (Cincinnati: C. S. Williams, 1858), 37.

43. Agate [Whitelaw J. Reid], Washington, D.C., August 1, "Letter from Washington. 'Gen. Bickley.' From Passages in the History of a Notorious Humbug," *Cincinnati Daily Gazette,* August 6, 1863, 1; George W. Bickley, editor of *Scientific Artisan,* boarding at Gibson House. *Williams' Cincinnati Directory, City Guide, and Business Mirror,* 37.

44. For this and the following two paragraphs, see Agate [Whitelaw J. Reid], Washington, D.C., August 1, "Letter from Washington. 'Gen. Bickley': From Passages in the History of a Notorious Humbug," *Cincinnati Daily Gazette,* August 6, 1863, 1.

45. Wyn Craig Wade, *The Fiery Cross: The Ku Klux Klan in America* (New York: Touchstone Book, 1987), 40.

46. On Aaron's death, see Evans, *History of Scioto County,* 753. Statements by Kinney and Cady, February 7, 1864, from Report on the Order of American Knights, Records of the Office of the Judge Advocate General, National Archives, cited in Klement, *Dark*

Lanterns, 8. Rachel Kinney Dobson Bickley's father, Aaron Kinney, had died April 11, 1857, and she had likely come into some inheritance distinct from what she had gotten through her marriage to Dobson.

47. Klement, therefore, errs in saying that the *Scientific Artisan* "dismissed" Bickley (*Dark Lanterns*, 8, 8n5), although he clearly knew this source. See Klement, *Dark Lanterns*, 9–10.

48. Ron Powers, *Dangerous Water: A Biography of the Boy Who Became Mark Twain* (New York: Basic Books, 1999), 241, 242, 243, 245–46.

49. Agate [Whitelaw J. Reid], Washington, D.C., August 1, "Letter from Washington. 'Gen. Bickley': From Passages in the History of a Notorious Humbug," *Cincinnati Daily Gazette*, August 6, 1863, 1.

50. *K.G.C.: An Authentic Exposition*, 10. Maxwell Whitman called this "the fullest contemporary account of the society." Whitman, *Gentlemen in Crisis: The First Century of the Union League of Philadelphia, 1862–1962* (Philadelphia: Winchell, 1975), 304n69.

CHAPTER 4. HIGHER LAWS

1. "Freedom's Railway," *Detroit Tribune*, January 17, 1887, 2; http://clarke.cmich.edu/undergroundrailroad/georgedebaptiste.htm. Lambert identified John Brown's associate Richard Realf as an unusual white member of the order.

2. "Obituary of Alexander Bearse, John Lockley, Eunice Ames, and John T. Hilton," *Liberator*, March 25, 1864, 51, also in *William Cooper Nell: Selected Writings, 1832–1874*, ed. Dorothy Porter Wesley and Constance Porter Uzelac (Baltimore: Black Classic Press, 2002), 644, 627–28; "Presentation of a Portrait to a Masonic Grand Lodge," *Liberator*, October 10, 1862, 4.

3. Edward N. Palmer, "Negro Secret Societies," *Social Forces* 23 (December 1944): 208–9; David G. Hackett, "The Prince Hall Masons and the African American Church: The Labors of Grand Master and Bishop James Walker Hood, 1831–1918," in *Religion and American Culture: A Reader*, ed. David G. Hackett (New York: Routledge, 2003), 289–314, originally in *Church History* 69 (December 2000): 770–802.

4. James Oliver Horton, *Free People of Color: Inside the African American Community* (Washington, D.C.: Smithsonian Institution Press, 1993), 35, 42–43, 45, 49, 101–10, 111, 153; Maurice Wallace, "'Are We Men?': Prince Hall, Martin Delany, and the Masculine Ideal in Black Freemasonry, 1775–1865," *American Literary History* 9 (Autumn 1997): 296; Caryn Cossé Bell, *Revolution, Romanticism, and the Afro-Creole Protest Tradition in Louisiana, 1718–1868* (Baton Rouge: Louisiana State University Press, 1997), 82, 83; James McCune Smith, "The Odd Fellows' Celebration," in *The Works of James McCune Smith: Black Intellectual and Abolitionist*, ed. John Stauffer (Oxford: Oxford University Press, 2006), 159–61.

5. Foner and Walker, *Proceedings of the Black State Conventions*, 1:36n3 (see chap. 2, n. 32); Palmer, "Negro Secret Societies," 208; R. R. Wright, "The Negro in Unskilled Labor," *Annals of the American Academy of Political and Social Science* 49 (September 1913): 19, 24.

6. "Death of George DeBaptiste," *Detroit Daily Post*, February 23, 1875; "George De-Baptiste: His Death Yesterday," *Detroit Advertiser and Tribune*, February 23, 1875, posted at Clarke Historical Library, Central Michigan University http://clarke.cmich.edu/undergroundrailroad/georgedebaptiste.htm; Patrick Rael, *Black Identity and Black Protest in the Antebellum North* (Chapel Hill: University of North Carolina Press, 2002).

7. William J. Simmons, *Men of Mark: Eminent, Progressive, and Rising* (Cleveland: G. M. Rewell, 1887), 546–48; Palmer, "Negro Secret Societies," 209. Description of Lambert from "Freedom's Railway," *Detroit Tribune,* January 17, 1887, 2.

8. Simmons, *Men of Mark,* 547; W. H. Gibson, "Historical Sketch of the Progress of the Colored Race, in Louisville, Ky.," 42–43, independently paged in *History of the United Brothers of Friendship and Sisters of the Mysterious Ten, in Two Parts: A Negro Order, Organized August 1, 1861, in the City of Louisville, Ky.* (Louisville: for the author by Bradley & Gilbert, 1897).

9. "Order of the United Brothers of Friendship," 7–9, independently paged in ibid.

10. *Manual of the International Order of Twelve of the Knights and Daughters of Tabor, Containing General Laws, Regulations, Ceremonies, Drill, and a Taborian Lexicon* (St. Louis: A. R. Fleming, 1891), 7–9. For the importance of barbers such as Dickson and DeBaptiste, see Douglas W. Bristol's *Knights of the Razor: Black Barbers in Slavery and Freedom* (Baltimore: John Hopkins University Press, 2009).

11. Mackenzie, *Royal Masonic Cyclopaedia,* 504, 457, 328, 453 (see prologue, n. 16); Simmons, *Men of Mark,* 729–31. Rev. Patrick Henry Alexander Braxton also became a member (1051). See also Betty M. Kuyk, *African Voices in the African American Heritage* (Bloomington: Indiana University Press, 2003), 53–59, 63, 66–67.

12. Albert L. Rawson, *Pronouncing Bible Dictionary,* quoted in *The Negro in Revelation, in History, and in Citizenship . . . with Introduction by Gen. John B. Gordon,* by Rev. J. J. Pipkin (St. Louis: N. D. Thompson Publishing, 1902), 35–36; Martin Delany, *The Origin and Objects of Ancient Freemasonry: Its Introduction into the United States and Legitimacy among Colored Men . . .* (Pittsburgh: Haven, for the author, 1853). For Rawson's career, see Mark A. Lause, *The Antebellum Crisis and America's First Bohemians* (Kent: Kent State University Press, 2009), 61–62.

13. "Obituary of Alexander Bearse, John Lockley, Eunice Ames, and John T. Hilton," *North Star,* July 6, 1849, 3, also in Nell, *William Cooper Nell,* 229.

14. Marconis, *Sanctuary of Memphis,* 3–4 (see prologue, n. 16); Calvin C. Burt, *Egyptian Masonic History of the Original and Unabridged Ancient and Ninety-six Degree Rite of Memphis* ([Utica, N.Y.: White & Floyd], 1879), 203–4, 205, 206, 207, 314–17. For the British dimension of this impulse, see Betty Fladeland, *Men and Brothers: Anglo-American Antislavery Cooperation* (Urbana: University of Illinois Press, 1972), and her *Abolitionist and Working-Class Problems in the Age of Industrialization* (Baton Rouge: Louisiana State University Press, 1984).

15. Larry Gara, *The Liberty Line: The Legend of the Underground Railroad,* 2nd ed. (Lexington: University Press of Kentucky, 1996), 30, 37–38. Literature on the subject is voluminous, if usually repetitive, but, for recent titles, see Betty DeRamus, *Forbidden Fruit: Love Stories from the Underground Railroad* (New York: Atria Books, 2005); Jacqueline L. Tobin, *From Midnight to Dawn: The Last Tracks of the Underground Railroad* (New York: Anchor Books, 2008); and Tricia Martineau Wagner, *It Happened on the Underground Railroad* (Guilford, Conn., and Helena, Mont.: Twodot, 2007).

16. "Freedom's Railway," *Detroit Tribune,* January 17, 1887, 2.

17. Bell, *Revolution, Romanticism, and the Afro-Creole Protest Tradition,* 83, 84.

18. "Freedom's Railway," *Detroit Tribune,* January 17, 1887, 2, with "Death of George DeBaptiste," *Detroit Daily Post,* February 23, 1875, and "George DeBaptiste: His Death

Yesterday," *Detroit Advertiser and Tribune,* February 23, 1875; Katharine DuPre Lumpkin, "'The General Plan Was Freedom': A Negro Secret Order on the Underground Railroad," in *John Brown Mysteries: Allies for Freedom,* ed. Jean Libby (Missoula: Pictorial Histories Publishing, 1999), 89. See also Foner and Walker, *Proceedings of the Black State Conventions,* 1:181–87, 190, 196.

19. "Freedom's Railway," *Detroit Tribune,* January 17, 1887, 2.

20. Ibid.; Allan Pinkerton, *The Spy of the Rebellion: Being a True History of the Spy System of the United States Army during the Late Rebellion Revealing Many Secrets of the War Hitherto Not Made Public, Compiled from Official Reports Prepared for President Lincoln, General McClellan, and the Provost-Marshal-General* (New York: G. W. Dillingham Col., 1883), 354–57; *Manual of the International Order of Twelve,* 9–10; "Freedom's Railway," *Detroit Tribune,* January 17, 1887, 2.

21. Foner and Walker, *Proceedings of the Black State Conventions,* 1:43–52; Nell, *William Cooper Nell,* 18n, 23n, 99–100, 278–79, 281, 432, 590.

22. Mary Kay Ricks, *Escape on the Pearl: The Heroic Bid for Freedom on the Underground Railroad* (New York: Harper Perennial, 2008), 77–78.

23. William Monroe Cockrum, *History of the Underground Railroad as It Was Conducted by the Anti-slavery League: Including Many Thrilling Encounters between Those Aiding the Slaves to Escape and Those Trying to Recapture Them* (Oakland City, Ind.: J. W. Cockrum Printing, 1915), 13–14.

24. Stanley J. Robboy and Anita W. Robboy, "Lewis Hayden: From Fugitive Slave to Statesmen," *New England Quarterly* 46 (December 1973): 591, 593, 595–98, 607–11; Nell, *William Cooper Nell,* 194–95, 622, 632.

25. "Freedom's Railway," *Detroit Tribune,* January 17, 1887, 2.

26. Simmons, *Men of Mark,* 202; Benjamin Quarles, *Black Abolitionists* (New York: Oxford University Press, 1969), 7, 25, 26; "Beneficial Societies," *Register of Pennsylvania* 7 (March 1831): 163–64. For the NIC, see Lause, *Young America,* 107–8 (see chap. 1, n. 14).

27. "National Colored Convention, Held in Rochester, N.Y., on the 6th, 7th, and 8th of July '53" (from *Frederick Douglass' Paper*), *Liberator,* July 22, 1853, 1; "National Convention of Colored Men," *National Era,* July 28, 1853, 117; *Proceedings of the Colored National Convention, Held in Rochester, July 6th, 7th, and 8th* (Rochester: Frederick Douglass' Paper, 1853).

28. "Meeting of the [Massachusetts] State Council, in Behalf of Colored Americans," *Liberator,* February 24, 1854, 30, in "State Council of Colored People of Massachusetts, Convention, January 2, 1854," in *Proceedings of the Black State Conventions,* ed. Foner and Walker, 2:90, 92; Nell, *William Cooper Nell,* 368–69. See also Horton, *Free People of Color,* 47–49.

29. Fred W. Allsopp, *Albert Pike: A Biography* (Little Rock: Parke-Harper, 1928), 221, 231.

30. *Authentic Exposition of the "K.G.C.,"* 70 (see chap. 3, n. 4); T. F. Robley, *History of Bourbon County, Kansas, to the Close of 1865* (Fort Scott, Kans.: Monitor Book & Printing, 1894), 58.

31. For the presence of social radicals in the settlement of Kansas and the struggle over its future, see Mark A. Lause, *Race and Radicalism in the Union Army* (Urbana: University of Illinois Press, 2009), 9–24.

32. "Kansas: Convention of Kansas Aid Committees at Buffalo," *New York Times,* July 11, 1856, 8; "Republican Convention at Pittsburgh," the call for a national Radical Abolitionist convention, in "Minutes of the National Abolition Convention," "Discussions in the National Abolition Convention," "The Republican Convention at Philadelphia," "The Platform Examined," and "The Candidates," *Radical Abolitionist* 1 (April 1856): 65–66, 68–69; (May 1856): 78–80; (June 1856): 94–95; (July 1856): 97–104, 105–6, 106–8, 108–11; M. Leon Perkal, "American Abolition Society: A Viable Alternative to the Republican Party?" *Journal of Negro History* 65 (Winter 1980): 60–61; "Radical Abolition Convention," *National Era,* May 1, 1856, 70; James McCune Smith, "Horoscope," in *Works of James McCune Smith,* 147, and, for his discussion with Peter H. Clark on "Our Leaders," 126, 125, 127. Henry Louis Gates mistakenly implied that Smith "organized the New York City Abolition Society, a group made up of blacks who vowed to abolish slavery 'by means of the Constitution; or otherwise.'" J. M. Smith, *Works of James McCune Smith,* xxvii.

33. T. Smith, *Liberty and Free Soil Parties,* 274, 280, 281, quote from 282 (see chap. 1, n. 40); Bovay quoted in Flower, *History of the Republican Party,* 152 (see chap. 1, n. 40); Joshua K. Ingalls, *Reminiscences of an Octogenarian in the Field of Industrial and Social Reform* (New York: M. L. Holbrook, 1897), 53. On the 1854 and 1855 NIC, see Lause, *Young America,* 114; and Boyd S. Stutler, preface to *Provisional Constitution and Ordinance for the People of the United States by John Brown* (Weston, Mass.: M & S Press, 1969), 4–5, originally published in 1858 by Day at St. Catherine's, Ontario.

34. Lause, *Young America,* 119; *Cleveland Plain Dealer,* June 4, 6, 1855, 3; and the most complete accounts as both "National Industrial Congress," *Cleveland Morning Leader,* June 8, 1855, 3; *Cleveland Morning Leader,* June 9, 1855, 3.

35. "National Radical Abolition Convention," *New York Daily Tribune,* May 29, 1856; *New York Daily Tribune,* May 29, 1856; "Radical Abolition State Convention," *New York Daily Tribune,* September 19, 1856.

36. *Life and Public Services of James Buchanan of Pennsylvania* (New York: Livermore & Rudd, 1856). Printer alleged to be W. H. Tinson (same as Forbes). Holst, *Constitutional and Political History of the United States,* 44n–45n (see chap. 3, n. 25). Lause, *Young America,* 120–21; "The Mechanics' and Workingmen's Meeting in the Park," *New York Times,* October 29, 1856, 1.

37. "A Friend of Fremont: Colonel Richard J. Hinton's Military and Political Estimate of Him," *Brooklyn Daily Eagle,* December 8, 1894, 5; "The Working Men's Provisional Committee," *New York Herald,* September 12, 1855, 4; "The Softs" and "The Workingmen: The Union in Danger," both under "City Politics," *New York Times,* October 15, 1856, 1; "German Mass Meeting—Who Moulded Mills Jackson," under "City Politics," *New York Times,* November 1, 1855, 1; "Republican National Convention," *New York Times,* June 17, 1856, 1; "Republican National Convention: Mr. Seward's Name Withdrawn," *New York Times,* June 18, 1856, 1; "Republican National Convention: Second Day's Proceedings," *New York Times,* June 19, 1856, 1; "Great German Fremont Meeting," *New York Times,* August 22, 1856, 1; "Celebration of the Anniversary of the Proclamation of the French Republic of 1792," *New York Times,* September 23, 1856, 4. On Greeley's request, see Devyr, "American Section," 115, 107 (see chap. 2, n. 42). This work consists of a separately paged "Irish and English" section and an "American" section; references in this study cite the second p. 107. "Great Convention at Pittsburgh," *New York Daily Tribune,* September 18, 1856.

38. "Mechanics to the Rescue," *New York Times,* September 2, 1856, 3; "Free Terri-tory for Free Labor," *New York Times,* September 11, 1856, 6; "Free Territory for Free Labor," *New York Times,* September 22, 1856, 3; "Free Territory for Free Labor," *New York Times,* September 30, 1856, 3; *New York Times,* October 3, 1856, 4; "Huzza for the Natick Cobbler," *New York Times,* October 4, 1856, 6; "Free Labor: Senator Wilson before the Mechanics and Working-men of New-York," *New York Times,* October 6, 1856, 1; "Free Labor: Senator Wilson before the Mechanics and Working-men of New-York," *New York Times,* October 11, 1856, 4; "Mechanics and Workingmen, to the Rescue!" *New York Times,* October 21, 1856, 3. See also "Doings of the Chivalry: Irishmen Banished from South Carolina for Their Political Opinions" (from *Cheraw [S.C.] Gazette*), *New York Times,* September 17, 1856, 2.

39. James Frederick, *To the Friends of the Five Point Mission* (New York: n.p., not after 1860); William Oland Bourne, *History of the Public School Society of the City of New York* (New York: W. Wood, 1870). For his views, see "We Hold These Truths to Be Self-Evident," *American Brotherhood,* September 15, 1855, 2; "Prospectus of the *Iron Platform,*" "Appeal of the Association for Improving the Condition of the Poor," "The Kansas Rally," and "How to Get Rid of Slavery," *Iron Platform,* May 1, 1856, 1–2, 2, 4; and the broadsides *The Crisis and the Cure: Correspondence between General Duff Green and William Oland Bourne* (New York: n.p., 185?) and *The Democratic Party and Its "Iron Platform"* (New York: n.p., 1857). For Poer, see *New York Daily Tribune,* October 5, 1860, 5, October 20, 1860, 5, October 23, 1860, 5, October 26, 1860, 5, October 27, 1860, 3; and his association with William Oland Bourne, "Officers of the Workingmen's Democratic Republican Association," *Iron Platform: Extra,* no. 39 (February 1864): 4.

40. They understood the importance of the new party's name without the explanation of the classically educated—Hine's "*re,* affairs, *publico,* by the public" or Bovay's "*Res Publica*—the common weal." Lucius A. Hine, *A Lecture on Garrisonian Politics: Before the Western Philosophical Institute, Delivered in Cincinnati, Sunday, April 24th, 1853* (Cin-cinnati: printed by A[lcander] Longley for the Western Philosophical Institute, 1853), 8; Bovay in "Emigration to Oregon," *Workingman's Advocate,* December 28, 1844, 2; and "Remarks of Mr. Commerford," *Workingman's Advocate,* April 6, 1844, 4.

41. Hardy, *History and Adventures of the Cuban Expedition,* 22 (see chap. 2, n. 44). For more on the association with Kansas, see "Filibustering," 429–30 (see chap. 3, n. 34).

42. "The Principles of the European," *Liberator,* December 5, 1856, 194; *European,* Janu-ary 10, 17, 24, February 14, 1857, with contents cited in the *New York Times,* January 10, 17, 24, 1857, 5, and February 14, 1857, 6; Marraro, *American Opinion on the Unification of Italy,* 176n, 180–81.

43. Ingalls, *Reminiscences of an Octogenarian,* 35, 49.

44. The proceedings are in Osborne P. Anderson, *A Voice from Harper's Ferry: The Unfinished Revolution* (1861; reprint, New York: World View Publishers, 1974), 39–43; Reynolds, *John Brown,* 261–64, but see also 113–14, 191, 234, 240–44, and 258 (see chap. 2, n. 1).

45. Hinton, "John Brown and His Men," 695, and, for the later New York City connec-tion, Hinton, *John Brown and His Men,* 162–63 (for both, see chap. 2, n. 1); James McCune Smith, "Human Brotherhood and the Meaning of Communipaw," in *Works of James Mc-Cune Smith,* 92.

46. "Anniversary of British West India Emancipation," *Liberator,* August 13, 1858, 132; also in Nell, *William Cooper Nell,* 520.

CHAPTER 5. DECISIVE MEANS

1. Item noted (from *Vicksburg Sun*), *Yazoo (Miss.) Democrat,* April 7, 1860, 2; "Guns to Take Mexico," *Baton Rouge Daily Gazette & Comet,* April 19, 1860, 2; "From Washington," *New York Times,* March 28, 1860, 1; "Threatening Condition of Our Mexican Relations" (from *Charleston Mercury*), *New York Times,* April 11, 1860, 4; commentary on a letter, "Mexican Affairs," to the *New Orleans Delta, New York Times,* May 5, 1860, 4; Thomas W. Cutrer, *Ben McCulloch and the Frontier Military Tradition* (Chapel Hill: University of North Carolina Press, 1993), 171, 173, 197; May, *Southern Dream of a Caribbean Empire,* 144–46 (see chap. 3, n. 23).

2. Lehning, "International Association," 179–80, 180–81, 187–88, 198–99n1, citing the first number of the *Bulletin International,* as quoted in *Le Prolétaire,* June 17, 1857; Lehning, "International Association," 326 (see prologue, n. 8). See also Billington, *Fire in the Minds of Men,* 326–29 (see prologue, n. 6); "Address to Bedini," *New York Daily Tribune,* February 1, 1854; "Universal Democratic Republicans," *New York Daily Tribune,* March 7, 1855, 7; and "Italian National Society," *New York Daily Tribune,* November 23, 1859.

3. "Freedom by Means," *New York Independent,* November 15, 1855, 363. See also Thomas R. Marshall, "When Kansas Bled," *New York Times,* September 16, 1925, 27.

4. Forbes to Dr. S. G. Howe, May 14, 1858, and Forbes to F. B. Sanborn, April 24, 1858, in "Most Important Disclosures," *New York Herald,* October 27, 1859, 4; Jeffery Rossbach, *Ambivalent Conspirators: John Brown, the Secret Six, and a Theory of Slave Violence* (Philadelphia: University of Pennsylvania Press, 1982).

5. Franklin B. Sanborn, *Recollections of Seventy Years* (Boston: R. G. Badger, 1901), 135; Nat Brandt, *The Town That Started the Civil War* (Syracuse: Syracuse University Press, 1990), 200.

6. "Garibaldi and His Former English Lieutenant," *New York Times,* June 24, 1859, 2; "A Roman," letter to the editor dated June 25, "Garibaldi and Colonel Forbes," *New York Times,* June 28, 1859, 1.

7. To limit ourselves to English sources, see *Memoirs and Adventures of Felice Orsini Written by Himself,* ed. Ausonio Franchi, 2nd ed. (Turin, 1858).

8. "The Orsini and Pierri Demonstration: Grand Torchlight Procession of Frenchmen, Germans, Italians, Hungarians, and Other Foreigners; Large Gathering in the Park," *New York Times,* April 23, 1858, 1; "The World at Large," *National Magazine: Devoted to Literature, Art, and Religion* 12 (June 1858): 571; Allen quoted in "National Reform Banquet" (from *Cincinnati Daily Herald*), *Harbinger* 7 (June 10, 1848): 45–46; "The 'Regicides,'" *New York Herald,* April 8, 1858, 3; "Funeral Demonstration" and "The Orsini Demonstration," *Farmer's Cabinet,* April 14, 28, 1858, 2.

9. "Appendix VIII: A Manifesto by the Central International Committee Sitting in London, June 24, 1858," in Lehning, "International Association," 241–46, also on Garrison letter, 245–46; "Orsini and Pierri Meeting in Boston," *New York Times,* May 1, 1858, 1; Garrison quote from "Personal," *New York Times,* May 3, 1858, 1; "The Orsini Conspiracy in England," *New York Times,* May 3, 1858, 4; "Orsini Demonstration in Chicago," *New*

York Times, May 21, 1858, 2; Detroit in "Demonstrations of the Unemployed," *New York Times,* June 8, 1858, 5.

10. "The International Revolutionary Association," *New York Herald,* May 27, 1858, 5; Fifth Resolution of the International Meeting at New York, April 22, 1858; Lehning, "International Association," 199n2, citing the English text of the manifesto of the Central Committee of June 24, 1858, and 199n4, 199–200n1, citing the Kommunistenklub founded on October 25, 1857, with background on its president Kamm, 326–27. See also Hermann Schlüter, *Die Anfaenge der deutschen Arbeiterbewegung in Amerika* (Stuttgart: Verlag von J. H. W. Dietz Nachfolger, 1907), 160–62.

11. "News of the Day" and "The Republican Celebration by the International Society," *New York Times,* June 24, 1858, 4; "Le 10° Anniversaire," *Le Libertaire,* June 29, 1858, 3.

12. Lehning, "International Association," 200n2, 200n3, 200n4, 327–28; "Anniversary of the French Revolution of 1792," *New York Herald,* September 23, 1858, 4.

13. Valentin Pelosse in both "Mais qui est Déjacque?" 9–14, and "Essai de Biographie de Joseph Déjacque," in *Joseph Déjacque: La question révolutionnaire, l'humanisphere, a bas les chefs! La liberation des noirs Americains,* ed. Valentin Pelosse (Paris: Editions Champ Libre, 1971), 15–28; *Dictionnaire biographique du mouvement Ouvrier Français,* ed. Jean Maitron, 5 vols. (Paris: Editions Ouvrières, 1964), available at http://maitron-en-ligne.univ-paris1.fr/.

14. "Esclavagie" (from *Revue de l'Ouest*), *Le Libertaire,* January 31, 1860, 3; "Negrophobie" (from *Revue de l'Ouest*), *Le Libertaire,* February 27, 1860, 4; "Fear of Insurrection among Poor Whites in Virginia," *European,* November 29, 1856, 34; "Rights of Colored People to Ride in Railroad Cars," *European,* December 27, 1856, 108; "A Fremont Man Murdered in Mississippi," *European,* January 3, 1857, 118; "Assassination of White Men in the South," *European,* February 7, 1857, 194; "Emigration to Virginia," *European,* March 7, 1857, 262; "Emancipation in Missouri," *European,* March 14, 1857, 284.

15. "Petite Revue," *Le Libertaire,* February 5, 1859, 3; "Anniversaire du 24 Février," *Le Libertaire,* March 5, 1859, 1–2, 3; "Manifestation of the Solidarity of the Nations," *New York Times,* January 18, 1859, 5; "City Intelligence," *New York Times,* January 18, 1859, 5; "Letter from New York," *Philadelphia Press,* January 28, 1859, 2.

16. James L. Huston, *The Panic of 1857 and the Coming of the Civil War* (Baton Rouge: Louisiana State University Press, 1987), 25–28, 36–37, 220–21; Kenneth Stamp, *And the War Came: The North and the Secession Crisis, 1860–61,* 2nd ed. (Baton Rouge: Louisiana State University Press, 1970), 124–25, 126, 181, 253, 259, 296.

17. See *New York Daily Tribune,* February 2, 18, 1859; Wade quoted in William K. Wyant, *Westward in Eden: The Public Lands and the Conservation Movement* (Berkeley and Los Angeles: University of California Press, 1982), 60; "Land Reform Association," *New York Herald,* January 17, 1858, 3; untitled notice under "City Intelligence," *New York Herald,* January 29, 1858, 8; "The Homestead Land Bill," *Charleston Mercury,* March 19, 1859, 1; and "'Land for the Landless vs. Niggers for the Niggerless'" (from *New York Tribune*), *Charleston Mercury,* March 19, 1859, 1. See also "Grow in New York," *Agitator,* May 26, 1859, 2; and "Letter from New York," *Philadelphia Press,* July 22, 1859, 2.

18. "The Organs of Modern Socialism," *New York Herald,* July 14, 1858, 4; "Anniversary of the French Revolution of 1792," *New York Herald,* September 23, 1858, 4. Déjacque ob-

jected to the date as a date of the middle-class moderate elements. "La république comme la voulaient nos pères," *Le Libertaire,* October 25, 1858, 1.

19. "Anniversaire du 24 Février," *Le Libertaire,* March 5, 1859, 3; "Interruptions châtiées," *Le Libertaire,* June 15, 1859, 3; "City Intelligence: Funeral of Dr. Louis Szpaczek," *New York Times,* April 11, 1859, 4; Lehning, "International Association," 203–5, 206, 329n1, citing Bernhard Hamann's letter from New York, May 12, 1859, in *Das Volk* (London), June 11, 1859. On October 5, 1860, Giuseppe Garibaldi announced plans for an International Legion to aid the Italian cause.

20. Agate [Whitelaw J. Reid], Washington, D.C., August 1, "Letter from Washington. 'Gen. Bickley': From Passages in the History of a Notorious Humbug," *Cincinnati Daily Gazette,* August 6, 1863, 1; "A New Filibustering Expedition" (from *New York Tribune*), in *West Point (Miss.) Southern Broad-Axe,* July 20, 1859, 2; "Our Relations with Mexico," *New York Times,* March 31, 1860, 4; Greeley, "'Columbia, the Land of the Free,'" 1 (see chap. 3, n. 1).

21. The technique was nothing new. It most obviously recalled the way the smooth-talking Palermo peasant Giuseppe Balsamo remade himself as Count Cagliostro and invented a secret society as a means of making money. However, the times in which Bickley attempted to do so were not those of Cagliostro, and such things had a tendency to assume a life of their own.

22. "Obituary: George N. Sanders," *New York Times,* August 13, 1873, 8. See also Kline, *Baltimore Plot,* 380–81 (see prologue, n. 1).

23. W. Stephen Belko, *The Invincible Duff Green: Whig of the West* (Columbia: University of Missouri Press, 2006), xxx; William S. Pretzer, "'The British, Duff Green, the Rats, and the Devil': Custom, Capitalism, and Conflict in the Washington Printing Trade, 1834–36," *Labor History* 27 (Winter 1985): 5–30. Some observers traced the secession scheme back to Aaron Burr. See H. W. P. letter, "The Disunion Plot in 1806," *New York Times,* May 13, 1861.

24. "The Illustrious Blanton Duncan Getting Up Fashion Plates for Rebel Traitors," *Nashville Daily Union,* July 2, 1862, 2; letter from Duncan, "Messrs. Duncan and King," *Spirit of the Times,* December 22, 1855, 534; letter from W. King, "Col. B. Duncan—Death of Poor Old 'Major,'" *Spirit of the Times,* June 8, 1861, 280; "Col. Blanton Duncan Dead: He Was a Favorite of Napoleon III and Opposed the Civil War," *Washington, D.C., Evening Times,* April 10, 1902, 3.

25. "The Knights of the Golden Circle" (from *London Spectator,* August 17), *New York Times,* August 30, 1861, 2; Bickley from Fort Lafayette, "Department of the East," *New York Times,* March 21, 1865, 4. Articles on the KGC are common in newspapers of 1859–60, as any search of the historical newspaper databases provided by ProQuest demonstrates. Greeley, "'Columbia, the Land of the Free,'" 1; Agate [Whitelaw J. Reid], Washington, D.C., August 1, "Letter from Washington. 'Gen. Bickley': From Passages in the History of a Notorious Humbug," *Cincinnati Daily Gazette,* August 6, 1863, 1.

26. "The K.G.C.'s," *West Baton Rouge Sugar Planter,* April 7, 1860, 2; Tidwell, with Hall and Gaddy, *Come Retribution,* 228, 263 (see chap. 3, n. 26). Ferrandini's KGC commission dated from August 8, 1859, and was signed by Bickley. U.S. Census Maryland, Baltimore, 6th Ward, 1870, 461. On Ferrandini, see Kline, *Baltimore Plot,* 112–14, 125, 424n48, 485n57.

27. Kline, *Baltimore Plot,* 25, 60, 76, 112, 174, 415n54, 433n64, 475.

28. "A Soldier of Fortune," *New York Times,* April 7, 1860, 4; "A K.G.C." wrote a letter

to the editor defending Bickley dated April 13, "The Knights of the Golden Circle," *New York Times,* April 17, 1860, 10.

29. *Rules, Regulations & Principles of the KGC* (New York: Benjamin Urner Printers, 1859); Agate [Whitelaw J. Reid], Washington, D.C., August 1, "Letter from Washington. 'Gen. Bickley': From Passages in the History of a Notorious Humbug," *Cincinnati Daily Gazette,* August 6, 1863, 1; *K.G.C.: An Authentic Exposition,* 10 (see chap. 3, n. 50); Arnoldo De León, *They Called Them Greasers: Anglo Attitudes toward Mexicans in Texas, 1821–1900* (Austin: University of Texas Press, 1983); Jerry Thompson, Juan Nepomuceno (Cheno) Cortina (Cortinas), http://www.tsha.utexas.edu/handbook/online/articles/view/CC/fco73.html; Charles W. Goldfinch and José T. Canales, *Juan N. Cortina: Two Interpretations* (New York: Arno Press, 1974).

30. *Indianola (Tex.) Courier* (from *La Grange True Issue*), November 24, 1860, 3; Christopher Long, "Knights of the Golden Circle," http://www.tsha.utexas.edu/handbook/online/articles/view/KK/vbk1.html, citing Ollinger Crenshaw, "The Knights of the Golden Circle: The Career of George Bickley," *American Historical Review* 47 (October 1941).

31. "George DeBaptiste," *Detroit Advertiser and Tribune,* February 23, 1875. Lambert's statement that John Brown drew upon "this body" before the Harpers Ferry raid, easily misunderstood as a claim about the influence of the specific secret society, actually seems to refer to the fugitives in Canada, as his next remarks are on the Chatham convention. "Freedom's Railway," *Detroit Tribune,* January 17, 1887, 2.

32. Tidwell, with Hall and Gaddy, *Come Retribution,* 255, 256. See also Leonard, *Lincoln's Avengers,* 35, 64 (see chap. 3, n. 26); Winkler, *Lincoln and Booth,* 35 (see chap. 3, n. 26); and William A. Tidwell, *April '65: Confederate Covert Action in the American Civil War* (Kent: Kent State University Press, 1995), 116.

33. Lehning, "International Association," 203–5, 206n1, 329, citing Bernhard Hamann's letter from New York, dated May 12, 1859, in *Das Volk* (London), June 11, 1859; J. K. Hudson, "The John Brown League: An Unwritten Chapter of History," and O. E. Morse, "An Attempted Rescue of John Brown from Charleston, Va., Jail," John Brown Papers, Kansas Historical Society, Topeka. See also *The Narrative of John Doy of Lawrence, Kansas* (New York: T. Holman, for the author, 1860); and Hinton, *John Brown and His Men,* 512, 520–25 (see chap. 2, n. 1). Also involved were Joseph Gardner, Silas S. Soule, and J. A. Pike.

34. "The John Brown Revolution," *New York Herald,* April 20, 1860, 2; "The Kansas War," *Boston Herald,* April 11, 1860, 4; *Louisville Daily Journal,* February 17, 1860, 3; "Telegraph to the Herald," *New York Herald,* February 22, 1860, 4; "Another Insult to Virginia" (from *Petersburg Express*), *Memphis Daily Appeal,* April 13, 1861, 2; "A New John Brown Party in Massachusetts" (from *Boston Traveler*), *New York Herald,* April 20, 1860, 2; "The Kansas War," *Boston Herald,* April 11, 1860, 4. See also Lause, *Race and Radicalism in the Union Army,* on the John Brown connections (see chap. 4, n. 31).

35. "Twenty-ninth Anniversary of the Polish Revolution," *New York Herald,* November 30, 1859, 5; "Spiritual Lyceum and Conference [One Hundred and Fourth Session]," *Herald of Progress,* July 7, 1860, 3–4; "La Guerre Servile," *Le Libertaire,* October 26, 1859, 1–2. Forbes, as part of his immersion into American radicalism, also attended spiritualist activities. See Harrison D. Barrett, *Life Work of Mrs. Cora L. V. Richmond* (Chicago: Hack & Anderson, Printers, for the National Spiritualists Association, 1895), 131.

36. Hudson, "John Brown League."

37. "Guns to Take Mexico," *Baton Rouge Daily Gazette & Comet,* April 19, 1860, 2; (from *Vicksburg Sun*), *Yazoo (Miss.) Democrat,* April 7, 1860, 2; "From Washington," *New York Times,* March 28, 1860, 1; "Threatening Condition of Our Mexican Relations" (from *Charleston Mercury*), *New York Times,* April 11, 1860, 4; commentary on a letter, "Mexican Affairs," to the *New Orleans Delta, New York Times,* May 5, 1860, 4; Cutrer, *McCulloch and the Frontier Military Tradition,* 171, 173, 197; May, *Southern Dream of a Caribbean Empire,* 144–46.

38. "The K.G.C." (from *New Orleans Courier*), *Alexandria Louisiana Democrat,* March 21, 1860, 4; "The K.G.C.s," *Little Rock Old-Line Democrat,* April 5, 1860, 3; "The Knights of the Golden Circle," *New York Times,* April 4, 1860, 8; "The Knights of the Golden Circle," *New York Times,* April 5, 1860, 5; "The Knights of the Golden Circle," *New York Times,* April 9, 1860, 5.

39. "Our Relations with Mexico," *New York Times,* March 31, 1860, 4; "Filibuster-ism Again: Organization for the Armed Invasion of Mexico—Pronunciamento for the Knights of the Golden Circle" (from *Richmond Whig*), *New York Times,* July 23, 1860, 3; *K.G.C.: An Authentic Exposition,* 3–4, 4–5, 6, 7, 8, 9, excerpt from *Louisville Journal,* July 18, 1861. "The 'K.G.C.'" (from *Austin Southern Intelligencer*), *San Antonio Alamo Express,* November 5, 1860, 1; Agate [Whitelaw J. Reid], Washington, D.C., August 1, "Letter from Washington. 'Gen. Bickley': From Passages in the History of a Notorious Humbug," *Cincinnati Daily Gazette,* August 6, 1863, 1; "The K.G.C." (from *New Orleans Courier*), *Alexandria Louisiana Democrat,* March 21, 1860, 4; "The K.G.C.: A Few Re-marks Thereon" (from *Vicksburg Sun*), *Natchez (Miss.) Daily Free Trader,* March 30, 1860, 2; (from *Vicksburg Sun*) *Yazoo (Miss.) Democrat,* April 7, 1860, 2; Frazier, *Blood and Treasure,* 14 (see chap. 3, n. 21).

40. "From Washington: The Safety of Passengers on Vessels Propelled by Steam," *New York Times,* March 28, 1860, 1; "Affairs in Mexico," *New York Times,* June 28, 1860, 4; "The Knights of the Golden Circle," *New York Times,* July 27, 1860, 1; "Knights of the Golden Circle" (from *New Orleans Courier*) on Doblado, *New York Times,* August 2, 1860, 2; "The Knights of the Golden Circle" (from *London Spectator,* August 17, 1861), *New York Times,* August 30, 1861, 2; "The K.G.C.," *Corpus Christi Ranchero,* September 22, 1860, 2; "The Extraordinary Life of an American Adventurer," *Abingdon Virginian,* October 4, 1867, reprinted in Felter, *History of the Eclectic Medical Institute,* 112 (see chap. 3, n. 3).

41. "The 'K.G.C.'" (from *Austin Southern Intelligencer*), *San Antonio Alamo Express,* November 5, 1860, 1.

42. Bickley, dated Austin, October 9, 1860 (from *Galveston News,* October 20), in "K.G.C.," *Corpus Christi Ranchero,* October 27, 1860, 2; *K.G.C.: An Authentic Exposition,* 8, from *Louisville Journal* of 1861, which mistakenly believes the date of this plan to be a misprint that anticipates a future event rather than the chaotic Texas venture in the fall of 1860; "Knights of the Golden Circle" (from *Norfolk Day Book*), *Little Rock Old-Line Democrat,* September 20, 1860, 2; "News Items" (from *Memphis Avalanche*), *Saturday Evening Post,* October 13, 1860, 7.

43. "K.G.C.," *Corpus Christi Ranchero,* September 15, 1860, 2; "The K.G.C.," *Corpus Christi Ranchero,* September 22, 1860, 2; "The Knights," *Corpus Christi Ranchero,* Septem-ber 29, 1860, 2; "K.G.C.," *Corpus Christi Ranchero,* October 13, 1860, 2; "K.G.C.," *Corpus*

Christi Ranchero, October 27, 1860, 2. See also "An Expedition Comes to Nothing" (from *Corpus Christi Ranchero,* originally *Galveston Civilian), Baton Rouge Daily Gazette & Comet,* October 12, 1860, 2.

44. Bickley, dated Austin, October 9, 1860 (from *Galveston News,* October 20), in "K.G.C.," *Corpus Christi Ranchero,* October 27, 1860, 2, and in "Knights of the Golden Circle," *Des Arc (Ark.) Constitutional Union,* November 16, 1860, 3; Chaffin, *Fatal Glory,* 175 (see chap. 2, n. 44); "The Extraordinary Life of an American Adventurer," *Abingdon Virginian,* October 4, 1867, reprinted in Felter, *History of the Eclectic Medical Institute,* 113; Bickley, dated Austin, October 9, 1860 (from *Galveston News,* October 20), in "K.G.C.," *Corpus Christi Ranchero,* October 27, 1860, 2, and in "Knights of the Golden Circle," *Des Arc (Ark.) Constitutional Union,* November 16, 1860, 3; May, *Southern Dream of a Caribbean Empire,* 129–31.

45. "A Soldier of Fortune," *New York Times,* April 7, 1860, 4.

46. *Rules, Regulations & Principles of the KGC*; Union League, *Address of the National Executive Committee of the Union League, to the Citizens of the United States* (New York: Ben J. Urner, 1860), with the declaration of grievances on 9–10. C. E. Havens, signer of "Union League," said there were no bounds to California and American future unless we "corrupt our manhood and sink into premature decay." David Goodman, *Gold Seeking; Victoria and California in the 1850s* (Stanford: Stanford University Press, 1994), 52.

47. "Juin 1848," *Le Libertaire,* August 17, 1860, 3–4.

48. "Social Equality," *Herald of Progress,* July 7, 1860, 5; "Social Equality," *Herald of Progress,* July 14, 1860, 5; "Social Equality," *Herald of Progress,* July 21, 1860, 5, 8; "Social Equality," *Herald of Progress,* August 4, 1860, 2–3; *Herald of Progress,* August 11, 1860, 5; *Herald of Progress,* August 25, 1860, 5; "The Industrial Congress," *Herald of Progress,* December 1, 1860, 4.

49. *Biographical Directory of the American Congress, 1774–1971* (Washington, D.C.: Government Printing Office, 1971), 556, 1229; *The "Tribune" Almanac for 1860* (New York, 1859), 19, included in *The "Tribune" Almanac for the Years 1838 to 1868, Inclusive: Comprehending the Political Register with the Whig Almanac . . .* 2 vols. (New York, 1868), vol. 2; For the evolution of this campaign, see the accounts in the *New York Daily Tribune,* October 5, 1860, 5, October 11, 1860, 7, and November 2, 1860, 8; Commerford to Johnson, in *The Papers of Andrew Johnson,* ed. LeRoy P. Graf and Ralph W. Haskins, 20 vols. (Knoxville: University of Tennessee Press, 1967–), 3:358.

50. *New York Daily Tribune,* October 20, 1860, 5.

51. The call appeared in the *Herald of Progress,* October 13, 1860, 5; Fifth Resolution of the International Meeting at New York, April 22, 1858; Lehning, "International Association," 245–46; "Appendix VIII: A Manifesto by the Central International Committee Sitting in London, June 24, 1858," in Lehning, "International Association," 241–46. See also "Letter from New York," *Philadelphia Press,* November 23, 1860, 2.

52. William L. Barney, *The Secessionist Impulse: Alabama and Mississippi* (Tuscaloosa: University of Alabama Press, 1974), 171–73, 177, 176 (quote) (emphasis in the original).

53. Barney, *The Secessionist Impulse,* 207–19, 206 (quote).

CHAPTER 6. THE COUNTERFEIT NATION

1. *San Antonio Tri-Weekly Alamo Express,* February 4, 1861, 3; William A. Phillips, *The Conquest of Kansas, by Missouri and Her Allies: A History of the Troubles in Kansas, from the Passage of the Organic Act until the Close of July, 1856* (Boston: Phillips, Sampson, 1856), on the flag, 45–46, 193.

2. "Filibusterism Again," *New York Times,* July 23, 1860, 3.

3. *K.G.C.: An Authentic Exposition,* 4–5, 6, 7, 8 (see chap. 3, n. 50); *Authentic Exposition of the "K.G.C.,"* 86 (see chap. 3, n. 4).

4. Bickley, *Adalaska,* 102 (see chap. 3, n. 17); Bickley, *History of the Settlement and Indian Wars,* 120, and generally 118–21 (see chap. 3, n. 9); "The Knights of the Golden Circle" (from *Houston Telegraph* of November 1), *Liberator,* November 23, 1860, 1.

5. Bickley, *History of the Settlement and Indian Wars,* 260, 261; Annie Able, *The American Indian in the Civil War, 1862–1865* (Lincoln: University of Nebraska Press, 1992), 110–11n.

6. Bickley, *History of the Settlement and Indian Wars,* 112; quoted in Haller, *Profile in Alternative Medicine,* 97 (see chap. 3, n. 40), from Bickley, "Female Medical Education," *Eclectic Medical Journal* 1 (1857): 117–20. Still, insofar as a correspondent of the *Cincinnati Commercial* could be believed, the authorities of 1861 captured a "female spy" as "a member of the Knights of the Golden Circle." "A Female Spy," *Augusta Daily Constitutionalist,* August 6, 1861, 3; *Augusta Daily Chronicle and Sentinel,* August 7, 1861, 1; *Atlanta Southern Confederacy,* August 7, 1861, 3; *Memphis Daily Appeal,* August 7, 1861, 2.

7. Felter, *History of the Eclectic Medical Institute,* 111 (see chap. 3, n. 3); *Authentic Exposition of the "K.G.C.,"* 85; *K.G.C.: An Authentic Exposition,* 4–5, 6, 7, 8; Bickley from Fort Lafayette, "Department of the East," *New York Times,* March 21, 1865, 4.

8. "Filibusterism Again: Organization for the Armed Invasion of Mexico—Pronunciamento for the Knights of the Golden Circle" (from *Richmond Whig*), *New York Times,* July 23, 1860, 3; Bickley from Fort Lafayette, "Department of the East," *New York Times,* March 21, 1865, 4.

9. "The 'K.G.C.'" (from *Austin Southern Intelligencer*), *San Antonio Alamo Express,* November 5, 1860, 1.

10. "K.G.C.," *Leavenworth Daily Times,* August 4, 1861, 2; *Cincinnati Daily Nonpareil,* April 17, 1852; *K.G.C.: An Authentic Exposition,* 10; ms. roll of the Brotherhood of the Union, Brotherhood of America Papers, Historical Society of Pennsylvania, Philadelphia (emphasis in the original).

11. "Knights of the Golden Circle" (from *Norfolk Day Book*), *Little Rock Old-Line Democrat,* September 20, 1860, 2; A K.G.C., "The Knights of the Golden Circle," *New York Times,* April 17, 1860, 10; "More Filibustering" (from the Washington correspondent of the *Philadelphia Inquirer*), *National Era,* September 8, 1859, 144; *Authentic Exposition of the "K.G.C.,"* 73.

12. *Authentic Exposition of the "K.G.C.,"* 86; "The Knights of the Golden Circle" (from *London Spectator,* August 17), *New York Times,* August 30, 1861, 2.

13. *K.G.C.: An Authentic Exposition,* 7; *Authentic Exposition of the "K.G.C.,"* 86, 88; "The Extraordinary Life of an American Adventurer," *Abingdon Virginian,* October 4, 1867, reprinted in Felter, *History of the Eclectic Medical Institute,* 112; "K.G.C.," *Leavenworth Daily Times,* August 4, 1861, 2.

14. *K.G.C.: An Authentic Exposition,* 8; *Authentic Exposition of the "K.G.C.,"* 87; Bickley from Fort Lafayette, "Department of the East," *New York Times,* March 21, 1865, 4.

15. "The 'K.G.C.'" (from *Austin Southern Intelligencer*), *San Antonio Alamo Express,* November 5, 1860, 1; *Authentic Exposition of the "K.G.C.,"* 65.

16. "Filibusterism Again," *New York Times,* July 23, 1860, 3.

17. *Authentic Exposition of the "K.G.C.,"* 87; Crenshaw, "Knights of the Golden Circle," 37 (see chap. 5, n. 30); "Filibusterism Again: Organization for the Armed Invasion of Mexico—Pronunciamento for the Knights of the Golden Circle" (from *Richmond Whig*), *New York Times,* July 23, 1860, 3.

18. Bickley from Fort Lafayette, "Department of the East," *New York Times,* March 21, 1865, 4; *K.G.C.: An Authentic Exposition,* 8, 7.

19. *Authentic Exposition of the "K.G.C.,"* 87, 72.

20. *K.G.C.: An Authentic Exposition,* 7; *Authentic Exposition of the "K.G.C.,"* 50–51, 65, 85, 86, 69.

21. Dale Baum, *The Shattering of Texas Unionism: Politics in the Lone Star State during the Civil War Era* (Baton Rouge: Louisiana State University Press, 1998), 76; "The 'K.G.C.'" (from *Austin Southern Intelligencer*), *San Antonio Alamo Express,* November 5, 1860, 1.

22. "Manifest Destiny: The 'Knights of the Golden Circle'" (from *Baltimore Daily Exchange*), *New York Times,* August 23, 1859, 2; "The Extraordinary Life of an American Adventurer," *Abingdon Virginian,* October 4, 1867, reprinted in Felter, *History of the Eclectic Medical Institute,* 113.

23. "A Slave League," *Leavenworth Daily Times,* December 21, 1861, 2; "The K.G.C.'s," *Marshall Texas Republican,* November 17, 1860, 2; "Filibusterism Again: Organization for the Armed Invasion of Mexico—Pronunciamento for the Knights of the Golden Circle" (from *Richmond Whig*), *New York Times,* July 23, 1860, 3; "The 'K.G.C.'" (from *Austin Southern Intelligencer*), *San Antonio Alamo Express,* November 5, 1860, 1.

24. For coverage of this meeting, see "The 'K.G.C.'" (from *Austin Southern Intelligencer*), *San Antonio Alamo Express,* November 5, 1860, 1.

25. "The K.G.C.'s," *Marshall Texas Republican,* November 17, 1860, 2; David S. Heidler, *Pulling the Temple Down: The Fire-Eaters and the Destruction of the Union* (Mechanicsburg, Pa.: Stackpole Books, 1999), 185.

26. Jerry D. Thompson and Lawrence T. Jones III, *Civil War & Revolution on the Rio Grande Frontier: A Narrative and Photographic History* (Austin: Texas State Historical Association in cooperation with the Center for Studies in Texas History at the University of Texas, 2004), 31–32; *San Antonio Tri-Weekly Alamo Express,* February 4, 1861, 3; "Major Clark Addresses the Alamo Rifles," *San Antonio Tri-Weekly Alamo Express,* February 13, 1861, 3; Cutrer, *McCulloch and the Frontier Military Tradition,* 179–81 (see chap. 5, n. 1).

27. *San Antonio Tri-Weekly Alamo Express* (from *San Antonio Herald*), February 25, 1861, 3; "Texas K.G.C. State Convention," *LaGrange (Tex.) State Rights Democrat,* March 7, 1861, 3; "War Declared," *San Antonio Tri-Weekly Alamo Express,* March 22, 1861, 3; Jewett, *Texas in the Confederacy,* 64 (see chap. 3, n. 2).

28. "Election in San Antonio," *San Antonio Tri-Weekly Alamo Express,* February 25, 1861, 2; Baum, *Shattering of Texas Unionism,* 76; "The K.G.C." (from *Mobile Mercury,* April 3), *Natchez (Miss.) Daily Free Trader,* April 11, 1860, 3.

29. "Ominous," *San Antonio Tri-Weekly Alamo Express,* March 4, 1861, 3; "Look to the Army," *New York Times,* March 7, 1861, 4; Frazier, *Blood and Treasure,* 36 (see chap. 3, n. 21).

30. "The Knights of the Golden Circle" (from *Houston Telegraph* of November 1), *Liberator,* November 23, 1860, 1; *Authentic Exposition of the "K.G.C.,"* 23–24; "Newspaper Indications," *New York Times,* January 19, 1861, 11; Jewett, *Texas in the Confederacy,* 50–51.

31. *New York Times,* July 28, 1860, 7; *Cleveland Leader,* July 26, 1860, 2.

32. "More Filibustering" (from *Philadelphia Inquirer*), *National Era,* September 8, 1859, 144; "The Knights of the Golden Circle," *New York Times,* July 28, 1860, 7; Greeley, "'Columbia, the Land of the Free,'" 1 (see chap. 3, n. 1).

33. "Col. Blanton Duncan's Lithographic Establishment in Columbia," *Charleston Mercury,* August 1, 1862; "Col. Blanton Duncan Dead: He Was a Favorite of Napoleon III and Opposed the Civil War," *Washington, D.C., Evening Times,* April 10, 1902, 3; Clement Anselm Evans, ed., *Confederate Military History,* 23 vols. (Atlanta: Confederate Publishing), 9:34.

34. "K.G.C.," *Leavenworth Daily Times,* August 4, 1861, 2. Summarized material from the *Louisville Journal* in "Newspaper Indications," *New York Times,* January 19, 1861, 11; and Pontiac, "From Louisville," *New York Times,* March 21, 1861, 2; *K.G.C.: An Authentic Exposition,* 9–10; "Topics of the Day," *Brooklyn Daily Eagle,* May 4, 1861, 3.

35. *Louisville Journal* quoted in "K.G.C.," *Leavenworth Daily Times,* August 4, 1861, 2; "The Treasonable Plot Confessed," *Frankfort Commonwealth,* June 4, 1861, 3; "Filibusterism Again: Organization for the Armed Invasion of Mexico—Pronunciamento for the Knights of the Golden Circle" (from *Richmond Whig*), *New York Times,* July 23, 1860, 3; *K.G.C.: An Authentic Exposition,* 10. The local Union Leagues printed only the documents of the order as *K.G.C.: An Authentic Exposition of the Origin, Objects, and Secret Work of the Organization Known as the Knights of the Golden Circle.* Newspapers across the Union carried the story in one form or another.

36. *Authentic Exposition of the "K.G.C.,"* 57.

37. "The K.G.C.: A Few Remarks Thereon" (from *Vicksburg Sun*), *Natchez (Miss.) Daily Free Trader,* March 30, 1860, 2; *Authentic Exposition of the "K.G.C.,"* 25–26, 29–30, 49, 57; "The 'K.G.C.'" (from *Austin Southern Intelligencer*), *San Antonio Alamo Express,* November 5, 1860, 1; "The Knights of the Golden Circle" (from *London Spectator,* August 17), *New York Times,* August 30, 1861, 2; Robert Emmett McDowell, *City of Conflict: Louisville in the Civil War, 1861–1865* (Louisville: Louisville Civil War Round Table, 1962), 17.

38. *Authentic Exposition of the "K.G.C.,"* 49.

39. Item from *Louisville Journal,* June 14, 1861, in "Diary of Events," in *Rebellion Record,* ed. Frank Moore (New York: G. P. Putnams, 1861), 1:94. See also "'Knights of the Golden Circle,'" *Brooklyn Daily Eagle,* June 4, 1861, 1.

40. C. A. Russell, "An Address to the Knights of the Golden Circle in Texas," *LaGrange (Tex.) State Rights Democrat,* May 15, 1861, 1; "Grand Split in the Southern Confederacy," *New York Times,* October 17, 1861, 8.

41. Don Alberts, *The Battle of Glorieta: Union Victory in the West* (College Station: Texas A&M University Press, 1998), 20; Frazier, *Blood and Treasure,* 37, 43, 50, 83, 118, 139, also noting that the U.S. government before the war had dismissed Baylor from the Office of Indian Affairs for having a conflict of interest (27).

42. Alberts, *Battle of Glorieta*, 8; Teel quoted in Robert Scott, *Glory, Glory Glorieta: The Gettysburg of the West* (Boulder: Johnson Books, 1992), 35.

43. Frazier, *Blood and Treasure*, 197, which points out that this was not formally Confederate policy. However, this misses the way the Confederacy did such things. *The War of the Rebellion: A Compendium of the Official Records of the Union and Confederate Armies, Published under the Direction of the . . . Secretary of War . . .* (Washington, D.C.: Government Printing Office, 1880–1901), ser. 1, 50, pt. 1, 942, hereafter cited as *O.R.*

44. Thompson and Jones, *Civil War & Revolution*, 49–51.

45. William C. Whitford, *The Colorado Volunteers in the Civil War: The New Mexico Campaign in 1862* (Denver: State Historical and Natural History Society, 1906, reissued Glorieta: Rio Grande Press, 1971), 137, 138–40. Teel returned in 1892 to excavate the guns, which were moved, a few years later, to a Colorado museum.

46. Frazier, *Blood and Treasure*, 15; Scott, *Glory, Glory Glorieta*, 13–16, 23–24; Alberts, *Battle of Glorieta*, 7–8; Whitford, *Colorado Volunteers in the Civil War*, 11–12; Martin Hardwick Hall, *Sibley's New Mexico Campaign* (Austin: University of Texas Press, 1960), 85.

47. "Massacre of Confederate Officers" and "Massacre of Confederate Officers: The Sequel," *Osage Magazine* 2 (February–May 1910), posted online, http://www.anpa.ualr.edu/digital_library/Osage_Sketch/osage_sketch_7.htm and http://www.anpa.ualr.edu/digital_library/Osage_Sketch/osage_sketch_8.htm. Related to the general legacy of the KGC, the idea that these were high-ranking Confederate officers is a groundless myth embedded in sources from Frazier, *Blood and Treasure*, 15, to Kansas historical markers. In July 1864, Jim Reynolds brought a more successful band of guerrillas into Colorado, where a company of miners ran them down. William C. Ferril, *Sketches of Colorado in Four Volumes* (only one volume published) (Denver: Western Press Bureau, 1911), 33.

48. Robert J. Chandler, "An Uncertain Influence: The Role of the Federal Government in California, 1846–1880," *California History* (Winter 2003); "California Gossip," *New York Times*, April 5, 1861, 2.

49. Showalter letter, February 8, 1864, *O.R.*, ser. 1, pt. 2, 1079; Aurora Hunt, *The Army of the Pacific, 1860–1866* (Mechanicsburg, Pa.: Stackpole Books, 2004), 72–75, 342. They were known as the Knights of the Columbian Star as well as the KGC. El Monte, San Bernardino, Los Angeles, San Luis Obispo, Mariposa, Stockton, Sacramento, and San Francisco were said to have castles of the KGC, 342–44.

50. "Filibusterism Again: Organization for the Armed Invasion of Mexico—Pronunciamento for the Knights of the Golden Circle" (from *Richmond Whig*), *New York Times*, July 23, 1860, 3.

51. Felter, *History of the Eclectic Medical Institute*, 111; Haller, *Profile in Alternative Medicine*, 28; May, *Southern Dream of a Caribbean Empire* (see chap. 3, n. 23); Bickley, poem "The Andalusian's Love," *Godey's Lady's Book and Magazine* 65 (December 1862): 567.

52. "Arrest of Gen. Geo. W. L. Bickley," *Louisville Daily Journal*, July 28 or 20, 1861, 3; *Louisville Daily Journal*, July 20, 1863, 3.

53. For the story of his arrest, see *New York Times*, July 28, 1863, cited in Hagy, "George Washington Lafayette Bickley" (see chap. 3, n. 5); G. W. L. Bickley to Lincoln, December 18, 1863, Bickley Papers, National Archives, Washington, D.C., cited in ibid.; *Louisville Daily Journal*, March 22, 1864, 2; "Department of the East," *New York Times*, March 21, 1865, 4; "The Bickley Case before the Court," *New York Times*, May 11, 1865, 4.

54. "Col. Blanton Duncan's Lithographic Establishment in Columbia," *Charleston Mercury,* August 1, 1862; Confederate Bond Engravers, http://www.Confederatebonds.com/printers.htm. Duncan fled with Hampton's cavalry; the Federals occupied his home as headquarters.

55. S. H. D., "Inside Views of Dixie: By the Northern Spy, Duff Green," *New York Times,* May 1, 1864, 5. See also Harold S. Wilson, *Confederate Industry: Manufacturers and Quartermasters in the Civil War* (Jackson: University Press of Mississippi, 2002), 18–19, 22; and Duff Green, *Facts and Suggestions Relative to Finance and Currency: Addressed to the President of the Confederate States* (Augusta: J. T. Paterson, 1864).

56. Historicus, "The Duties of Neutral Nations," *Times* (London), October 2, 1863, 4; Sanders, "To the Editor of the *Times*" in response, *Times* (London), October 30, 1863, 10; Ann Larabee, *The Dynamite Fiend: The Chilling Tale of a Confederate Spy, Con Artist, and Mass Murderer* (New York: Palgrave Macmillan, 2005).

CHAPTER 7. THE REPUBLIC SAVED

1. Goldfinch and Canales, *Juan N. Cortina* (see chap. 5, n. 29); J. Fred Rippy, "Border Troubles along the Rio Grande, 1848–1860," *Southwestern Historical Quarterly* 23 (October 1919): 91–111; Paul Schuster Taylor, *An American-Mexican Frontier: Nueces County, Texas* (Chapel Hill: University of North Carolina Press, 1934); Jerry Don Thompson, *Sabers on the Rio Grande* (Austin: Presidial, 1974).

2. Kline, *Baltimore Plot,* 88–89, 112–13, 118, 379–81, 485–86n60 (see prologue, n. 1); "A Plot at Baltimore against President Lincoln's Life," *Agitator,* April 16, 1862, 2, which also noted the recent trial at Richmond of a man named Byrne, said to be the captain of the band of assassins there. Among the radicals active against the plot were John Brown's associate George Stearns, who warned about Baltimore, and William E. Doster, the provost at Washington. Winkler, *Lincoln and Booth,* 88–89, 281, 282, 417, 418 (see chap. 3, n. 26).

3. George C. Odell, *Annals of the New York Stage* (New York: Columbia University Press, 1931–), 7:334; Marconis, *Sanctuary of Memphis,* 3–4 (see prologue, n. 16); Burt, *Egyptian Masonic History,* 203–4, 205, 206, 207, 314–17 (see chap. 4, n. 14). Seymour prepared the special rites for the new order on November 1, 1861. Mark E. Neely Jr., *The Fate of Liberty: Abraham Lincoln and Civil Liberties* (New York: Oxford University Press, 1991).

4. *Authentic Exposition of the "K.G.C.,"* 56, 23, 62, 52, 22, 34 (see chap. 3, n. 4). The organization he called the KGC had circles in the counties of Spencer (forty-five members), Davies (ten), and Gibson (seven), and the towns of New Albany (twenty-five) and Vincennes (fourteen). Indiana was the strongest KGC state. Wade, *Fiery Cross,* 219 (see chap. 3, n. 45).

5. *Authentic Exposition of the "K.G.C.,"* 23, 34, 56, 61–62, 63–64. The politics of the newspapers had much to do with their reporting. In Illinois, the *Carbondale Times* reported ten thousand KGCs in the southern part of the state, and the *Springfield Daily Journal* noted "a lodge of this order in this city, numbering a hundred or more," but the *Chicago Times* doubted "whether lodges of the Knights of the Golden Circle exist in this State." "Knights of the Golden Circle" *Springfield Illinois Daily State Journal,* December 7, 1861, 1; "The Golden Circle," *Springfield Illinois Daily State Journal,* December 12, 1861, 1, both posted at Abraham Lincoln Historical Digitization Project, Northern Illinois University Libraries, http://lincoln.lib.niu.edu/file.php?file=isjournal12121861.html.

6. *Authentic Exposition of the "K.G.C.,"* 58–59; *Brooklyn Daily Eagle,* April 27, 1867, 2. "May be there never was any organization known as the Knights of the Golden Circle." *Brooklyn Daily Eagle,* March 29, 1893, 4.

7. *Authentic Exposition of the "K.G.C.,"* 79. "A Knights of the Golden Circle Trial" (from *Cincinnati Enquirer*), *Memphis Daily Appeal,* February 26, 1862, 2.

8. Tidwell, with Hall and Gaddy, *Come Retribution,* 189 (see chap. 3, n. 26); Mark E. Neely Jr., *Southern Rights: Political Prisoners and the Myth of Confederate Constitutionalism* (Charlottesville: University Press of Virginia, 1999), 36–42.

9. *Nashville Daily Union,* May 16, 1862, 3.

10. Original roster of the John C. Brown Camp, United Confederate Veterans, No. 468, established at El Paso, 1892. Died October 16, 1904. Confederate Burials, Concordia Cemetery, El Paso, Texas (two cards on him), Charles Longuemare, Co. K, 1st Missouri, Office of Adjutant General, Index of Service Records, Confederate, 1861–1865, Box 106, Reel s734; Thomas de la Hunt, *Perry County: A History* (Indianapolis: W. K. Stewart, 1916), 278.

11. Tidwell, with Hall and Gaddy, *Come Retribution,* 182–83, 209; de la Hunt, *Perry County: A History,* 278; Mary K. Maule, "A Chapter of Unwritten History," typescript, n.d., Western Reserve Historical Society, Cleveland, Ohio. All from file F 1483, Missouri's Union Provost Marshal Papers: 1861–1866, http://www.sos.mo.gov/archives/provost/.

12. http://www.newadvent.org/cathen/09506a.htm. Extent: 3.5 linear feet. James Alphonsus McMaster Papers, University of Notre Dame Archives, Notre Dame, Ind.

13. Rothensteiner, *History of the Archdiocese of St. Louis,* 2:211–12, and for Hunt, 1:807, 2:272, 273 (see prologue, n. 32). As early as the fall of 1863, the eastern press discussed a conspiracy around King Leopold. "A 'Latin' Plot to Subjugate the United States," *Philadelphia Inquirer,* October 23, 1863, 4.

14. J. P. Sanderson signed parole, July 23, 1864, box 2, Hunt Family Papers. Missouri History Museum Library, St. Louis. Charles L. Hunt enrolled in the militia. March 13, 1865, Box 2, Hunt Family Papers.

15. See Larabee, *Dynamite Fiend* (see chap. 6, n. 56).

16. *Authentic Exposition of the "K.G.C.,"* 50, 86. See also Neely, *Southern Rights;* Georgia Lee Tatum, *Disloyalty in the Confederacy* (Chapel Hill: University of North Carolina Press, 1934); and Albert Burton Moore, *Conscription and Conflict in the Confederacy* (Columbia: University of South Carolina Press, 1996).

17. On Louisville, see Daniel J. Ryan, *The Civil War Literature of Ohio: A Bibliography* (Cleveland: Burrows Brothers, 1911), 310–11, citing Item 572, *Proceedings of the State Union Clubs of Ohio* (Cincinnati: Union Clubs, 1862). On Tennessee, see I. Winslow Ayer, *The Great Treason Plot in the North during the War* (Charlotte, Mich.: Eaton County Republican, 1895), 242. On St. Louis and elsewhere, see Clement M. Silvestro, *Rally Round the Flag: The Union Leagues in the Civil War* (East Lansing: Historical Society of Michigan, 1966), 4.

18. Paul R. Dotson, "Sisson's Kingdom: Loyalty Divisions in Floyd County, Virginia, 1861–1865" (master's thesis, Virginia Poly Tech Institute, 1997); Daniel Ellis, *Thrilling Adventures of Daniel Ellis* (Johnson City, Tenn.: Overmountain Press, 1989); Edmund Kirke, *On the Border* (Boston: Shepherd, 1867); Ralph Mann, "Family Group, Family Migration, and the Civil War in the Sandy Basin of Virginia," *Appalachian Journal* (Summer 1992); Kenneth Noe, "Red String Scare: Civil War Southwest Virginia and the Heroes of

America," *North Carolina Historical Review* (July 1992); Henry T. Shanks, "Disloyalty to the Confederacy in Southwestern Virginia, 1861–1865," *North Carolina Historical Review* (1944).

19. On the challenges of Southern Unionism generally, see Victoria E. Bynum, *The Long Shadow of the Civil War: Southern Dissent and Its Legacies* (Chapel Hill: University of North Carolina, 2010), and for the specific importance of the military contribution, see Richard N. Current, *Lincoln's Loyalists: Union Soldiers from the Confederacy* (Boston: Northeastern University Press, 1992).

20. "Our Washington Correspondence," *New York Times,* March 28, 1861, 1; David Pickering and Judy Falls, *Brush Men & Vigilantes: Civil War Dissent in Texas* (College Station: Texas A&M University Press, 2000), 157n39, citing Roy Sylvan Dunn, "The KGC in Texas," *Southwestern Historical Quarterly* 70 (April 1967): 556.

21. "A Slave League," *Leavenworth Daily Times,* December 21, 1861, 2.

22. Pinkerton, *Spy of the Rebellion,* 354–57 (see chap. 4, n. 20).

23. Victor Vifquain, *The 1862 Plot to Kidnap Jefferson Davis,* ed. Jeffrey H. Smith and Phillip Thomas Tucker (Mechanicsburg, Pa.: Stackpole Books, 1998). In general, see Edwin C. Fisher, *The Secret War for the Union: The Untold Story of Military Intelligence in the Civil War* (Boston: Houghton Mifflin, 1998); and Donald E. Markle, *Spies and Spymasters of the Civil War* (New York: Hypocrene Books, 2004).

24. Silvestro, *Rally Round the Flag,* 5–6; Ayer, *Great Treason Plot,* 241, 242–43, mentions the clandestine Copperhead organizations, listing the "Circle" or "Knights of the Mighty Host," "Southern League," "Order of the Sons of Liberty," "Order of the American Knights," and, most famously, Beckley's "Knights of the Golden Circle."

25. Silvestro, *Rally Round the Flag,* 6. The old National Reformers played little role in such locally elite associations. Melinda Lawson, "The Civil War Union Leagues and the Construction of a New National Patriotism," *Civil War History* 48 (December 2002): 338–62; Henry W. Bellows, *Historical Sketch of the Union League Club of New York: Its Origins, Organization, and Work, 1863–1879* (New York: Club House, 1879).

26. "New-York Workingmen's Association," *New York Daily Times,* August 20, 1864, 8.

27. Jean-Charles Houzeau, *My Passage at the New Orleans "Tribune": A Memoir of the Civil War Era,* ed. David C. Rankin, trans. Gerard F. Denault (Baton Rouge: Louisiana State University Press, 1984), 2, 5, 7, 9, and, for his friendship with Durant, 38–39. Born in 1820, Houzeau would have been Déjacque's age. For the persistent memory of Orsini, see "The Conspiracy against the Emperor," *New York Times,* December 6, 1862, 1.

28. Rossbach, *Ambivalent Conspirators,* 247 (see chap. 5, n. 4); Viotti, *Garibaldi,* 108, 112 (see chap. 2, n. 8); *The Memoirs of Garibaldi,* ed. Alexander Dumas, trans. P. S. Garnett (New York: D. Appleton, 1931), 350–53; "To the London Garibaldi Committee, Colonel Forbes Report respecting the British Legion in those points which came under his immediate attention," dated Naples, November 28, 1860, bound with two cover letters, both dated January 2, 1861, the first to his acquaintance, the earl of Clarendon, through whom he forwarded the second to Lord Russell in the Foreign Office. "Italy (Miscellaneous) 1859 to 1863," Item 73, Series 22, PRO 30, National Archives, Kew, UK. Trevelyan hoped to write of Forbes's later activities in Italy in a future volume. Trevelyan, *Garibaldi's Defence of the Roman Republic,* 350–51 (see chap. 2, n. 2). See also "America," under "Latest and Telegraphic News," *Liverpool Mercury,* November 19, 1859.

29. Zamoyski, *Holy Madness*, 400 (see prologue, n. 1). William de Rohan to Abraham Lincoln, November 20, 1864, Series 1, General Correspondence, 1833–1916, Abraham Lincoln Papers, Library of Congress, available at http://memory.loc.gov/ammem/index .html. On Stevens, see George E. MacDonald, *Fifty Years of Freethought*, 2 vols. (1921; reprint, New York: Truth Seeker, 1929), 2:482. "Sicily," *Daily News* (London), August 4, 1860; "Garibaldi's Englishmen," *Bristol Mercury*, August 18, 1860; "English Volunteers for Garibaldi," *Reynolds's Newspaper*, August 26, 1860.

30. "To the London Garibaldi Committee"; "Naples (from Our Own Correspondent)," *Times* (London), November 8, 1860, 10; *Compendio del Volontario Patriotico* (Naples: Dalla Stamperia Nazionale, 1860); Trevelyan, *Garibaldi's Defence of the Roman Republic*, 358. See also W. Baring Pemberton, "Garibaldi's Englishman: The Story of Colonel John Peard," *History Today* 9 (December 1959): 783–90; Charles Stuart Forbes, *The Campaign of Garibaldi in the Two Sicilies* (Edinburgh and London: William Blackwell and Sons, 1861), 89, 220–21; "Giuseppe Garibaldi," *American Phrenological Journal* 33 (January 1861): 2; "The British Legion in Italy," *Daily News*, October 15, 1860; and "The Italian Struggle," *Lloyd's Weekly Newspaper*, November 11, 1860.

31. "The British Legion at Naples," *Daily News*, November 22, 1860; "Ill-Treatment of the British Legion," *Lloyd's Weekly Newspaper*, November 25, 1860, summarized in "Mismanagement of the British Garibaldian Legion," *Reynolds's Newspaper*, November 25, 1860.

32. Trevelyan, *Garibaldi's Defence of the Roman Republic*, 286; "To the London Garibaldi Committee." Garibaldi persuaded Lord John Russell that the Neapolitan Bourbons could no longer survive. D. Mack Smith, *Cavour and Garibaldi, 1860: A Study in Political Conflict* (Cambridge: Cambridge University Press, 1954), 227.

33. "Miscellaneous," *Leeds Mercury*, December 15, 1860. See also "Extraordinary Story—Captain Styles and the Garibaldians," under "Foreign Intelligence," *Birmingham Daily Post*, January 10, 1861; "Captain Styles and the Garibaldians," *Belfast News-Letter*, January 11, 1861; and "Actions in Superior Courts," in "London Gazettes," *Era*, March 8, 1863.

34. *New York Tribune* item reprinted in "Personal," *Independent*, September 3, 1863, 3. On this basis, it was likely our subject who wrote "H. Forbes, B.A.," *Poland, and the Interests and Duties of Western Civilization, Together with an Appendix Containing Interesting Documents* (London: for the author, 1863). Trevelyan, *Garibaldi's Defence of the Roman Republic*, 351; notice at Portland Hotel, Southsea, noted the arrival of Mrs. Colonel Forbes in the country. "Local Intelligence," *Hampshire Telegraph and Sussex Chronicle*, June 14, 1862.

35. Two items under "Arts and Manufactures," *Birmingham Daily Post*, January 2, July 16, 1864; "General Garibaldi's Movements" and "Garibaldi in London," *Daily News*, April 22, 23, 1864. The English committee to meet Garibaldi included the Chartist poet John Bedford Leno, who discussed Gustave Paul Cluseret in his *The Aftermath with Autobiography of the Author* (London: John Bedford Leno published by Reeves & Turner, 1892).

36. Letters from "Carbon" to the *Liberator* quoted are from "To Workingmen," December 4, 1863, 195; "Louis Napoleon Flanked," April 3, 1863, 54; and "International Leagues," March 11, 1865, 44. Others include "To the American People," October 18, 1861, 166; "The Feeling in England," December 5, 1862; "France and Great Britain," November 21, 1863, 188; and "The Republic," November 27, 1863, 190. In 1865, he also seems to have attended a

protest meeting against repression in Jamaica. "The Irruption in Jamaica," *Derby Mercury,* December 13, 1865. In 1866, Cambridge gave an M.A. to one Hugh Forbes. "University Intelligence," *Daily News,* May 18, 1866.

37. "From New York," *Philadelphia Inquirer,* July 26, 1861, 5; Earnst A. McKay, *The Civil War and New York City* (Syracuse: Syracuse University Press, 1990), 97; "German Socialism and the War," *New York Daily Times,* August 12, 1861, 4; "Meeting of Workingmen—Destitution—Demand for Work—An Appeal to the Declaration of Independence" (from *New York Day Book*), *Memphis Daily Appeal,* August 3, 1861, 1; "Remarkable Demonstration of German Workingmen" (from *New York Express*), *Memphis Daily Appeal,* August 4, 1861, 4; "The Shadow on the Wall" (from *Courier des Etats Unis*), *Brooklyn Daily Eagle,* August 16, 1861, 2; "The German Workingmen in New York," *Richmond Daily Dispatch,* August 26, 1861, 2; "From New York," *Philadelphia Inquirer,* July 26, 1861, 5; quoted lines "by Argus," "Our New York Letter," *Philadelphia Inquirer,* July 29, 1861, 5; "Fallacies of the Workingmen," *New York Herald,* August 24, 1861, 4.

38. Gustave Paul Cluseret, "American Military Sketches" (translated from *Revue Nationale*), *New Nation,* March 5, 1864, 1–2, March 12, 1864, 1.

39. "Ultimate Reconstruction," *New Nation,* March 5, 1864, 4–5; "What We Are and What We Want," *New Nation,* March 5, 1864, 8.

40. Claude Pelletier under "Communications: Philosophy of Strikes," *New Nation,* March 5, 1864, 3; "Finance and the Finances," *New Nation,* March 5, 1864, 3–4; "Finance and the Finances," *New Nation,* March 12, 1864, 1; Fitzhugh Ludlow, "Frank Wood," *New Nation,* April 2, 1864, 12–13; Stephen Pearl Andrews, "A Private Chapter of the Origin of the War: Second Paper," *New Nation,* April 9, 1864, 3–4; "A Distinguished Radical in Danger for 'Free Speech,'" including letter from Thomas J. Durant, *New Nation,* April 9, 1864, 12; C[laude] P[elletier], "The Labor Question," *New Nation,* April 23, 1864, 3–4; Ed Laboulate, "On the Condition of the United States," *New Nation,* June 18, 1864, 1–2; Albert Brisbane, "The Philosophy of Money," *New Nation,* June 25, 1864, 2–3.

41. "What We Are and What We Want," *New Nation,* March 5, 1864, 8; "The Black Parade," New Nation, March 12, 1864, 10–11; "First Commission to a Colored Officer," *New Nation,* April 2, 1864, 11; "The Atrocities of Fort Pillow," *New Nation,* April 30, 1864, 11–12; "The White Side of the Black Question," *New Nation,* July 30, 1864, 6; "Why Should Black Men Fight for the Republic" (from *Boston Commonwealth*), *New Nation,* August 27, 1864, 6–7. David R. Roediger, *The Wages of Whiteness: Race and the Making of the American Working Class* (London: Verso, 1991).

42. "Candidates for the Presidency," *New Nation,* March 5, 1864, 8; "Political: The Fremont Movement," *New Nation,* March 12, 1864, 12; "The Missouri Radical Convention" under "Political: General National Convention," *New Nation,* March 19, 1864, 1; "Radicalism in the Senate," *New Nation,* March 19, 1864, 7; "The *New Nation,*" *New Nation,* March 19, 1864, 8; "Correspondence: The Presidential Nomination," *New Nation,* March 26, 1864, 3–4; "Political: Formation of a Fremont Campaign Club," *New Nation,* March 26, 1864, 5–6; "Platform of the Fremont Campaign Club" under "Political: Formation of a Fremont Campaign Club," *New Nation,* March 26, 1864, 6; "Municipal Affairs: City, Governmental, and Sanitary Reform," *New Nation,* March 26, 1864, 12; "Political: The Pomeroy-Chase," *New Nation,* April 2, 1864, 6; reprints of the Cleveland convention, *New Nation,* May 28, 1864, 8.

43. "The Union Forever! Immense Demonstration in This City," *New York Times*, April 21, 1861, 1; "The Enthusiasm in New York," *Independent*, April 25, 1861, 1. See also "La Question Américaine," *Le Libertaire*, February 4, 1861, 3.

44. "Tax-Payers' Union Party," *New York Times*, October 4, 1861, 5; "Workingmen's League," *New York Times*, October 20, 1861, 5; Joshua K. Ingalls, "Land Reform in 1848 and 1888: George Henry Evans and Henry George," *Truth Seeker* 15 (April 28, 1888): 258.

45. Bellows, *Historical Sketch of the Union League Club*, 46, Goodwin on 46, 83, on Kapp and Skidmore, 47; *Proceedings of the Organization of the Loyal National League at the Cooper Institute, Friday Evening, March 20th, 1863* (New York: C. S. Westcott, Printers, 1863), on Goodwin, Hunt, and Bryant, 48, and on Minturn, 5; "The Union: Monster Mass Meeting of the Loyal Citizens of New York," *New York Times*, March 7, 1863, 6; "Tremendous Union and War Meeting in New York," *Farmer's Cabinet*, March 12, 1863, 2; *Farmer's Cabinet*, March 19, 1863, 2; "The Union Mass Meeting," *Farmer's Cabinet*, June 25, 1863, 2.

46. "The Future of the Democratic Republican Party" (letter to Fernando Wood), *Iron Platform: Extra*, no. 24 (November 1862): 1–4; "The Democratic League," *Iron Platform*, no. 26 (January 1863): 7; "Letter to the Workingmen of Chicago" under "Workingmen's Correspondence," *Iron Platform*, no. 39 (February 1864): 3; "Address to Southern Workingmen" under "Workingmen's Correspondence," *Iron Platform*, no. 39 (February 1864): 4. See also Bourne's broadsides *To the Laboring Men of New York* (New York: n.p., July 18, 1863); *Don't Unchain the Tiger!* (New York: n.p., July 24, 1863); *A Challenge* (New York: n.p., August 25, 1863); *An Abolition Traitor* (New York: n.p., August 29, 1863); *Dan'l O'Connell on Democracy!* (New York: n.p., October 13, 1863); and *A Traitor's Peace* (New York: n.p., October 30, 1863); and his book *White Slaves* (New York: sold by Sinclair Tousey, 1863).

47. "A Call for Volunteering," *New York Daily Times*, November 15, 1863, 8; "Grand War Meeting," *New York Daily Times*, November 30, 1863, 7.

48. "From Washington," *New York Daily Times*, March 22, 1864, 1; "New-York Workingmen's Association," *New York Daily Times*, August 20, 1864, 8; "Reply of President Lincoln," *Iron Platform: Extra*, no. 40 (March 1864): 1–2; "President Lincoln and the Workingmen" (the latter from *New York World*), *Iron Platform: Extra*, no. 40 (March 1864): 4–5; "The President—the Workingmen—and 'the Nigger' of the 'World,'" *Iron Platform: Extra*, no. 40 (March 1864): 6–7.

49. "Workers in Wood: Mass Meeting at the Cooper Institute" and "Grand Mass Meeting: Printers and the Book Trade; Rally at Cooper Institute," *New York Daily Times*, September 2, 1864, 8; "Printers, Bookbinders, Engravers, Lithographers, and the Book Trade" with "Reform Mass Meeting," *New York Daily Times*, September 4, 1864, 8; "The Syracuse Convention," *New York Daily Times*, September 11, 1864, 1; "Stand Number One," *New York Daily Times*, September 28, 1864, 1; "The Union Demonstration," *New York Daily Times*, September 28, 1864, 4; "No Interference with Trades Unions," *New York Daily Times*, September 29, 1864, 4; "Twentieth Ward: Union Mass Meeting," *"New York Daily Times*, October 6, 1864, 5; "City Politics: Union Primaries," *New York Daily Times*, November 23, 1864, 8; "Local Intelligence: The Charter Election—Apathy in Regard to the Result—List of Candidates," *New York Daily Times*, December 5, 1864, 1864, 8.

50. Three items titled "Brotherhood of the Union," *United States Mechanics' Own* (Phila-

delphia), March 10, April 7, May 26, 1860, all 2; George E. McNeil, *The Labor Movement: The Problem of To-Day* (New York: M. W. Hazen, 1887), 397, 399, 610.

51. "First Annual Report of the American Freedman's Union Commission," *American Freedman* 1 (November 1866), 117; John Relly Beard and James Redpath, *Toussaint L'Ouverture: A Biography and Autobiography* (Boston: Redpath, 1863); "Touissant L'Ouverteur," *North American Review* 98 (April 1864): 595–602; *First Annual Meeting of the National Equal Rights League, Held in Cleveland, Ohio, October 19th, 20th and 21st, 1865* (Philadelphia: E. C. Markley & Sons, Printer, 1865), 5–6; "Death of George DeBaptiste," *Detroit Advertiser and Tribune*, February 23, 1875. On Redpath, see Elizabeth G. Rice, "A Yankee Teacher in the South," *Century Illustrated Magazine* 62 (May 1901): 151–54.

52. Houzeau, *My Passage at the New Orleans "Tribune,"* 29, 134; *Printer* 2 (July 1859): 55; *Printer* 2 (September 1859): 111; *Printer* 2 (October 1859): 135; *Printer* 2 (February 1860): 208; *Printer* 3 (November 1860): 128. John Laizer was listed in the rolls of the National Typographical Union, Local No. 17, New Orleans. *Printer* 2 (July 1859): 55; *Printer* 2 (February 1860): 208; Paschal Beverly Randolph, *The Rosicrucian's Story* (New York: Sinclair Tousey, 1863). On Durant, see Foner and Walker, *Proceedings of the Black State Conventions*, 2:246 (see chap. 2, n. 32); and John P. Deveney, *Paschal Beverly Randolph: A Nineteenth-Century Black American Spiritualist, Rosicrucian, and Sex Magician* (Albany: State University of New York Press, 1997).

53. Winkler, *Lincoln and Booth*, 28–29; Tidwell, *April '65*, 116–17, 139–41 (see chap. 5, n. 32); John B. Castleman, *Active Service* (Louisville: Courier-Journal, 1917), 67–68, 131, 137, 184, 209, 211, 223; Jennifer L. Weber, *Copperheads: The Rise and Fall of Lincoln's Opponents in the North* (Oxford: Oxford University Press, 2008), 149–51, 166.

54. Tidwell, with Hall and Gaddy, *Come Retribution*, 196, 202.

EPILOGUE

1. Leonard F. Guttridge and Ray C. Neff, *Dark Union: The Secret Web of Profiteering, Politicians, and Booth Conspirators That Led to Lincoln's Death* (Hoboken: John Wiley & Sons, 2003), 66–68, 72–73, 77, 81–88; Leonard, *Lincoln's Avengers*, 49–51 (see chap. 3, n. 26). See also William Hanchett, *The Lincoln Murder Conspiracies* (Urbana: University of Illinois Press, 1983), which provides solid grounding for the often speculative conspiracies. See also James L. Swanson, *Manhunt: The 12-Day Chase for Lincoln's Killer* (New York: William Morrow, 2006). On Booth, see Michael W. Kauffman, *American Brutus: John Wilkes Booth and the Lincoln Conspiracies* (New York: Random House, 2004).

2. Winkler, *Lincoln and Booth*, 36–38, 166–67 (see chap. 3, n. 26); Tidwell, *April '65*, 69–70, 73–75, 2324–35n (see chap. 5, n. 32); Tidwell, with Hall and Gaddy, *Come Retribution*, 19–22, 281–83, 292–95, 307–16, 318–20, 463–65 (see chap. 3, n. 26).

3. Winkler, *Lincoln and Booth*, 38–39; Guttridge and Neff, *Dark Union*, 19–26; Leonard, *Lincoln's Avengers*, 64, 84–85; Tidwell, *April '65*, 234–35n35; Tidwell, with Hall and Gaddy, *Come Retribution*, 329–33; Edward Steers, *Blood on the Moon: The Assassination of Abraham Lincoln* (Lexington: University Press of Kentucky, 2001), 71–72, and *The Lincoln Legend: Myths, Hoaxes, and Confabulations Associated with Our Greatest President* (Lexington: University Press of Kentucky, 2007), 169; Kline, *Baltimore Plot*, 381–83 (see prologue, n. 1).

4. For this and the next three paragraphs, see Winkler, *Lincoln and Booth*, 43–46, as well as any of those cited above.

5. Betty J. Ownsbey, *Alias "Paine" Lewis Thornton Powell, the Mystery Man of the Lincoln Conspiracy* (Jefferson, N.C.: McFarland, 1993).

6. Winkler, *Lincoln and Booth*, 151–70; Guttridge and Neff, *Dark Union*, 52–54; Tidwell, with Hall and Gaddy, *Come Retribution*, 135–43.

7. Guttridge and Neff, *Dark Union*, 106–8; Leonard, *Lincoln's Avengers*, 52–53

8. Tidwell, *April '65*, 182–84; Tidwell, with Hall and Gaddy, *Come Retribution*, 418–21; Winkler, *Lincoln and Booth*, 62–64, 168, 171, 192, 195, 249, 319.

9. Winkler, *Lincoln and Booth*, 168–69; Tidwell, *April '65*, 169–70; Tidwell, with Hall and Gaddy, *Come Retribution*, 414.

10. See also James L. Swanson, *Manhunt: The 12-Day Chase for Lincoln's Killer* (New York: Harper Collins Publishers, 2008).

11. Swanson, *Manhunt*, 112, 146–47, 190; Leonard, *Lincoln's Avengers*, 34; Guttridge and Neff, *Dark Union*, 106–8, 151.

12. Jeffrey William Hunt, *The Last Battle of the Civil War: Palmetto Ranch* (Austin: University of Texas Press, 2002); Phillip Thomas Tucker, *The Final Fury: Palmito Ranch, the Last Battle of the Civil War* (Mechanicsburg, Pa.: Stackpole Books, 2001). For a continuation of the Anglo "pacification" of the valley, see Benjamin H. Johnson's *Revolution in Texas: How a Forgotten Rebellion and Its Bloody Suppression Turned Mexicans into Americans* (New Haven: Yale University Press, 2003).

13. Ford, *Rip Ford's Texas*, 365–66, 368–69, 370–71, 372–73, 374, 389 (see chap. 3, n. 27).

14. Hunt, *Last Battle of the Civil War*; Tucker, *Final Fury*.

15. Tucker, *Final Fury*, 120–21; Hunt, *Last Battle of the Civil War*, 171.

16. Hunt, *Last Battle of the Civil War*; Tucker, *Final Fury*.

17. Albert Mathews's explicit repudiation of "The Right of Revolution" in William Oland Bourne's new publication, *Soldier's Friend* 1 (May 1865): 1.

18. "Mazzini and the Socialists," *New York Times*, April 7, 1852, 2.

19. French officials, reluctant to draw the old radical too closely to their new government, authorized his recruitment and tendered him command of the tiny Army of the Vosgues.

20. *Dictionnaire Biographique Mouvement Ouvrier Mouvement*, http://maitron-en-ligne .univ-paris1.fr/. Removed and jailed by political opponents, he won his release as the troops overwhelmed the barricades of the Communards. Remarkably, Cluseret escaped the massacre that followed. He eventually returned to France in 1884, wrote *Mémoire*, and won election as a socialist to the Chamber of Deputies before his death at the turn of the century.

21. Alexander Saxton, "George Wilkes: The Transformation of a Radical Ideology," *American Quarterly* 33 (Autumn 1981): 453–55.

22. Trevelyan, *Garibaldi's Defence of the Roman Republic*, 351 (see chap. 2, n. 2); "Letters from Eastern Europe," *Liverpool Mercury*, December 8, 1875; Daniel Pick, "Transcript of Lecture 14 May 2003 'Roma o morte': Garibaldi, Nationalism, and the Problem of Psycho-Biography," *History Workshop Journal* 57 (Spring 2004): 7, http://muse.jhu.edu/journals/ history_workshopjournal/v057/57.lpick.html. Marriage arranged between A. Forbes, second son of Colonel Forbes, of the Coldstream Guards, and Miss Home Drummond Moray, daughter of Mr. and Lady Anne Home Drummond Moray. "Court and Fashion" under

"Correspondence," *Belfast News-Letter,* June 9, 1881. On the drowning of his son Alfred Forbes, see "The Country," *Adelaide (South Australia) Advertiser,* November 4, 1902, 7.

23. The 1880 U.S. Census lists eighty-year-old John Ferrall as living with his son, Robert Ferrall, of the Supreme Court. The elder Ferrall regularly corresponded from this city with the *Boston Investigator.*

24. Yearley, "Thomas Phillips" (see chap. 1, n. 12); *Tenth Annual Report of the Bureau of Statistics of Labor and Industries,* 146 (see chap. 1, n. 21).

25. *Philadelphia Inquirer,* March 12, 1870, 2; *Tenth Annual Report of the Bureau of Statistics of Labor and Industries,* 146, description on 146–47. For more on the Brotherhood of the Union and Wahnetas, see Seymour M. Lipset, "Democracy in Private Government (a Case Study of the International Typographical Union)," *British Journal of Sociology* 3 (March 1852): 49–50.

26. "The Moral Police Fraternity," *Friend of Progress* (June 1865): 90–93; Andrew Jackson Davis, *Arabula; or, The Divine Guest, Containing a New Collection of Gospels* (Boston: W. White; New York: Banner of Light Office, 1868), 118–19, 124; Emma Hardinge Britten, *Modern American Spiritualism: A Twenty Years' Record of the Communion between Earth and the World of Spirits,* 3rd ed. (New York: the author, 1870), 275, 276, 278, 539–39; "Fourth National Convention of Spiritualists, Held at Cleveland, Ohio, September 3rd, 4th, 5th, and 6th, 1867," *Banner of Lights,* October 19, 1867.

27. Solon Buck, *The Granger Movement: A Study of Agricultural Organization and Its Political, Economic, and Social Manifestations, 1870–1880* (Cambridge: Harvard University Press, 1913), 78, 58ff; D. Sven Nordin, *Rich Harvest: A History of the Grange* (Jackson: University Press of Mississippi, 1974), 29, 146, who also noted that the loss of twenty thousand dollars through speculation by the state treasurer forced serious cutbacks in the cooperative plans for the year (144).

28. http://www.woodmen.com/news/news/magazines/magarticle.cfm?anum=115; Kevin Warneke, "Father of Fraternalism: A Working Man with a Plan," *American Heritage* (January–February 2003).

29. J. M. Smith, "Horoscope," in *Works of James McCune Smith,* 145–46 (see chap. 4, n. 4).

30. "The Royal Masonic Rite," *New York Daily Times,* January 31, 1885, 2. In addition to many other works, Massey wrote two volumes: *Ancient Egypt, the Light of the World* and *A Book of the Beginnings: Containing an Attempt to Recover and Reconstitute the Lost Origins of the Myths and Mysteries, Types and Symbols, Religion and Language, with Egypt for the Mouthpiece and Africa as the Birthplace.* He visited the States several times, lecturing on his views. On Pink, see "Williamsburgh," *New York Daily Tribune,* May 28, 1852. After returning to Britain, he wrote *The Angel of the Mental Orient* (London: William Reeves, 1895), discussed in Richard M. Bucke, *Cosmic Consciousness* (Philadelphia: Inness & Sons, 1901), 299–303. His nephew was J. William Lloyd, the anarchist. See his letter to *Liberty* 3 (June 20, 1885): 5.

31. On race, see Buck, *Granger Movement,* 74n1. In parts of Mississippi, the Ku Klux Klan reportedly used the Grange as a cover for its activities, but Nordin thought some of the Louisiana lodges became integrated. Nordin, *Rich Harvest,* 32–33. See also, on class, John R. Commons et al., *History of Labour in the United States,* 2 vols., 2nd ed. (New York: Macmillan, 1946), 2:162–64, 196; Norman J. Ware, *The Labor Movement in the United*

States, 1860–1895 (New York: D. Appleton, 1929), 15, 17, 60, 76; Philip S. Foner, *History of the Labor Movement in the United States* (New York: International Publishers, 1947), 1:441; Foster Rhea Dulles, *Labor in America: A History,* 3rd ed. (New York: Crowell, 1966), 111, 131; David Montgomery, *Beyond Equality: Labor and the Radical Republicans, 1862–1872* (New York: Vintage Books, 1967), 194–95.

32. On class, see William Earl Parrish, *Missouri under Radical Rule, 1865–1870* (Columbia: University of Missouri Press, 1965), 218–19, 222–24; A. Warner St. John, "Origin, Objects, and Plan of the Industrial Brotherhood," *People's Press,* July 16, 1874; Malcolm G. McGregor, *The Biographical Record of Jasper County, Missouri* (Chicago: Lewis Publishing, 1901), 443–44, 241; *The History of Jasper County* (Des Moines, Iowa: Mills, 1883), 369–70; *Workingman's Advocate,* July 26, 1873; untitled notice and "Industrial Congress," *People's Press,* April 23, 1874, 2, 4; "Industrial Brotherhood and Sovereigns of Industry," *People's Press,* July 9, 1874, 4.

33. Root in "Indorsements of the Industrial Brotherhood," *People's Press,* March 19, 1874, 3; Peter J. Rachleff, *Black Labor in the South: Richmond, Virginia, 1865–1890* (Philadelphia: Temple University Press, 1984), 75–78. For the black Knights, see Phillip S. Foner, *Organized Labor & the Black Worker, 1619–1973* (New York: International Publishers, 1974), 49. Melton A. McLaurin discusses the particular strength of the order at Richmond in *The Knights of Labor in the South* (Westport Conn.: Greenwood, 1979), 40–42, 47–51, 64–67, 135–39, 142–47, 149–50, 169–70, 173–74, 184–85.

34. Jeffrey Ostler, "The Rhetoric of Conspiracy and the Formation of Kansas Populism," *Agricultural History* 69 (Winter 1995): 1–27. See also Hofstadter, *Paranoid Style in American Politics* (see introduction, n. 5).

35. This helped explain the renewed postwar hostility to secret societies as an inherent defiance of the state power. J. M. Foster, "Secret Societies and the State," *Arena* 19 (February 1898): 229–39.

36. "Department of the East," *New York Times,* March 21, 1865, 4; "General Order from Its President: The Order Suspended until 1870," *New York Times,* July 11, 1865, 1; *Brooklyn Daily Eagle,* April 27, 1867, 2; "Sketch of George Bickley, the Originator of the Knights of the Golden Circle" (from *Memphis Avalanche*), *Brooklyn Daily Eagle,* September 26, 1867, 2; Christopher Long, "Knights of the Golden Circle," http://www.tsha.utexas.edu/handbook/online/articles/view/KK/vbk1.html, citing Crenshaw, "Knights of the Golden Circle" (see chap. 5, n. 30).

37. Item from *Louisville Journal,* June 14, 1861, in "Diary of Events," in *Rebellion Record,* ed. Frank Moore (New York: G. P. Putnams, 1861), 1:94.

38. Charles L. Sonnichsen, *I'll Die before I'll Run: The Story of the Great Feuds of Texas* (New York: Harper & Brothers, 1951), 170–72; Mary Harman and Elmo Ingethron, *Bald Knobbers: Vigilantes on the Ozark Frontier* (Gretna, La.: Pelican Publishing, 1994), 6.

39. William Dugas Trammell, *Ça Ira: A Novel* (New York: United States Publishing, 1874). After a distressingly short interval, George N. Sanders sent out probes to see if it would be safe to return to New York. The *Times* advised him "not to come to this city *just yet.*" "A Sensitive Rebel," *New York Daily Times,* April 23, 1865, 4. At the Lincoln funeral, Thomas H. Robinson, marshal for Capital Circle No. 1, Brotherhood of the Union. *The Lincoln Memorial* (New York: Bunce & Huntington, 1865), 132. Leonard, *Lincoln's Avengers,* 147, 189.

40. Karen Halttunen, *Confidence Men and Painted Women: A Study of Middle-Class Culture in America, 1830–1870* (New Haven: Yale University Press, 1982), 205.

41. Harman and Ingethron, *Bald Knobbers*, 6–7.

42. Pope Brook, *Charlatan: America's Most Dangerous Huckster, the Man Who Pursued Him, and the Age of Flimflam* (New York: Crown, 2008), 7–9, 101. See also R. Alton Lee, *The Bizarre Careers of John R. Brinkley* (Lexington: University Press of Kentucky, 2002). A quick search through Confederate service records for the Carolinas and their neighboring states reveals no surgeon named Brinkley.

43. Brook, *Charlatan*, 136–37, 155–63, 182–88; Christopher Lasch, *The Culture of Narcissism: American Life in an Age of Diminishing Expectations* (New York: W. W. Norton, 1978).

44. T. J. Jackson Lears, *Rebirth of a Nation: The Making of Modern America, 1877–1920* (New York: HarperCollins, 2009), but see also his *No Place of Grace: Antimodernism and the Transformation of American Culture, 1880–1920* (Chicago: University of Chicago Press, 1994) and *Something for Nothing: Luck in America* (New York: Viking, 2003).

INDEX

MARK LAUSE is a professor of history at the University of Cincinnati and the author of numerous books, including *Young America: Land, Labor, and the Republican Community* and *Race and Radicalism in the Union Army.*

THE UNIVERSITY OF ILLINOIS PRESS
is a founding member of the Association of American University Presses.

Composed in 10.5/13 Minion Pro with Avenir display by Celia Shapland at the University of Illinois Press. Manufactured by Sheridan Books, Inc.

University of Illinois Press
1325 South Oak Street
Champaign, IL 61820-6903
www.press.uillinois.edu